D0984711

JUST ANOTHER DAY IN VIETNAM

COL (RET) KEITH M. NIGHTINGALE

Published in the United States of America and Great Britain in 2019 by
CASEMATE PUBLISHERS
1950 Lawrence Road, Havertown, PA 19083, USA
and
The Old Music Hall, 106–108 Cowley Road, Oxford OX4 1JE, UK

Hardback Edition: ISBN 978-1-61200-785-4
Digital Edition: ISBN 978-1-61200-786-1

A CIP record for this book is available from the British Library

Printed and bound in the United States of America

Typeset in India for Casemate Publishing Services. www.casematepublishingservices.com

For a complete list of Casemate titles, please contact:

CASEMATE PUBLISHERS (US)
Telephone (610) 853-9131
Fax (610) 853-9146
Email: casemate@casematepublishers.com
www.casematepublishers.com

CASEMATE PUBLISHERS (UK)
Telephone (01865) 241249
Email: casemate-uk@casematepublishers.co.uk
www.casematepublishers.co.uk

Dedicated to my wife Vicki,
who served a much longer tour than I.

Contents

Acknowledgments

This book is the residue of a very long day and night spent in the darker parts of War Zone D, III Corps, South Vietnam. The core of the book is in regard to the people that served in that spot on that day: Captain Al Shine, Senior Advisor to the 52nd Ranger Battalion, SFC Swyers, and Elephant—our radio operator. Most of all I would wish to thank Major Nguyen Hiep, Commander 52nd Ranger Battalion, whose example, competence, and sheer will allowed us to return. Hiep was later killed in a "re-education camp" due to his intransigence. All of us and his nation are sorrier for the loss.

I would be remiss if I did not acknowledge the people that did all the heavy lifting in making this book possible. My editors, Sharon Gaul, Claudia Leufkens, and Forrest Smith; and my agent at Princeton International, Gayle Wurst, who refused to accept rejections and fixed her bayonets to the throats of publishers and like all good soldiers, took the hill.

Most of all, I wish to acknowledge my wife Victoria, who soldiered through much more than I can describe to make these words live.

About this Book

A compilation of fact and conjecture, this book tells a plausible story of what happened on that day. The book is not a personal author narrative, but is the combined stories of all who served that day. In a formal sense, it is fiction based on fact—much like Michael Shaara's *Killer Angels*—and other similar works with its foundation in facts extended for narrative purposes.

It is the story of an action that took place in June 1967 in the III Corps sector of South Vietnam between the 52nd Vietnamese Ranger Battalion and a main force Viet Cong (VC) regiment. Other participants included the spotter aircraft element based at Xuan Loc, South Vietnam; Vietnamese 18th Division, Army of the Republic of Vietnam (ARVN); the Vietnamese 5th Mechanized Regiment; the 42nd Vietnamese Infantry Regiment; the U.S. 11th Armored Cavalry Regiment (ACR); innumerable USAF tactical aircraft, and a U.S. heavy artillery battery (8-inch and 175mm guns). The battle was real as described.

The conjectural aspects were developed by me based on debriefings of our returned Ranger POWs during December of 1967. In the debriefs, conducted by the 52nd Battalion Commander, a story emerged independently consistent from each returnee. I saw the larger narrative in my mind very soon after my own exposure and wrote this based on my impressions as to what likely occurred. The key points indicated were as follows:

The action was planned at the highest level of the North Vietnamese government—the Politburo.

Its objective was to isolate an elite South Vietnamese unit and annihilate it in order to destroy southern morale. The beginning of a new strategic direction, this strategy would be the first of many similar efforts.

The 18th ARVN Division was targeted due to its proximity to Main Force VC elements, its proven battle ineptitude, and the belief that the commanding general would force the engagement of the 52nd Rangers rather than commit his own forces. Conjecture proved truth.

A VC soldier, who was a voluntary POW (Chieu Hoi), was a key part of the larger plan to dupe the 52nd to move to an unsupportable location in War Zone D. (I have named this voluntary POW Mr. Hu, as I do not recall his actual name. All descriptions of him and his thought process are conjecture).

This story is based on some degree of interpolation as to actions of the North Vietnamese, specifically the meeting at the Politburo to confirm the larger strategy by General Nguyen Chi Thanh, as well as the meticulous planning by the subordinate elements to make the battle unfold as it did. The interpolation follows the narrative described by the returned prisoners as was related to them by their guards and senior officers in the prison area.

The description of the effects of the B-52 strike, the death of General Thanh, and his transport to the North were as described independently by the returnees.

It is important to understand how the 52nd Ranger Battalion operated during this action. I have consolidated the actions of the then Senior U.S. Advisor (Captain Al Shine) and me (Lieutenant Keith Nightingale) into a single entity—"The Lieutenant"—for ease of continuity and flow. In fact, Captain Shine did virtually all of the heavy lifting associated with the action. I did adjust the artillery, the initial gunship run, and the elimination of the VC mortar position. Captain Shine was the principle conduit with the forward air control (FAC) bird overhead as well as the key support to Major Nguyen Hiep during the action.

In normal course, and in this action, the battalion was divided into two columns of two companies each as we traversed the ground. Captain Shine and Major Hiep went on the left column, and I went with the executive officer, Captain Tot, on the right. Captain Shine had Specialist Fourth Class Garrett as his radio operator, and I had Sergeant First Class Swyers as mine. We moved and fought in this configuration during this engagement.

The actions of the 11th ACR at the ambush site are as related by members of the 11th ACR in several After Action Reports and personal narratives. The thought process of the Commanding General, 18th ARVN Division, is conjecture based on a variety of sourcing.

The depiction of the USAF management of the tactical air strikes, as well as the actions on board the B-52 bomber are a combination of personal observation, in addition to a narrative from a senior USAF officer to me.

The real story is about the members of the 52nd Ranger Battalion and how they conducted themselves at a very high level under the fiercest personal odds and conditions. This conclusion is not conjecture.

Glossary

This is an informal glossary designed to explain certain terms used as well as to explain some specific military acronyms within the context of the story.

ACAV. Armored Cavalry Assault Vehicle. A vehicle with modified gun mounts. Usually, it was a standard M113 tracked carrier with two side-facing 7.62mm M-60 machine guns mounted on the rear deck and a pintle-mounted .50 cal machine gun operated by the vehicle commander. It usually had a crew of five: a driver, track commander, two M-60 gunners and a fifth man usually oriented to the rear with an M-79 grenade launcher. Some had more and some less. The floor was usually filled with sandbags to shield against mines and covered with plywood for flooring. The plywood was usually stacked with ammunition cans, grenades, food, water, batteries and individual living gear.

ACR. Armored Cavalry Regiment. In this case, the 11th ACR, a U.S. mechanized armor unit of brigade strength. It had three maneuver battalions as well as organic artillery (155mm), engineers, maintenance, and medical and other support elements. It was located at Blackhorse Basecamp south of Xuan Loc. The shoulder patch of the unit was a rearing Blackhorse.

APC. Armored personnel carrier, primarily the M113 tracked vehicle, designed to carry infantry.

Arc Light. The term used for a B-52 strike. Most standard strikes were performed by three B-52s flying in a V formation. Their bomb box was approximately a 1 by 3 kilometer rectangle.

ARVN. Army of the Republic of Vietnam.

Binh Tram. The North Vietnamese Army populated the supply trails with Binh Trams. These were self-supporting elements responsible for the care, feeding, and passage of infiltrating elements. They varied greatly in size depending upon local missions. Some had huge truck parks, engineer elements, and security. Others were quite small and configured for local missions.

CBU. Cluster bomb unit, an aerial bomb containing a large number of smaller munitions, designed as an anti-personnel weapon.

Cham/Nung/Montagnard. Specific ethnic populations within and close to Vietnam. The Montagnards were predominately hill tribes along the central massif of Vietnam whereas the Chams and Nungs were of more Thai and Laotian extraction from the Cambodia and Laotian areas. All three were heavily recruited by the U.S. due to their exceptional military acumen.

Chinese. This refers to alleged Chinese observers/advisors with the North Vietnamese during and after the ambush at Suoi Long. Throughout the Vietnam War, there have been anecdotal stories regarding Chinese and Russian advisors with high-level NVA elements. The Ranger POWs reported on their release that they saw both at General Thanh's camp.

CMH. Congressional Medal of Honor. The citation refers to Special Forces Captain Robert Q. Williams, who was awarded a CMH and rescued personally by Nguyen Hiep during an extraction under fire at Dong Xuai Base.

Corps. Vietnam was organized into four nominal Corps areas by the South Vietnamese and U.S. governments. They encompassed specific areas had widely varying troop strengths. Each was unique due to its geographical nature. I Corps was the northernmost area bordering North Vietnam and Laos. It was highly mountainous with a small coastal plain. II Corps encompassed the Central Highlands and was the historical invasion route into Vietnam. III Corps was a mix of deep triple-canopy jungle, densely populated coastal areas, and the national capital of Saigon. It also held the bulk of U.S. support and maintenance elements at Bien Hoa and Long Binh Junction. IV Corps was the very flat, waterlogged southern area of South Vietnam. It was also the primary rice-growing region for the nation. It abutted Cambodia and was the primary drainage basin for the Mekong River.

COSVN. Central Office for South Vietnam. This was the U.S. term for the North Vietnamese political and military headquarters inside South Vietnam.

CS. A gas causing tears, salivation, and painful breathing.

Dusters/Quad 50s. World War II-Korean War-era anti-aircraft weapons systems mounted on tracked vehicles and trucks and used for fire support. The quad 50 was four .50 cal machine guns on an electrically driven turret. The Duster was a tracked vehicle with 2 rapid-fire 40mm guns. In Vietnam, the U.S. usually had one quad 50 (often mounted on a truck) and one dual 40mm mounted on a light tank chassis assigned to a specific unit. Both were devastating ground support weapons.

FDC. Fire Direction Center.

KCS. Kit Carson Scouts. During the Vietnam War, U.S. elements used several forms of captured or turned VC or NVA personnel. They were interned under the Chieu Hoi program (voluntary surrender) and became KCS, assisting U.S. units in local culture, with translations, and as scouts and booby trap experts. They accompanied U.S. infantry, usually at the platoon level. The ARVN used LCS, who were deserters who had been captured or returned. These were primarily basic prison labor elements that would do the sandbag filling, bunker building, and wire-laying tasks. In the case of the Rangers, the 52nd used these personnel to carry heavy weapons such as the .50 cal machine gun and 81mm mortars and the ammunition.

LZ. Landing Zone.

NCO. Non-commissioned officer.

NCOIC. NCO in charge.

NDP. Night Defensive Perimeter.

NVA. The North Vietnamese Army.

PZ. Helicopter pickup zone.

Rome plow. Caterpillar D8 bulldozers with an angled blade with a long piercing steel blade attached on the forward angle. These were designed to clear trees on roadsides by shredding tree trunks and then collapsing them. All major roads throughout Vietnam used by U.S. forces were probably cleared initially by Rome plows.

RPG. Rocket-propelled grenade. Highly effective, Russian-designed, man-portable, anti-tank weapon.

Spooky. A C-47 transport aircraft converted into an aerial gunship. C-130s were also converted into gunships (AC-130s). The C-47 variant primarily used a gyroscopically mounted 20mm Gatling gun supplemented by two or more 7.62 mini-guns. The AC-130 has several configurations and included a dual 40mm Bofors or a 105mm howitzer, all gyroscopically mounted. The C-47 was primarily a ground combat support system while the AC-130 was used for road interdiction on the infiltration routes in western Vietnam, Laos, and Cambodia. The guns were side-firing, allowing the aircraft to circle a target, concentrating fire on a single point.

VC. Viet Cong. The communist guerrilla movement in South Vietnam.

WP. White phosphorus, an incendiary munition.

Maps

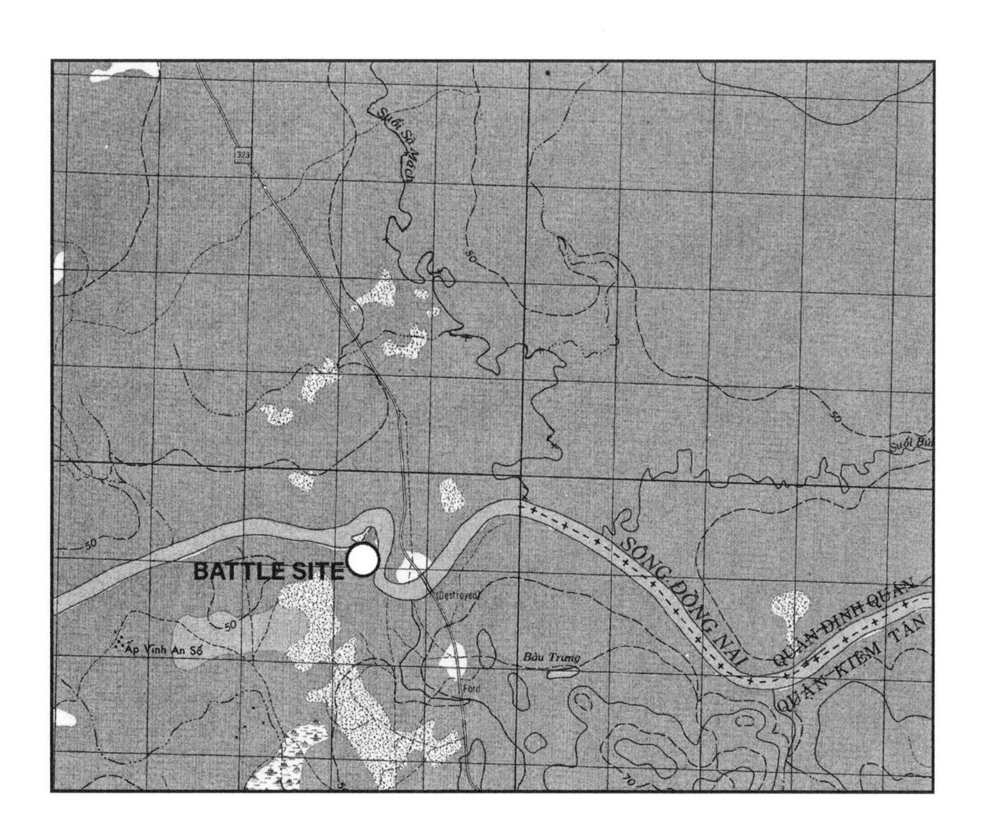

Suối Sà Mách
323
50
Suối Bù
BATTLE SITE
SÔNG ĐỒNG NAI
QUẬN ĐỊNH QUÁN
QUẬN KIỆM TÂN
(Destroyed)
Ấp Vinh An Số
Bàu Trưng
Ford
70

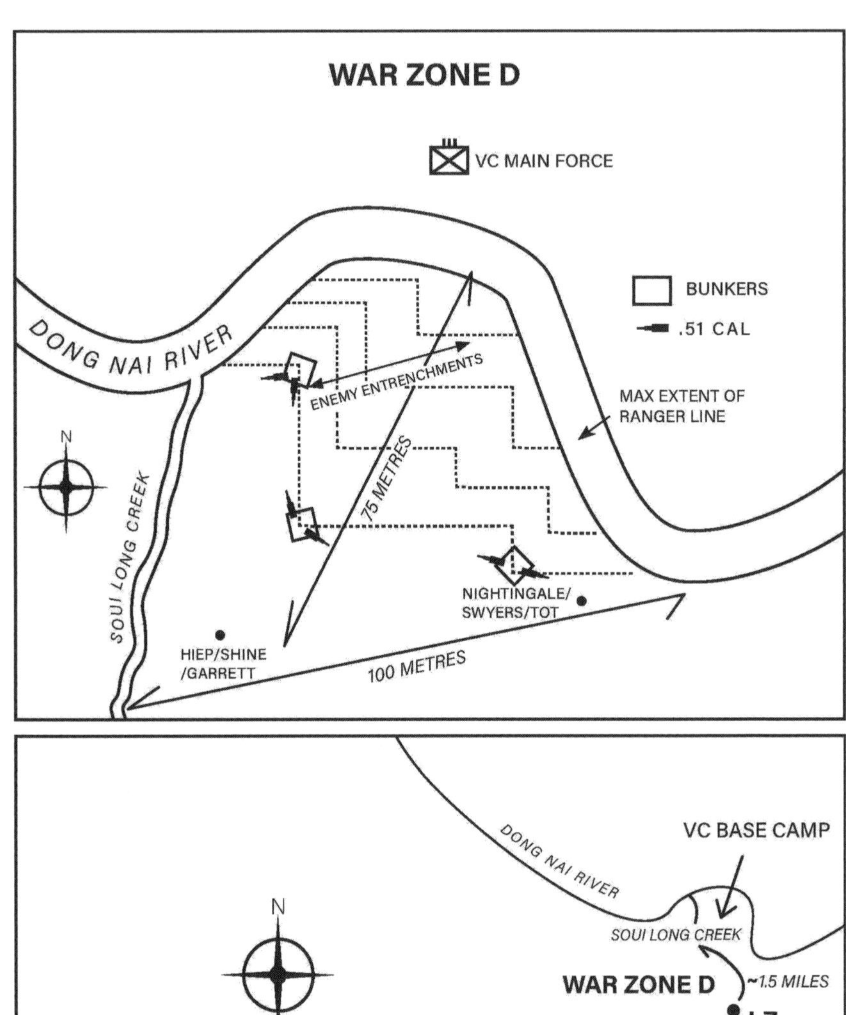
WAR ZONE D
VC MAIN FORCE
BUNKERS
.51 CAL
DONG NAI RIVER
ENEMY ENTRENCHMENTS
MAX EXTENT OF RANGER LINE
N
75 METRES
SOUI LONG CREEK
NIGHTINGALE/ SWYERS/TOT
HIEP/SHINE /GARRETT
100 METRES

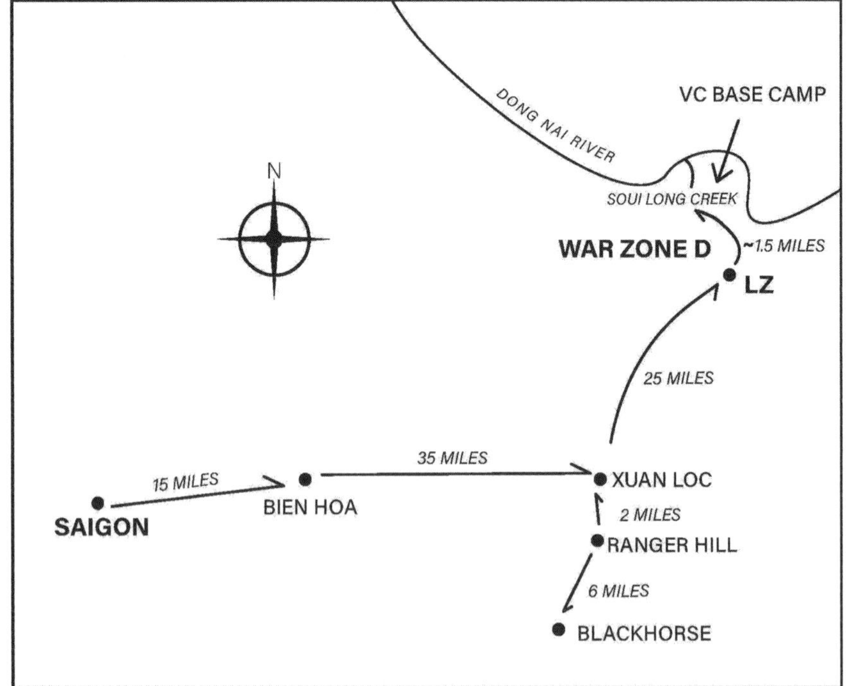
DONG NAI RIVER
VC BASE CAMP
SOUI LONG CREEK
N
WAR ZONE D
~1.5 MILES
LZ
25 MILES
15 MILES
35 MILES
SAIGON
BIEN HOA
XUAN LOC
2 MILES
RANGER HILL
6 MILES
BLACKHORSE

Introduction

The basis of this book is my initial introduction into combat in Vietnam as a 1st Lieutenant with the Vietnamese Ranger infantry. I was the Deputy Senior Advisor to the Vietnamese 52nd Ranger Battalion located at Xuan Loc, Long Kanh Province, III Corps, South Vietnam. The book is 95 percent fact and 5 percent speculation regarding a major action the battalion fought in June of 1967 near the Dong Ngai River, War Zone D.

The action was begun by a Viet Cong (VC) soldier who surrendered to U.S. elements in Long Kanh. He related that a VC company was building a base camp near the Dong Ngai along a stream named Suoi Long. The intelligence led the commanding general of the 18th ARVN Division to assign the task of finding and destroying the camp to the 52nd Rangers. The Rangers deployed in less than 24 hours from initial notification to a Landing Zone approximately 4 kilometers from the reported base camp.

The Rangers were immediately engaged and ambushed by a full-strength Main Force VC battalion backed by an entire VC regiment, which quickly engaged the trapped Rangers that night and early morning. No U.S. support was available other than long-range artillery. In desperation, the Ranger battalion commander, the following morning at dawn, ordered a covering assault into the attacking VC by one company to be followed by a withdrawal under pressure of the remainder of the battalion aided by more than 72 tactical airstrikes within a 45-minute period. As I regrouped into our new perimeter at around 10 a.m., I counted a total of 32 Rangers left from an original assault force of 450.

During the Christmas period in December 1967, a number of Ranger prisoners held by the VC during this action were released back to our control as a goodwill gesture. During the debrief of the ex-POWs, they independently related that they were told by their captors that the entire action was planned at the highest level in order to trap and destroy a major South Vietnamese unit. We had no reason to doubt the authenticity of the report and this book is based on the supposition that it is true.

The character of Hu, the informant, and his actions are real. The death of Gen Thanh, COSVN commander, and the effect of the B-52 Arc Light strike with subsequent movement into Laos, is as the former POWs related to us. The portrayal of Thanh and his planning briefings are conjecture. The remainder of the description is as I saw the action, the players, and the effects.

For this action, the 52nd Ranger Battalion was awarded a second U.S. Presidential Unit Citation, one of the very few Vietnamese units to garner two of the highest awards the U.S. can proffer upon a military unit, U.S. or foreign.

Col (Ret) Keith M. Nightingale

I

The Ground

The French term was *Mal d'Orient*—the sickness of the east. Indochina, our Vietnam, was a beautiful lady who easily obsessed the visitor with her quite deadly charms. Lush beauty, vast landscapes, and the combination of heat, danger, and exotica joined to create a mystique that quickly captured all but the most jaded of visitors. Viewed dispassionately from afar, or for only the briefest of stays, the charms could be overlooked. But for the relatively permanent observer, or for those that recognized the potential shortness of their mortality combined with youth and a sense of adventure, she exuded a lush, heavy anesthetic, much like the many creatures she harbored that injected painkillers as a masking prelude to withdrawing the host's blood to sustain the future. Such was Vietnam for much of her history—a beautiful woman with a terminal effect on those who attempted to possess her. As is the nature of women, she selected her best parts as an attractant and allowed a host to expose his vulnerabilities to her advantage.

The nature of the contested ground had not changed for a millennium. It was as flat as land could be. Had it been a desert, an observer could have seen the horizon from 360 degrees without the slightest interruption to the extent of his vision. Neither situation was possible, however, as the ground was covered with several hundred square kilometers of dense tropical rainforest. The actual battle ground encompassed less than 20 acres but it was reflective of the whole.

To the west was the Dong Nai River. It was approximately 50 meters wide and ranged in depth from 20 feet to fewer than 6 inches. It was a dark brooding river and rolled with a fast current. Where it broke over exposed rocks, it foamed and swirled into eddies next to the bank or swiftly joined the deeper water midstream. The bed of the river was primarily exposed granite, black and unforgiving to passing craft. Occasionally, sheets of sandstone were exposed, tan and flat, worked smooth by the flowing waters. The banks were generally steep and began with greasy laterite clay and descended to the water's edge where they were joined by the river rocks that formed the mother bed.

As the Dong Nai flowed swiftly south, its face was frequently broken by smaller streams that emerged from the maw of the jungle. These outflows created large eddies at their point of joining the larger flow where the milk chocolate jungle water mixed with the black tannin-laden river. Bits of foam, debris, and greenery constantly rotated in a circle as the larger, faster river consumed the contents of the smaller.

The southern border of the battlefield was formed by such a stream, the Soui Long. It was a very small stream in comparison to many that drained the jungle. It was just deep enough to make a man have to swim, and wide enough to prevent an easy passage, particularly for a soldier and his burdens. Its banks were covered with a thick thorn bamboo brush belt that reached several yards into the jungle.

The bamboo itself was unusual. It was not straight as most species, but very brushy, crooked, and twisting in uncontrolled directions very much like concertina wire. Along all the trunk and limb masses were long thorns that turned the entire arrangement into a closely matted thorn barrier denying passage to all but the most patient and determined transient. Interspersed within this protective barrier, spread out about every 12 feet like guard houses, were ant hills. They were a reddish brown clay of an upside-down ice cream sundae design rising to a height of 5 feet or more through the bamboo. The occupying ants were a deep burgundy color, about three-quarters of an inch in length with long mandibles that injected a very acute poison, drawing large welts on the human corpus.

The Soui Long was not straight but took several meanders through the flat jungle floor. From the confluence with the Dong Nai, it went straight east for about 50 meters and then took a sharp turn north, traveling for another 100 meters and then again coursed slowly back toward the east. The oxbow of land created by the stream's design constituted slightly less than 20 acres. None of this was visible from above as all was covered with the impenetrable carpet of jungle as far as the eye could see.

To the north of the battlefield lay triple-canopy jungle. The distance between the northern route of the Soui Long and the bank of the Dong Nai River encompassed about 200 meters of triple-canopy rainforest. The area of conflict would be surrounded on three sides by water and on one side by dense forest.

The rainforest possessed certain universal traits with its companions in other parts of the world. The trees, huge giants, rose several hundred feet to the sky. They had shallow roots, all that was necessary due to the high water table, but self-supported with great flying buttress root systems like medieval cathedral constructions that emerged midway up the trunk to the jungle floor itself.

The first third of the trunks grew neither leaves nor branches. Instead, they saved their growing and foliation for an altitude where there was reasonable probability of capturing the flickering sunlight. In the crotches of these trees, and on those portions of the limbs that paralleled the ground, there grew profusions of ferns, flowers, and other foreign elements that had migrated to that spot to take advantage of the favorable mating of water and sunlight. Only in the last 20 or so feet of the trees' full height did they spread limbs and thick leaf growth.

The intense competition for sunlight caused a great tangle of leaf growth at the top of the trees. A constant but subtle flow of dead and decaying leaves rained on the forest floor as the trees replaced their nurturing skins.

The ground beneath this green umbrella was unlike that known anywhere else on earth. It was almost liquid with accumulated vegetation, decaying matter, and moisture. It moved to the touch and could not be defined unless several inches of the covering was removed. Rising slowly above it, to a height of several inches, was an odor of decay and heat. The occasional spears of light that touched the floor showed the moisture and organic matter rising from the earth as it shimmered in a shaky blue-brown haze. Under the canopy, the temperature and humidity usually exceeded that of the air above the leafy cover. In daylight, the effect of the rainforest on the floor below could be plainly seen. Nothing small could grow effectively on the ground to obstruct movement. From the jungle earth, mammoth trunks with their buttressing support systems sprung in all directions. The whitish-blue, smooth-skinned trunks reflected the dim light and showed endless similar scenes in all directions. Occasional horizontal shapes would expose themselves to the viewer as fallen predecessors, aided by a milieu of fungi slowly evaporating into the earth. Mixing with the tree trunks were hundreds of vines that snaked from the canopy to the jungle floor. Many of them twisted into each other, attached themselves to the buttress roots and fell into tangled masses obscuring the division between parasite and host.

Irregularly spread throughout the area were spots where a large tree had recently died. Wherever this had occurred an explosion of growth and cellular energy was expended as vegetative newborns struggled to capture a place in the sun. In these spots, the floor of the jungle became an impenetrable mass of vines, flowers, bushes, and merging seedlings.

Throughout the forest, but barely perceptible to the casual observer, was a wealth of living things. High in the trees were birds and monkeys, their presence revealed only by an occasional cry or flash of exposure in a shaft of sunlight. Midway down the trunks of trees were lizards, mice, and small birds.

They lay in tree crotches and holes and waited for nature and its programmed chances to bring them meals. Interspersed among them and on the floor of the jungle was nature's army, the millions of pounds of insects that waited under leaves, within logs and beside rocks to eat, excrete, convert, and return the jungle vegetation and animal matter back to basic earth.

Night comes quickly to the area and without warning. The dappled light diffuses into nothingness and the hint of sounds begins to overtake the daylight silence. The floor of the jungle glows with phosphors and decaying matter. Insects initiate their love rituals with flashing lights. Moonlight catches the isolated raindrop as it falls through the leafy umbrella toward the earth. Everywhere, the living matter of the area begins to stir and make its presence felt. The observer, now robbed of his primary senses, is suddenly aware of the many other elements that are sharing the same space and begins to mentally enclose about himself.

The core of the jungle is the continuous cycle of life, death, and decay. Here, human combatants are unwelcome intruders. A man's blood is sucked by leeches and mosquitoes, his flesh is assaulted by centipedes, ants, and scorpions. All of the material possessions he depends upon, clothes, equipment, and baggage, are attacked by mold and mildew as they relentlessly reduce these items back to nature, one spore at a time. Given sufficient exposure to the atmosphere, man himself begins to erode with fungus, fatigue, and a myriad of infections that he continuously ingests from the fetid air he breathes. If he dies, his dirt mound, so fresh at its birth, is quickly reduced to nothingness by the inexorable impetus of this peculiar cycle of nature.

Into this cauldron of life, death, and limbo in between, two combatant elements moved to join together and perpetuate the *Mal d'Orient.*

2

The Initiation

The lady was neither married nor a mistress. To the adversaries for her possession, she was each their own. Her favors were dispensed with equanimity for those suitors willing to pay the price. It was the policy of both contestants to pursue her hand until ultimate ownership could be determined and she could shift from the role of possessor to possession. The issue for both adversaries was to select an approach that expedited the desired outcome.

Policy evolves. It is not made. Military policy is the foundation of strategy and indicates the approach that a force must take to achieve broad national objectives. Tactics are a subordinate to strategy. It is simply a means multiplied many times to achieve a strategic end. Within the North Vietnamese military leadership, this separation was always tenuous and often intertwined. Specific military actions were viewed as a necessary mix of both. In western militaries, in particular the United States, clear separation was a matter of both doctrine and policy. Military operations were conducted at the tactical level to execute national strategic policy. Rarely, if ever, would a force's actions be planned for or viewed as having strategic significance.

This approach was similar to that of the French who viewed Dien Bien Phu as a tactical issue until it became obvious that the Vietnamese viewed it as a strategic opportunity. Contemporaneously, this concept caused the U.S. to view the helicopter assault in Somalia on 3 October 1994 within the context of a low-level tactical operation until its failure caused a radical change in American strategic policy. In the fall of 1966, the design of tactical operations to achieve strategic objectives took center focus within the Hanoi policy deliberations.

General Nguyen Chi Thanh, one of a dozen premier leaders within the North Vietnamese structure, reviewed the course of the way in one of the interminable strategy sessions revered by his peers. Thanh was seated as one of a group around a long mahogany table on the ground floor of a stately French colonial house in the interior of North Vietnam. Here, in the mountains away from the routine American air strikes, the leadership could debate and decide policy in relative comfort.

Today was going to be particularly weighty as the issue was very simply, "How do we pursue the war?" The group was of approximately middle age. Most wore plain cotton uniforms or civilian clothes with open collars. Though there was a near total absence of rank, all were well aware of the acknowledged pecking order. Conversation followed a hierarchical scheme. All smoked cigarettes virtually incessantly and occasionally sipped cold tea from small porcelain cups with ceramic fly covers. Thanh, one of the more senior, was, however, younger than the rest. He was unusually large for a Vietnamese, a hint of his ancestral connections to Manchuria. By local standards he was almost fat and decidedly more jovial than the others. Occasionally, when he wanted to conduct a sidebar conversation out of either interest or boredom, he would lapse into French. As were virtually all the Vietnamese leaders in both North and South, Thanh was internally grateful for the French culture and used that venue to establish his superior place in society. Like the French, he tended to appreciate large events as a form of theater; no less in real life than on the stage. When it came his turn to speak, Thanh, as all good actors do, waited for the audience's undivided attention and then, assured of concentration, delivered his carefully calculated presentation in a deceptively casual and non-threatening manner.

The senior North Vietnamese leadership had secured a major but exhaustive victory over the French in 1954. They had consolidated their position in the North and had achieved major inroads in the South. By 1964, allied with, and supporting the indigenous South Vietnamese communists, they had almost achieved strategic and tactical superiority in the south. This was through a combination of patience and a willingness to absorb seemingly endless casualties. In a long way in a poor country, people were the most important and sometimes the only instrument available in the strategic tool kit.

The intervention of the Americans had reversed their successes and forced a readdress of tactics within the context of strategic objectives. Some of the leadership desired to carefully attrit the Americans over time with husbanded resources causing every battle to be a program of a strategic exhaustion—the tactical equivalent of *the death of a thousand cuts*. Eventually, the Americans, like the French, would reach a point of emotional and policy exhaustion that would exceed any residue of tactical superiority they may have acquired. The expense of maintaining the chase would exceed the value of capturing the prize. Patience and people would carry the issue. In this approach, casualties inflicted against the southern elements returned equal or greater value than those losses incurred. Commanders should seek opportunities to fight and bleed both sides.

The other view was that forces must be husbanded carefully against the great fire superiority of the Americans. Battles must be selectively chosen to provide the greatest possibility of success. This would translate into long-term strategic and moral superiority and place the north in a favorable position to conduct the final push against the south.

Ultimately, both views sought the same objective—the policy exhaustion of the United States. The former believed it could force such a condition earlier than the more patient strategy of the latter. General Nguyen Chi Thanh, as he paused to inhale his cigarette, espoused a variant of the former. With a mildly arrogant wave of the cigarette in his hand, he swirled the smoke about his wrist and stated with emphasis that not only did he have a strategic bias but, unlike many others, he had the experience, authority and organization to demonstrate the model action that would showcase his strategic view. The manpower would come from the 5th Viet Cong Division—a tactical instrument to execute his strategic vision. Several members demurred. Never had this group descended to unit-level discussions in developing strategic policy. The success of the leadership to this point had been in maintaining the capability to ignore any human element it had slaughtered on behalf of greater strategic interests. In Thanh's vision, the division was a bit player that could make the star—a tactical Yoric playing to a strategic Hamlet.

The term Viet Cong Division was recognized by all the members of the discussion group as a subterfuge. Most of the members were ethnic North Vietnamese who had never ventured further south than the Red River Delta. However, it was valuable to refer to the unit as Viet Cong—VC—emphasizing the political aspects of the struggle when it emerged in the south. Some of the VC were true southerners while others had extensive family ties below the 1954 Demarcation Line. Allowing the buzz and expletives to die down and their attention now assured, Thanh continued.

In the early portions of the communist general offensive in the south, just prior to the U.S. intervention, the local Viet Cong leadership was able to recruit substantial quantities of true Southern Vietnamese into their ranks. Fighting against South Vietnamese military forces unaided by significant American assets, these VC units were able to do better than hold their own. With the introduction of American forces and firepower, the indigenous elements were soon reduced to small units fighting to survive.

By 1966, the units were increasingly stocked with North Vietnamese recruits—a move not favorably received by the southern cadre who viewed the north with the same suspicion that the north viewed the Chinese. Nevertheless, survival required integration and acceptance insured a steady flow of people and supplies to maintain important local programs.

By the end of 1966, the north had established training camps for soldiers destined to replenish southern units. These were separate and distinct from drafts used to fill North Vietnamese army units. Dropping his voice for emphasis and carefully enunciating every point in short stark sentences, General Thanh now thrust to his main point which was to gain approval for the Big Battle Strategic Attrition viewpoint. He had selected a forming unit as his tactical instrument to make a strategic point. He believed it was but one of many such instruments that would have to be created in the time it took to convince the American public it could not win.

As Thanh explained to the Party policy makers, a well-orchestrated battle, designed to decimate South Vietnamese units in a very public way, would accelerate the policy of strategic exhaustion. The demonstrated inability of units, South Vietnamese or American, to overcome significant communist incursions, would eventually bankrupt the allied political base. While no one battle would achieve moral strategic victory, a series of such actions would counter-balance the tactical battle successes the American intervention had created. In Thanh's mind, the citizenship of the casualties was less important than the fact that they were casualties.

As the Commander of the Central Office of South Vietnam, COSVN, and responsible for the conduct of the war in the south, his viewpoint carried great weight in council; particularly because, to this point, he had said little in other discussions. Also, as most of the members knew, he was one of the few participants who actually routinely occupied a battlefield. After some desultory discussion and a lack of objection from the chairman of the group, General Hien, it was approved that Thanh would have his instrument and an opportunity to test his strategic view. With minimal follow-on discussions, the group approved the concept, making the southern battleground a theater for an American audience.

In the early spring of 1967, the conscripts for the 5th VC Division began gathering near Dien Bien Phu for extended training and outfitting. Here, they drew their weapons and uniforms and began forming into cohesive units. Training was delayed due to lack of cadre as members of other previously decimated units were filtered and coalesced in the Laotian sanctuaries—some had to return to local units engaged in the constant fighting against the U.S.-occupied tri-border area firebases or the intermittent siege operations in the A Shau Valley.

The site of the last French strategic defeat was ideal for training and assembly. It was close to Laos and rarely visited by American air strikes. The excellent road network established after the French occupation insured a steady stream of supplies from China as well as Laos and the western factory bases of North Vietnam. It was astride the principal road network that fed the operations in the south. Most importantly, from Thanh's viewpoint, it provided opportunities to filter the best of everything transiting in either direction. This was a strategy not universally agreed upon by all the local leadership.

The Party Commissar cadre strived to return the best remaining soldiers to the local fighting units as constant pressure on the Americans insured routine Western press publicity. General Thanh found himself in daily fights with the senior political leadership as he struggled to create a capability from drafted youth and the physically-exhausted survivors of decimated units now aged beyond their years.

By late April, the division, actually a reinforced regiment in strength, began its southward move. Thanh intentionally departed the Laotian area before the division was really prepared. But his logic was quite simple—a southern movement avoided the routine B-52 strikes that interrupted training and severely demoralized the draftees. By departing, he insured that what structure he had, would not be re-diverted by the political cadre and he reasoned that he could accumulate soldiers and cadre as he moved south. Of equal import, but a thought kept to himself, was that once he departed he was accountable only to Hanoi High Command and they had a lot on their minds. So long as he fed them daily messages and cultivated his accompanying commissars, he would be left alone.

The division was organized into three regiments with three battalions apiece. Each was equipped with basic infantry weapons ranging from AK-47s to heavy 51-caliber machine guns and 82mm mortars. The almost total absence of administrative overhead was common throughout the structure. Most communications were by courier and supplies were carried by the individual or brought by the endless ant army of laborers moving between the supply depots (referred to as Binh Trams) and the transient infantry base camps.

These units were composed of soldiers too old or too wounded to fight; entire units impressed into short-term carrying parties or coolies imported from the multitude of hill tribes that populated the length of the trail. Less visible in daylight but extremely active after dark, were hordes of trucks that moved the really large tonnage between Binh Trams to feed the insatiable appetite of the total effort. Despite the very basic nature of the army, Thanh's strategy of maintaining constant battlefield pressure demanded an infrastructure to sustain the campaign that would equal or exceed in efficiency most other existing armies.

The cadre were a mix of true VC and Northerners; soldiers were virtually all from the North. These cadre were hard, quality soldiers who had endured, survived, and possessed a deep residue of spirit that served them well. The constant rain of bombs and endless exposure to the elements in the roughest of jungle conditions had long ago filtered out the physically and mentally weak. What remained as Thanh's subordinate leadership knew very much what they were about.

As he had surmised, Thanh was able to accumulate strength as the unit moved down the trail. He intentionally selected the eastern-most of the many highway systems that sustained the war effort paralleling the border. This provided the opportunity to inspect every unit and organization that traversed the trail going into or out of South Vietnam. As he did so, Thanh diverted some elements into his own forces by confiscating equipment and supplies as he went.

When the division finally reached Binh Tram 42 in June, it numbered almost 2,000 personnel and was splendidly equipped in comparison with most communist units. Most important, from Thanh's perspective, was that the soldiers were fresh, well-fed, and had not undergone a direct air strike. In sum, he saw them as healthy idealists with high morale and little inkling of what lay ahead for them in this very ambitious and risky strategy. Now, as they reposed in the dappled shade of the western edge of War Zone D in Long Kanh Province, Thanh was anxiously awaiting the results of Comrade Nguyen Hu's carefully planned encounter.

3

The Beginning

Nguyen Hu carefully spread the brush until he could clearly see the soldiers. They were conducting their normal morning routine of cleaning the .50 calibers on top of the armored cavalry attack vehicles, or ACAVs as they were known, drinking coffee, and spreading their rain ponchos and poncho liners against the rays of the sun to dry off the evening's accumulated moisture. Small groups of men were listlessly talking and watching the sun slowly rise—already hot, steamy and enveloping—over the tanks and carriers of L Troop, 3d Squadron, 11th Armored Cavalry Regiment—the Cav.

The troop had drawn up in its normal laager position the night before and arranged itself for the evening. In the way of all soldiers and organizations through history, this unit had its manner of doing things and its accumulation of special baggage and accouterments that marked it as a combat unit. Much of its present routine would have been unacceptable in stateside garrison life, but was a matter of course at Grid Square PC 358254. Hu was aware of this and took advantage for his own ends. He had been studying this unit for some time and was confident of its reactions. In fact, the successful accomplishment of his plan depended upon its anticipated reaction.

The troop had been moving up Highway 20 all the previous week as part of a major road-clearing operation to connect Saigon with Dalat and the highlands in the North. K Troop's job was to act as advance security and to protect the Rome plow crews as they slowly worked their way north piercing tree trunks with the sharp angled blades and clearing the roadside jungle.

Hu had left his own base camp, deep in the jungle of War Zone D, and worked his way along familiar trails until he could track the armor elements at work. He selected overwatch positions in the hills that looked down on Highway 20 and carefully noted the rate of progress of the plows and estimated their evening halt position. Hu had guessed correctly last night and now took advantage of his insight.

The troop had avoided the open paddy field next to the village as he knew they would. This permitted him to enter the village after dark and to eat dinner and converse with the villagers. Following traditional American dislikes of co-locating with the population, the troop had occupied a partially cleared field near a bend in the road about 3 kilometers north of the village. The field was too small for the troop so the tanks and Rome plows drove in circles around the encroaching bamboo until an area of several hundred square meters had been cleared to bare laterite earth. The troop then moved to the center of the field and formed in a circle with the plows and support vehicles in the center. Between the leading edge of the armored personnel carriers—APCs—and tanks and the edge of the bamboo, there was now about 75 meters of open ground.

L Troop began its routine about an hour before dusk. The commander, a lieutenant, well-liked and respected, began to make his adjustments. Tanks and ACAVs alternated around the circle. Concertina barbed wire was spread about 20 meters in front of the vehicles and Claymore mines were emplaced behind sandbags within the protective canopy of the wire. Pairs of men, under the watchful eyes of squad leaders manning the 50-caliber cupola guns on the ACAVs, advanced into the green to string noise-maker cans on communication wires. This process took about 30 minutes and then the soldiers turned to their own individual tasks.

Each ACAV had its own beach umbrella and most also had lawn chairs and drink coolers. These were erected behind the vehicles whose ramps were now lowered for easy access. With the exception of the man in the cupola, the rest of the troop began to dissolve into small groups—writing letters, smoking, drinking homemade coffee, or talking. The lieutenant looked at his watch and the sky and began to talk into his radio handset. Hu knew this would happen and had left the laager area and returned to the village.

The first event came without warning. The villagers heard only a dull boom in the distance, followed by a large white cloud that appeared about 400 meters in the air near the laager position. The lieutenant made some comments into his handset, observed the next white cloud and then with a grunt of satisfaction, marked the final white burst on his map. He did this four times until all the cardinal points of the compass were covered. His artillery plots for the evening were now registered. The villagers asked Hu about this and he explained carefully what the Americans were doing. He had to be very elementary because even though they were familiar with the war itself and Americans in general, they had virtually no concept of technology or the tactics that it had developed.

The next event struck like a thunderclap. The villagers, though frightened, were considerably less so than they might have been because Hu had warned them it was coming. On a signal from the lieutenant, every weapon in the laager position began to fire. The tracers from the machine guns arced across each other and reached out into the sky and bamboo to disappear into time and foliage. The leaves rocked, swayed, and fluttered to the ground as main gun rounds from the tanks struck tree trunks, exploded wood, and sent shattered limbs crashing to earth. Interspersed among this cacophony, individual 40mm rifle grenades exploded with distinctive crumps and sent an oily black smoke snaking through the canopy. This entire sequence took less than 30 seconds to complete. The jungle and the night began to quickly descend upon the group and silence fell all around. The birds and lizards which had been frightened away by the firing, began to return and converse with one another. Bats began to make solitary arching swoops around the open field and mosquitoes swarmed around the warm odor-exuding human bodies.

The soldiers slowly ceased their conversations and began to fall asleep in their lounge chairs, the floors of the ACAVs, the interiors of the tanks or along the fenders, or in small hammocks strung between the corners of the ACAVs. Sleep in the laager position was always fitful at best. The temperature dropped only the slightest amount and the humidity remained the same. If it began to rain and thunder, everyone would be wakened and have to make shelter. The mosquitoes constantly swarmed and could be driven off with only marginal success. The issue repellent easily wore off and stung the eyes when mixed with sweat. The Pyrithiamine spray used under the mosquito net asphyxiated the occupant and provided only temporary relief.

Throughout the night, the troop retained its normal procedures. About every 15 minutes, a dull plunk would be heard, followed by a louder pop, followed in turn by a bright flash as a yellow-green flare burst high over the position. The light swayed and drifted with the winds at altitude and provided a wavering illumination of shifting shadows and substances to the men on guard. The flare would grow progressively duller until it suddenly terminated with a shower of sparks under its small white parachute. The area would then again be bathed in the inky black velvet night that characterized the land.

When the flare was expended from its carrying canister, the canister itself continued along its predictable arc to impact with the ground. In this case, its destiny with gravity caused it to enter the top of the canopied jungle growth. The metal cylinder, about 18 inches long and 155 millimeters wide, successively crashed through various limbs and leaves until, velocity expended, it came to rest on the soft, moist earth of the jungle floor. There, its edge contacting the wet earth, it exuded a light wisp of steam as it evened the temperature imbalance. A large candle bug warily paused at its lip, its antennas rapidly treading the air before it plunged inside the container looking for a new home or attracted by the sweet smell of cordite. The noise of the descending metal had shaken the local population and the birds had flown off with loud calls echoed by the lizards who scrambled to safe holes in tree trunks and limbs. With the noise now ended, the birds, who were circling, now returned to roost in silence once again. The guards noted all this and mentally returned to their boyhood memories of campfires and ghost stories and old horror movies. For a short while, each man was more alert than he had been. Something visceral had been activated within each. Hu was very familiar with all this and had fallen into a deep sleep just after the first flare had been fired.

The morning was not yet a fact when Hu woke. He quickly washed his face at the house well as the chickens pecked around the concrete well ring hoping to find some scrap that might have washed off. Hu, like all Vietnamese, was very modest and retained his black shorts as he soaped and rinsed his entire body. He had no towel so he simply shook himself off like a dog and walked into the house where the old woman had fixed him a hot glass of green tea. The glass was a shock to his fingers and he quickly guarded them with his cotton hat. Holding the glass between both hands, cradled inside the hat, he quickly consumed the tea and silently left after thanking the woman. She acknowledged the courtesy with a low grin that exposed her remaining teeth, almost black with years of accumulated betel nut stain.

Hu worked his way out of the village and followed a work trail that he knew would bring him close to the American position. The trail had been used by charcoal burners who had dug shelters to protect their product from the rains. About a kilometer and a half from the U.S. position, Hu stopped at a shelter and sat inside and waited for what he knew was coming. It came suddenly, virtually simultaneously with the early morning light.

The perimeter exploded in a crescendo of noise, light, and smoke. The weapons discharges of the previous evening were replayed again but with a larger chorus. The explosions, preceded by steel and wafts of cordite, coursed through the air and injured the soft jungle. This time, artillery and Claymores were added to the score and the site quickly became obscured with smoke, flame, and drifting jungle debris. The calls of birds and other creatures were lost in the background. Just as suddenly, it ceased, and with the exception of the sound of small fires feeding on the damaged residue, silence returned. Hu now left the sheltered charcoal stack, departed from the trail, and moved deftly on a straight azimuth to the laager site.

He stopped about 200 meters from the edge of the jungle and waited. He carefully located the wire and can noisemakers, lowered himself behind the outspread tree roots and waited. Within five minutes his intent came into view.

Three soldiers broke into the sun-fed dense green curtain that shields the perimeter of the true jungle. Pausing momentarily to rest from the exertions of clearing, they cautiously stepped inside a much different world.

The light, once hot and direct, was now obscured and filtered through the multiple layers of vegetation that towered above them. Occasional shafts of light broke through the top illuminating their beams with a bluish-green haze. Outside this world, noise and a sense of expanse ruled the senses. Here, the silence and confinement of a cloister reigned.

The trio stood momentarily fixed in the shifting patterns of dappling light as they adjusted their senses to the new conditions. Each had learned to plumb his primordial core very early upon arrival to the unit. Hearing and intuition became dominate factors of discernment that could be called upon very quickly to supplant the more common senses of twentieth-century civilization. That was why they were alive after several months in the bush. Though they could not articulate this transition, each was very respectful of the necessity to draw upon its strengths.

The first soldier was bare to the waist and immersed in a sheen of sweat. A machete was held loosely in a black-gloved hand. The leather tips had been cut off revealing water-dimpled fingertips. The cuffs of the gloves were ringed white with salt. Sweat rolled off his arm and streamed down the flat edge of the blade and collected in an expanding drip spot on the damp, rotten leaf mold. Already, leeches began to periscope their heads through the jungle floor and begin their rapid inchworm movements toward the new heat source.

The dancing colors of the jungle swayed across him. Alternating patches of white, blue, and green played in glistening dances across his torso. In his left hand he held an M-16 in a defensive gesture bisecting his left waist and right shoulder. The other soldiers were slightly behind him and fully dressed. One had no weapon and the other had a grenade launcher that he was holding with one hand and pointing to his lower right side. The unarmed man seemed to be in charge. Hu noted that they were more anxious than alert and continued to watch them without fear. After a pause, the unarmed man pointed toward the wire noisemaker and the three moved in a single file toward it.

Upon reaching the wire, the leader stood against while the other two men removed its two ends which were connected to tree branches. The cans fell to the earth with an audible clatter but the noise was quickly lost. The leader made a mental note to place the cans closer to the jungle edge next time. The wire was rapidly rolled up and the cans stuffed in a sandbag. Without hesitation, and with an air of relief, the three men rapidly returned to the light that beckoned them in the clearing.

As soon as Hu saw the men turn their back, he quietly but quickly followed directly in their path. He stayed about 15 feet behind them and waited on the rim of the forest as soon as they broke into the clearing. He waited until they progressed about halfway across the cleared area toward their tracks and then he boldly stepped out in the open ground, took three steps forward, and raised his hands and called out.

The laager position stood silent for a moment and then a collective scramble energized the entire scene. Shouts were sounded, magazines hastily inserted into weapons and soldiers not otherwise directly engaged stopped their activities to observe the cause of the noise.

The lieutenant, who had been sitting in his track reading a map and talking to his commander, looked out, saw the activity and moved immediately to the core of the scene. He placed his hand on top of a raised M-16 of a soldier next to him and shouted for everyone to hold fire.

The three soldiers that Hu was following looked first toward the noise emanating from their own positions and then, in a panic-stricken manner, directly behind themselves where their compatriots were pointing. As if charged by some form of mysterious telepathy, the three began to run as fast as they could to the safety of the circled steel. Hu slowly but deliberately followed in the vortex of their movement until he stood on the edge of the jungle barrier with his bare feet on the exposed red mud of the laager site. As the U.S. force shouted and moved with unfocussed energy, Hu stood stock still, breathed normally, and waited for calm to return.

Inside Hu's brain rested the information that he knew the Americans wanted to have. General Thanh had explained the plan and its details in the quiet solitude and peace of the Binh Tram base camp. He had walked for three days to arrive at this point and was confident that he would be successful. To this point, all had gone according to plan.

The lieutenant made a call on the radio and told his Kit Carson scout (KCS), a Vietnamese, to bring the man in the shorts and hat into the perimeter.

The KCS and two soldiers from the observation post at the wire gap moved toward Hu from the flank. The entire perimeter leaned forward and focused their weapons on the small, slight man now standing in the bright sunlight. With a word, the Americans stopped and dropped to a knee and pointed their weapons at Hu. Careful not to block either his guards' or the perimeter weapons' view of the standing man, the KCS stepped to the edge of the brush line and stopped a few feet from Hu's left side and began to speak.

For the first time since stepping through the jungle wall, Hu now shifted his focus from the perimeter to the scout. As he answered the man's questions, he fixed his gaze and tried to determine his countryman's origin and history. The scout spoke in a clear Hanoi dialect with none of the slurring common to the South. He guessed he was an NCO from an NVA unit that had been captured within the year.

Hu knew from his own unit's experiences that after capture, such people would volunteer to become scouts for the U.S. to avoid having to join the South Vietnamese Army. Occasionally, a scout would defect back to the North with good information on U.S. operations. Usually, before a large assault on U.S. field units, Hu's commanders would assemble ex-scouts and debrief them in great detail on U.S. security habits and dispositions. Once, he saw an ex-scout sit with General Thanh in his command post and analyze U.S. actions as the attack took place. General Thanh used this information to make adjustments. Still, firepower often overcame the best of intelligence.

The scout placed Hu at the head of their small column and walked the group back to the perimeter. At the wire gap, the lieutenant met them and instructed the scout to interrogate Hu in the center of the perimeter. Soldiers eyed Hu with a combination of anxiety and interest.

For most, this was the first time they had seen the enemy in any form other than dead. Here, they became intensely curious about the life and energy of Hu and tried to look inside the man that they envisioned had so often shot and mortared them. "He looks so small." "He looks so thin." As fear and anxiety waned and curiosity grew, the soldiers began to lose their intensity and broke into desultory conversation and smoke-laden discussions and reflections on past encounters.

The scout told Hu to sit down and offered him a cigarette that Hu promptly took with great appreciation. It was an American Pall Mall and much better than the tobacco provided by army supplies or the occasional Ruby Queen taken from dead South Vietnamese Army personnel. Hu sucked at the cigarette and carefully reflected on each question posed before responding. He also smiled and took on a somewhat pleading tone in his voice. It was important that Hu transmit a sense of scared sincerity. The guards, unable to understand the conversation, stood aside with a mixed ambivalence somewhere between duty and curiosity.

Slowly, the picture was painted. Hu told the scout that he had news of a new VC base camp near the Dong Nai River. He would be willing to lead soldiers there. He had a sister in the Delta and wanted to visit her and quit fighting. The scout narrated all this to the lieutenant and the judgment was that Hu was speaking the truth.

Almost as an afterthought, the guards tied Hu's hands and sat him behind the command track after lighting another Pall Mall for him. The scout had told them that Hu was a deserter from the VC and had family in the Delta. Like most soldiers viewing a helpless non-threatening human on the battlefield, the guards began to view him as a victim of circumstances rather than the enemy. Hu was perceptive enough to sense this and went to some lengths to perpetuate his persona of submission and relief.

All of this the scout passed to the lieutenant who dutifully transmitted the analysis to his senior on the radio and waited for instructions. Hu, now squatting on his heels, hands behind his back, still retained his normal breathing pattern and spoke politely to the scout. Instead of an interrogation, however, the discussion covered family and politics and the condition of each other's family. Neither Hu nor the scout felt any particular enmity toward the other. After several generations of warfare, uniforms and situations were simply conditions of the moment, subject to rapid change. Only death brought a halt to the constant mixing of choices.

Soon, a helicopter passed over the laager position and circled slowly. A soldier threw out a green smoke grenade and the color began to grow in billowing waves through the sky. The helicopter began to lose both altitude and air speed as it slipped gracefully toward the smoke. About 20 feet off the earth, the wind effect of the blades took hold and the smoke was beaten into the ground, swirled outside the arc of the blades and curled back in on top of them, rapidly dissipating into nothingness.

With the blades slowly turning, Hu was moved toward the helicopter by two soldiers. This time he had a cloth over his head. He was placed on the cold beaded aluminum floor of the helicopter and sandwiched between the guards. He heard the RPM quickly rise and could feel the effect of the lessening pull of gravity as the aluminum bird slowly broke with the earth, made a shuddering quarter turn and began to gather speed and altitude. For the first time Hu was apprehensive. This was the first time he had not experienced what his mind had foreseen.

4

The Interrogation

The helicopter arrived at the 11th ACR base camp amidst a swirl of yellow smoke that coursed over and through the blades. Joined with the loose laterite dust of the ground, the air beat and abraded against Hu's face. Unable to see due to the cloth covering his eyes, Hu could sense the wind and smell the mixture of smoke and jet fuel as it filled his nose. Shortly before the helicopter landed the guards, sensing the probability of higher headquarters officers accompanying the escort, had placed the mask over his eyes with some gestures of apology. They had enjoyed talking with him through the Kit Carson scout and did not perceive him as a danger as he had, unarmed and voluntarily, presented himself.

Hu cultivated this perception with his abject appearance and submissive personality. He rarely looked directly into the interrogator's eyes and when he did so it was always with a long imploring childlike look. When offered a cigarette, which was virtually continuously as soldiers sought to get inside the mind of a Vietnamese, Hu took it with a grateful gesture of clasping his hands together in a prayer-like form and touching his nose in the traditional Asian gesture of thanks.

Over the course of his incarceration by the cavalry troop, virtually every soldier passed by his location and stopped to listen to the discussions. At one point, Hu had indicated a desire to relieve himself and was accompanied to the edge of the perimeter. During his passage through the center of the perimeter, the troop commander noticed that he was more of a drum major leading his band than a prisoner and ordered that his wrists be rebound when he returned to the inner circle.

This act was done apologetically by the guards and with as much comfort as possible under the circumstances. The wrists were loosely tied and his eyes were covered with the large green wound bandage found in individual aid kits. After that, conversation died down and Hu stoically squatted on his haunches with his back against the APC. Shortly after, the helicopter appeared.

As predicted, several officers arrived with the helicopter. They jumped off and moved directly to the troop commander who was standing next to Hu.

They asked the commander some perfunctory questions and then posed with Hu and the troop commander while the helicopter crew chief took pictures. The key portion of the trip accomplished, they moved to the aircraft and gestured for the POW to join them.

Hu stood just inside the primary rotor wash, dwarfed by the much-larger Americans at his side. He leaned against one to brace himself against the buffeting winds. The American responded by placing his hand on Hu's shoulder and leaning toward him. From a distance, it appeared that the large and small man were engrossed in a deep and personal conversation.

Hu was led to the helicopter and lifted onto the floor by the guards. The door gunner placed handcuffs on Hu and attached a short length of chain with snaps at both ends to the cuff chain and a large aluminum ring on the floor. This forced Hu to sit cross-legged in the center of the aircraft with his back to the cockpit. The two visiting officers sat on either side of him and took pictures of the cavalry perimeter as the helicopter slowly gained altitude.

Hu had expressed considerable anxiety about this phase of his instructions to his handler/instructor. He was aware of helicopters and understood the concept but was uncertain as to how the helicopter would relate to him. As a rural peasant raised in an Anamist family, the relationship between man and his instruments was crucial. Hu could see the analogy between a bird and an airplane—both had wings. A helicopter had nothing like that. Therefore, it was subject to violating natural laws and could cause his death.

Hu was also aware of the rumors that Americans interrogated prisoners by throwing them out of helicopters. In his mind, he was relatively certain that some of the Vietnamese left the helicopter because their presence violated the natural order of things.

The colonel who had briefed Hu on his mission was a lapsed Catholic from the North and a mathematician by previous occupation. He was selected by General Thanh, the head of all communist operations in the South, because of his history in successfully transmitting complex concepts and instructions to simple, near-illiterate soldiers. Thanh recognized that for this mission to be successful, Hu, the messenger, would have to be elaborately coached and conditioned without a hint of preparation evident to Hu's intended captors. This required a messenger who possessed not only great simplicity and presence but also absolute unfeigned sincerity. Concurrently, the colonel must be skilled enough to convey the necessary facts and innuendos without conditioning the messenger to appear to be a robotic transmitter of prepared information.

The colonel tried to reason Hu through his concerns using an explanation of mechanics but only partially succeeded. The colonel reported this partial failure as a long-term success as Hu would present himself with an air of true fright and unsophistication and would probably express that to his captors. Such a simple person could not be expected to lie about such important information as he would be presenting to the Americans.

To allay concerns about the rumored interrogation techniques, they agreed that the best solution was for Hu to volunteer some tantalizing tidbits of information, but, from the perspective of a not-very-bright laborer. The colonel was aware that the Americans could only be sufficiently convinced if Hu was allowed to tell his story to the higher echelons. At all costs, Hu had to insure that he wasn't questioned and released by his initial captors.

For several days, the colonel and Hu went over his instructions. Tell them this. Withhold that. Make them draw it out. If they show you a map, do this. If they don't give you a map, ask for paper and draw one in simplified form. If they hit you, do this. If a senior man enters, say this. American rank was reviewed as well as the order of battle of the American forces. As a final preparation, Hu was given the names of several trustworthy Vietnamese that worked at the 11th Cav base camp.

All of these discussions were held inside a newly built base camp. This insured that Hu could draw the camp from memory and could accurately describe the stage of construction and its appearance—sure to be object of great interest to the South Vietnamese and their allies. As a final step, the colonel had a squad of infantry walk Hu from the base camp to all the likely landing zones in the area. In the event that he was asked to act as a scout, Hu could correctly trace the ground route. All of these things passed through Hu's mind as he settled in the aircraft and the rhythmic vibration of the helicopter coursed through his body from the floor.

After a relatively short time, as judged by Hu, he could sense the helicopter slowing down and losing altitude. He was pushed as if by some unseen force that uplifted his body from the floor. In the short course of the flight, Hu began to feel at ease with the machinery as the warm air and the rhythmic vibration helped him overcome his anxiety. As the helicopter came to a halt and he again smelled the hot mixture of grass, dust, and diesel, he mentally rehearsed his lines.

Two military policemen released the tie chain from his handcuffs and lifted him out of the helicopter. He was placed on the ground, grasped by both arms, and propelled some distance away from the noise and into a cool dark space.

His blindfold was removed and his hands released. He found himself in a large room sitting at a table. Across from him were several men. Two were Vietnamese in civilian clothes and the rest were Americans. He was offered a cigarette and asked seemingly-indulgent, innocuous questions by the Americans through the Vietnamese interpreters.

He was asked about his background, biographical data, schooling, family associations, and political allegiances. As instructed, he indicated no political affiliations, simply a desire to remain a farmer and avoid political issues for the good of his family. Then, the questioning became more direct.

Questions were fired in a trip-hammer form regarding where he was found, what he was doing, how he came upon the Americans, why he turned himself in, what he hoped to gain?

Hu patiently and carefully answered each in a slow and halting manner. It was important that he present the image of a scared peasant of average- to below-average intellect. On the several occasions when the Vietnamese verbally assaulted him, he cowered, hung his head and whimpered his protestations. The Americans would intervene and adjust the technique using the "good cop/bad cop" approach.

After some time, Hu judged about a half-hour, the group began to approach the meat of the subject. Hu was asked to relate how he managed to reach the cavalry perimeter. He recounted how he was impressed into a labor force by the VC from his farm near Dinh Quan. He was taken through War Zone D by boat and then walked to a bend in the river. There, he joined others and began to clear a base camp. He described the construction. He made a passing reference to the local camp leadership and identified the commander as a major, an appropriate rank for a reinforced company position. He indicated that he had been told of other similar camps being constructed but that they were on the western side of the Dong Nai River. This last portion clearly aroused everyone's interest and a map was produced.

In the Americans' enthusiasm to solicit more information, they overrode sound interrogation techniques as their translators were overshadowed by the rapid-fire questioning of an almost direct dialogue approach, losing any opportunity to pursue their own line of questioning or intuitive validation. This was an important shift as Hu was well aware; given sufficient time, the Vietnamese could ferret out the holes in his story. It was important to get out the key information and to solicit action before he lost the Americans' attention and interest level and was turned over to the Vietnamese.

Hu took the proffered map and asked that his village be indicated. Next, he asked that the river be identified. His next question was to request the position of the sun against the village in the early morning, the time he said he was taken by the VC. One of the Americans placed a flashlight, symbolizing the sun, east of the village and Hu began to trace a route from the village to the river. His finger, dirty and cracked, then traced the river south until he came to a large oxbow bend. Here, at the point where the bow exposed itself to the north, he stopped his finger. This, he indicated was where the boat stopped and the camp began.

The map reference number was jotted down and a phone call made to the Regimental Operations Center. From there, the reference number was passed to the Aerial Reconnaissance Company that immediately launched a sortie to check the area. By this time, Hu's trainer had required that a dugout canoe be tied to a tree by the bank leaving just the long pipe-covered extension of the propeller shaft exposed. He also insured that several trees were felled making a small but discernible gap in the canopy. Neither of these would be spotted by a casual observer, but to the trained eye of an experienced pilot, they would be noted.

As he described the base camp, Hu indicated that he could probably lead the Americans back to it by retracing his route. This effectively ended the interrogation as he was then moved, this time absent cuffs and blindfold, to a jeep. He was placed in the back with a Vietnamese interpreter and driven off to the regimental command post. There, he was deposited under the shade of a banana tree with an MP and the interpreter while the senior American interrogator briefed the commander.

After a short while, the commander and the interrogator emerged from a side door. The commander, a large burly man, eyed Hu and asked him if he could retrace his path. Hu responded with an appropriate mix of fear and confidence that he could. The commander turned away and with his cigar, indicated that Hu was to join a battalion resting in the shade of a rubber plantation several kilometers to the south. He then turned back into the building and reached for a telephone.

5

The Plan

The phone call reached the command center of the American Advisory compound in the province capitol of Xuan Loc, approximately 95 kilometers northeast of Saigon. The compound was a typical facility of the time reflecting a mixture of previous French occupants, American-packaged construction, and Vietnamese variations. The original French house quartered the officers. A tennis court had been reconditioned to the side of a wooden fabricated mess hall and a large antenna tower sprang from the center of the area like a giant orange Christmas tree, absent the foliage. Directly beneath the antenna was a large square building half-in and half-out of the ground constructed of sandbags, concrete, and creosoted timbers—this was the central communications facility. Surrounding the assemblage was a cyclone fence topped by concertina and ringed with bunkers and sandbagged watchtowers.

The senior American, an older colonel near retirement age, was playing tennis and arrived in the cool concrete communications center dripping with sweat, still holding his racquet. He took the military phone and listened intently to the cavalry commander. He asked a few questions and then hung up the phone. His operations officer, a profusely sweating, overweight officer with drooping salt-and-pepper moustache, was waiting in the cool venturi-generated wind of the tunnel that led into the bunker. He started to inquire as to the nature of the call but was cut short by the colonel's rapid-fire orders. The pair then walked quickly to the tennis court where they halted by the shaded bench and waited for the players to finish the point. Several volleys ensued and then a return hit the net and fell to the baking asphalt. At that juncture, the colonel stepped into the sunlight and gestured respectfully to the player moving to retrieve the ball. Brigadier General Tanh was going to have to make some decisions.

General Tanh commanded the 18th Vietnamese Army Division headquartered in Xuan Loc. The 18th had a notoriously bad reputation. In fact, it was originally designated the 10th but underwent a number change when its performance lived up to the national slang term of Number Ten—the worst possible. To this point, Tanh had pursued a policy of non-engagement to avoid further national embarrassment. In the strange ethics of the war, ability to avoid losing was second only to winning. Tanh excelled in not losing by insuring that his elements carefully picked and chose their engagements and then only after the greatest deliberation and preparation. Comrade Hu's appearance on the scene was about to upset Tanh's program.

At the senior levels of Vietnamese military leadership, of which Tanh was a peripheral member, the logic of professional conduct was well-established. The arrival of the Americans had provided an opportunity for the army to retreat to the populated areas while the Americans were encouraged to engage the communists as far forward as possible. Meanwhile, the Vietnamese military would associate with the population, ensuring political compliance while developing its internal resources through the U.S. assistance plans.

Tanh had played this strategy well in Xuan Loc, in part, due to his ability to cooperate with the Americans on their insatiable desire to acquire land for troop basing and authority to violate cultivated farmland on operations. His cooperation, seemingly provided after great deliberation, had resulted in a wealth of American units either basing near Xuan Loc or routinely transiting his command. In either case, he gained prestige. The area became more secure and the local economy increased at all levels.

In addition to Tanh's military position, he was also the Province Chief of Long Kanh, of which Xuan Loc was the capital. The position meant that he was responsible for the civil management of the province in addition to his more traditional military role. As a province and as a capital, the command had been the moribund flotsam of a war that swirled and burned along its periphery, often touching but never burning the population with great intensity.

To this point, Tanh had been a great success from everyone's view. The population prospered, the Americans got what they desired with minimal difficulty, and the communists could be assured of minimal harassment.

Historically, the position of the province was equally ambivalent. In part, this was due to its position along the primary national artery, Highway One, the only true sinew of governmental infrastructure that bound the nation. Coursing from the southern tip of Vietnam, winding its way through Saigon, the political and economic capital of the south, the highway traced its way across the nation, pausing in Bien Hoa to move west through Xuan Loc, before it abruptly broke east to join the sea and continue its path north until it halted at Quang Tri, the northernmost city at the edge of the 1954 Demarcation Line. Originally packed clay, the French converted it to concrete and now the Americans had paved key stretches with ant armies of green Morison-Knudsen machinery.

The French had appreciated the position of the province and its well-drained flat land and communications infrastructure. In the 1920s they had developed four major rubber plantations astride the highway that now covered several hundred square kilometers of the province. Each plantation followed a similar pattern.

The central facility was composed of several two-story plaster houses with broad open windows and Spanish tile roofs. Patios girdled the lower floor and were covered by small roofs and cooled by ceiling fans. Later, pools were added to accommodate the children on their return from schools in France for the summer. Peripheral buildings were similarly constructed to house the immediate labor force and industrial necessities of the establishment. Adjacent to the primary house, a garage usually housed a Citroen or Diane to be used by the household for its frequent diversions to the comfortable colonial infrastructure of traditional Saigon or the cool air of Dalat or Vung Tau during the height of the dry season.

The living facilities were located in the center of the plantation with only the dimmest visibility from the highway. From experience, the inhabitants had learned to disguise their entranceway to guard against drunk or inquisitive armed travelers. Only at the last hundred or so yards did the road become the splendid original construction with sweeping gravel-laid curves and mature plantings of European poplars prefacing the traffic circle that announced the primary house.

From the air, the plantation cores were readily identifiable against the sea of blue green rubber and jungle that spread below. The local American pilots had named each colony and used them as reference points on their daily reconnaissance missions. New scout pilots were invariably introduced to the area by low passes over the central buildings. Since the American aircraft had arrived in Xuan Loc, the female French had learned to restrict their sunbathing to an undesirable amount of clothing.

The French rubber colonies were self-sufficient, quiet enclaves protected by their trees and accommodating abilities. Rarely did the French venture into Xuan Loc, instead preferring to conduct serious shopping in the more comfortable environs in the heart of the older sections of Saigon. Occasionally, a Diane would be seen parked in the Xuan Loc market driven by a Frenchman in shorts, sandals, cotton shirt, and smoking a pipe or cigarette. He rarely spoke with the Americans and dealt strictly and quickly with one of the Chinese or Indian merchants that dominated the local commerce.

Each plantation covered dozens of square kilometers. Supporting colonies were built throughout the acreage fanning from the core to house the workers and necessary industrial support. They were connected with roads developed through the core of the industry, the trees themselves. Here, the labor force, though part of the Vietnamese population, was able to isolate itself from the war around. It was if the concentration of trees acted as a defense from the physical and social forces that swirled around them.

Initially, the jungle had been ruthlessly cleared by the French from the outer periphery of Bien Hoa to Xuan Loc and then some portions to the east. This was an area of more than 160 square kilometers. The magnitude of this initiative could only be partially appreciated on the ground. From the air, the immensity of the development was clear. Even so, the light taupe leaves of the rubber trees seemed small and inconsequential against the sea of darker green marking the surrounding jungle which lapped at every side.

The clearing process traced the National Highway, which served as the delineation point for each plantation. Now, many years later, the rubber trees had grown to full maturity and economic return. Before the Americans began clearing the edge of the highway, it was possible to drive north from Bien Hoa almost to the sea and rarely be struck by direct sunlight. Instead, the flashing stroboscopic effect of the filtered sunlight fell with brilliant dancing light across the transiting vehicle. Stopped at the edge of the road, travelers could cool themselves in the shade of these immense plantings and relax in the silence and coolness of the encompassing umbrella above.

From any angle of view under the canopy, the trees, planted in engineer-precise rows, disappeared into nothingness adhering to the finest perspective lesson of Renaissance artists. The trees rose smoothly with straight creamy green trunks to a height of more than 100 feet. Only at the very last 10 to 20 feet, did the trunk erupt into limbs and leaf-covered branches. The ground underneath was kept clear by the workers, which heightened the effect of the vastness of the undertaking. This aspect was used to good advantage by all antagonists.

Due to the plantations' proximity to the National Highway, they became lodestones for transiting elements or those intending to disrupt the flow. The long clear rows made rapid transit possible and the breadth of cultivation insured excellent security. Communist units, like the scout planes, used the facilities as reference points in their movements and often stopped for succor at the nodes of civilization that sprang from the cultivated interior. American forces, knowing that the enemy rarely occupied the plantations, chose to watch the perimeters and only occasionally scouted under the canopy. The Vietnamese Army, conditioned by years of experience and unstated appreciation for the French, maintained social contacts with the ex-patriots but rarely trespassed.

The owners, both local managers and foreign investors, took great steps to insure the maintenance of their development. The plantations became a neutral ground, to be used but not abused. The communists routinely used the outlying villages for information and sustenance. Wounded could be accommodated in small numbers by local families and treated by the plantation staff. The French would not deny this support or directly acknowledge its existence. However, they paid taxes to both sides and as much as possible accommodated the present power of the moment to retain anonymity and neutrality.

The working population isolated itself from the surrounding realities. Rarely would anyone see them under the canopy. Occasional glimpses of a pair of rubber collectors could be snatched as they worked their trees, slashing the trunks in diagonal rows and collecting the milky white sap in tin tanks following small tractors or ox carts. Once they spotted intruders, the workers would quickly turn and fade away into the nothingness of retreating perspective. Sometimes, when a U.S. unit halted by the road, a small group of children would gather in the shadows and then dart like fish in a pond to gather candy and cigarettes from the soldiers and just as quickly disappear into the shadows. This island of tranquility, convenience, and accommodation was also part of General Tanh's responsibility but not of great personal interest.

Tanh had been increasingly aware of the sensitivity of his situation and of his province in particular. The activities of the past year had served notice that his policy of non-engagement would soon be rendered inappropriate. Quickly leaving the American compound in his jeep after talking to the Americans, he whirled through the central traffic circle en route to his headquarters.

From the traffic circle, it would be possible to consider the sensitivity of General Tanh's situation specifically and that of the province as a whole. To the north, Highway 20 snaked its way through the mountains to the Second Corps border where it connected Saigon with Dalat—the national holiday site and home of the military academy. This ground was conceded to the communists except the highway, which was mutually transited as a matter of joint convenience. Tanh had established several outposts among the villages that dotted the road but had insured they restrict their operations by stocking them with local untrained youths and obsolete weapons.

To the east was the vast trackless jungle that abruptly ended at the Pacific Ocean. In that sea of vegetation, the communists had established rest centers and supply points as they moved to circumvent the Saigon complex from the east and south. Through clever negotiation, Tanh had managed to cause the American 11th Armored Cavalry to establish its principal base camp between Xuan Loc and the eastern jungle, thereby protecting that open flank.

West was the area designated War Zone D. This spanned the 130 kilometers between Xuan Loc and the Cambodian border. Acknowledged as a communist stronghold, it was never visited by Vietnamese Army elements and only rarely by Americans. Even then, they ventured forth only in great force and for the shortest period of time. This complex provided support for communist forces transiting toward operations near Saigon or moving away from more aggressive American operations to the south.

South of the traffic circle, the road headed in a near-straight line to Saigon. This artery tied the nation together in many ways and required the utmost sensitivity in management. Tanh constantly maintained forces along the highway but in a circumspect manner. When possible, his elements operated with cooperating American units. This insured that VC units would avoid contact and he would gain credit with the Joint General Staff for mutual operations. When such an arrangement was not possible, army units were restricted to a distance of no more than a kilometer from the road. At night, they were instructed to laager at key road intersections with police outposts that provided some modicum of protection. This was a policy that was well-received by Tanh's subordinate elements.

Xuan Loc was not considered an important location by the Vietnamese government despite its strategic location. Tanh had been assigned to the division and the province as a reward for political loyalty. It was not expected that he would accomplish much besides anonymity. To this point, he had met all expectations while improving his local situation.

Tanh had quickly seen that the key to personal success lay in maintaining low visibility externally while adroitly managing local conditions. He had managed, through accommodations and cultivation, to attract the positioning of a number of small U.S. units to the city area. The large American advisory compound, a heavy artillery battery and its parent headquarters, a scout plane unit at the airfield and a construction engineer unit, were all evidence of his agreeableness. He excelled at assisting U.S. units when they desired to operate across the rich cultivated Chinese-owned land that lay north and west of Xuan Loc. In return for cooperation, the Americans would volunteer necessary local construction and amenities. A new market place, school, hospital, and refurbished division headquarters quickly followed Tanh's negotiations.

With the communists, Tanh adopted a policy of selective accommodation. He did not conduct aggressive or quick operations. His programs were noted for their deliberate planning and exhaustive preparation. This provided the maximum opportunity for the local VC infrastructure to develop intelligence and insure avoidance. To the Americans, he professed the necessity for quality planning as he and other officers had been taught at U.S. military schools.

Within a year of Tanh's assumption of command, Xuan Loc's economy markedly improved. The presence of the Americans provided both security and economic infusion. The de facto accommodation with the communists further insured the tranquility of the immediate area and they reciprocated with disguised shopping expeditions for their needs through second parties. Comrade Hu's invasion into this carefully created neutral zone could prove difficult.

The 18th Division headquarters was housed in what was previously a French hospital. It was arranged in a long U-shape with a two-story administration building as the base. The staff sections fanned out along the legs with American advisors and their counterparts interspersed like checkerboard squares. Large floor fans stood outside the doors of the principal staff and smaller fans rotated in the casemate windows of lesser officers and NCOs. With the exception of the national flags, it would be impossible to tell the difference between this and that of the previous French effort.

Tanh strode into the primary briefing room with a retinue of Americans trailing in his vortex. They all took seats at the foot of the large briefing map while Tanh retreated to his office to place a telephone call.

After some pause, the phone connected with a particularly important friend of Tanh on the Joint General Staff. Tanh relayed what he had been told by the Americans and the proposition that had been suggested by the cavalry commander. While the American colonel had suggested that Tanh conduct a search for the new base camp reported by Hu, Tanh thought it more prudent to support an American reconnaissance with visible but distanced Vietnamese support.

He noted that the area was in War Zone D and beyond any existing artillery support and could result in embarrassing consequences. Unfortunately, the cavalry colonel, taken by the significance of Hu's information, had reported his proposition to the American headquarters in Saigon, which promptly supported the concept to the senior Vietnamese leadership. Tanh would have no choice. His elements would have to take the lead. Tanh attempted to dissuade the speaker at the other end but was quickly cut off. Hanging up the phone, Tanh strode into the briefing room, determined to make the best of a bad situation.

6

Choices

The briefing room was contained in the remains of what once had been an elegant French colonial salon room. The ceiling was high and the room quite deep. In shade, it would have been cool and restful. Now, in its military garb, it was bright, hot and not at all attractive. It looked like what it had become, a dusty seedy caricature of its previous grace and quality. While the ownership covered up the reduction in elegance with intensity and energy, it never quite compensated for the shift in class; much like the new rich acquiring a grand home from old wealth.

The mahogany paneling had been stripped on the front and back revealing a flat puce-colored plaster now adorned with maps and charts. The remaining paneling on the sides had been tacked and scratched by a thousand campaign planning aids that spanned the history from the Japanese occupation to the discussion of the day. The windows, once elegantly shuttered in thick casemated walls, were now opened to the fitful air. The shutters, long since removed, now served as table tops along the side of the room. At the rear, two large American floor fans raged helplessly against the tropical torpor.

General Tanh strode into the room and sat down at his center chair. It was a large red divan covered in ersatz leather. An identical chair was to his right. This was normally reserved for the senior American advisor or distinguished guests. Today, the usual occupant had offered his place to the cavalry commander and seated himself to Tanh's left. Between the two red chairs, a small wooden table held two large glasses of iced tea that had been covered with a Chinese porcelain lid to discourage the constantly buzzing entourage of flies. Due to General Tanh's lateness, the glasses had condensed a great deal of moisture, which streamed down the glasses and puddled together forming a small pool of refreshment for the flies that now encircled it.

Tanh and his staff were habitually well-dressed and polished. The Americans reflected a variety of conditions. The senior advisor was well-starched and polished reflecting his desire to emulate his counterpart as well as to underscore his proximity to laundry and boot service. The cavalry colonel appeared somewhat worse for wear. His fatigues were well-rumpled from sweat as was his equipment, which he had to remove to comfortably sit in the deep divan. All the officers around the front row, American and Vietnamese, were well-scrubbed reflections of their local leadership. To the rear of the conclave, six Americans, clearly out of place, stood inquisitively leaning forward, straining to hear the proceedings over the roar of the fans. These were the cavalry colonel's staff, charged with turning the meeting into meaningful orders upon its conclusion.

The staff briefers, Vietnamese and American, stood behind their podiums and nervously fiddled with their papers while the leading personalities exchanged pleasantries. Officers displaced from their traditional positions bumped back their subordinates, which was reflected as a continuous ripple of shuffling seats until all was quiet. Tanh turned to the Vietnamese briefer and nodded.

The briefer, following the precise sequence charted on the podium to his front, went through the mechanical litany of presentation. At the conclusion of each paragraph, he would halt and allow his American counterpart to describe the same issue in English. Today, however, the presentation was not traditional.

The staff did not have a chance to digest the information and to develop it to a point of satisfaction. A great deal of the issue was unknown. The intelligence had come from the Americans and could not be corroborated or verified. Hu, the source, was in a rubber plantation under American control and the usual town sources were ignorant. In sum, the slow, methodical Kabuki dance of presentation was more speculation than developed intelligence. What was not speculation was the final presentation of available forces and the necessity of Tanh to select one or more of them so the cavalry colonel could be on his way. In approximately half the time of a normal morning brief, the presentation ended and Tanh was left to develop the situation.

He turned to the colonel and in excellent English, asked for his views. The colonel, rising from his chair and pulling his sweat-soaked fatigue shirt over his belt line, moved to the large map at their front and withdrew a telescoping pointer from his pocket. Speaking in a moderate, confident voice, he indicated on the map all the locations Hu had mentioned and then traced Hu's sojourn from his village to the VC base camp. He then discoursed on Hu's information with a tone that conceded the points as fact rather than speculation. He concluded with a review of the steps he had taken to place his forces at Tanh's disposal to exploit this situation. A polite gauntlet had been dropped. While this didn't register with the Americans, it was immediately sensed by the Vietnamese. A decision would have to be reached now that could not be politely avoided.

Tanh smiled and thanked the colonel for his presentation. Reaching over to his glass, he removed the lid and sipped it, careful to hold the base with a handkerchief to catch the moisture. He replaced the lid on the glass and asked the operations officer to review the available forces.

At this moment, Xuan Loc had only two operational forces available—the 48th Regiment of his division and the 52nd Ranger Battalion, a corps force that resided near Xuan Loc. Neither were satisfactory choices by Tanh's method of computation.

The 48th was the city security. Its soldiers were notoriously poor performers and the officers were riddled with politics and influence. If the unit was to take the lead, its ineptitude would quickly be recognized by the Americans and reported to Saigon. Tanh would be held accountable for choosing them as well as for their performance. Worse, Tanh might have an internal rebellion on his hands from the regimental officers if they felt they might be at serious personal risk. The phone lines to friends in Saigon would be continuously busy.

The Rangers presented an equally difficult case. As a corps asset, they technically did not work for him though he knew he could gain acquiescence in their use from Saigon. The Rangers were extremely good fighters but equally bad citizens. They were composed of the racial and cultural outcasts from a highly rigid class system that neurotically rejected any non-ethnic South Vietnamese. Much like the initial black levees in the American Civil War, the Rangers were officered by the socially acceptable to lead the unacceptable.

Raised on a tradition of rejection, the Rangers, peopled from hill tribes, Cambodians, Nungs, Chams and Laos, routinely acted as outlaws when returned to polite Vietnamese society. Thieving and banditry against the Vietnamese was a socially acceptable behavior form when returned from the field. Accordingly, the Rangers spent a disproportionate amount of time in the field compared to others. Ironically, this was their salvation as they learned to fight intelligently and with great skill against forces much larger and better equipped. Much like Geronimo had done against the cavalry, the Rangers did against the VC despite the best efforts of their senior leadership to get rid of them.

Much as Tanh would have liked to use them, the employment of the Rangers created a potentially serious set of problems. If they should become endangered, the 48th might have to come to their rescue, assuring its own exposure. Should the Rangers be successful, Tanh might be criticized by Saigon for not allowing traditional Vietnamese units to win the fight. Worse, if the Rangers won a major struggle, the Americans would seek to use them more often, reducing Tanh's influence and robbing the division of an important source of equipment and supplies.

Tanh reflected for a moment and then walked to the briefing stage, halting in front of the map. Carefully, he stood fully erect and faced the room. His hands were clenched around his swagger stick, which was perpendicular to his thighs. He swung the polished brass tip forward and slapped it against the list of forces under his control. While looking steadily at the list, avoiding any eye contact, he announced that the division operation, supported by the Americans, would be led by the 48th Regiment supplemented by the Rangers. This brought a nervous shuffling of feet and a thin hum of whispers until he completed his thought. The regimental headquarters would deploy forward to join the Americans. The Rangers as the lead force would make the initial insertion and "develop the situation." Once engaged, the regiment and the cavalry would accomplish the primary task, destroying the VC force. On that short summary, he swung off the stage and strode directly down the center aisle without acknowledging anyone. His movement had been so abrupt and without warning that many were not able to rise to attention before he had cleared the room and entered his office with a loud slam of the door.

Tanh satisfied himself that he had accomplished the best of a bad situation. The 48th was nominally in charge and could take credit for a victory without exposing itself. The Rangers would be properly subordinate to the division and regardless of outcome could probably be hidden from publicity. The Americans would be happy as he had committed on paper all the forces he had available. Should the Rangers get into serious trouble, Tanh could play the role of the prudent commander and back off commitment of more forces until the situation was better developed; i.e., the Americans reinforced the Rangers. He was confident, based on past experience, that the Americans would commit forces as soon as the Rangers made significant contact. This would transfer the responsibility for subsequent action to the Americans rather than his Division. He could then position forces on the safer flanks while the Americans reinforced their own engaged forces.

7

The Ranger Battalion

The Ranger battalion was different from most Vietnamese units in that it had a polyglot of ethnic groups and it liked to fight. It was, in fact, very good at what it did by any measure. Advisors liked to serve with it because they had a better than even chance of going home alive. Additionally, unlike many Vietnamese units, an advisor could learn a great deal simply by watching and talking. The ability to speak Vietnamese was essential because only a few of the officers could speak English. The battalion had already won a United States Presidential Unit Citation for saving a newly arrived U.S. unit from annihilation.

The battalion had three rifle companies and a headquarters company. Each rifle company had three platoons of about 20 to 40 personnel per platoon depending on the time of year and the level of recent combat. The companies had one reliable officer—the company commander. There were few NCOs worthy of the name. Headquarters Company was composed of the command radio operators, supply personnel, medics, and a heavy weapons element. Many stayed behind in the battalion compound when the unit deployed to insure that the unit forward was properly supported. Through experience, the unit knew that it could not depend on any outside assistance regardless of promises to the contrary.

The weaponry within the battalion was obsolete compared to that of the enemy. Soldiers were armed with the WWII-era M-1 carbine, the Browning Automatic Rifle and the .30 caliber machine gun. If it weren't for their physical appearance, the troops could have walked out of a black and white film on Merrill's Marauders. Depending on the circumstances, the battalion might take an 81mm mortar to the field. Usually, this would be carried on a long pole by recaptured deserters and would be fired free hand without benefit of a fire direction center. The mortar crew was very accurate and very fast, to the amazement of U.S. observers. Recently, the battalion had acquired two brand-new M-60 machine guns—a gift from the 11th Cavalry. These were given to the best machine gunners in the battalion—both Montagnards—who never let the weapons leave their grasp.

The battalion lived on an isolated ridge outside of the province capitol of Xuan Loc. The local leadership would not entertain the thought of the Rangers living in close proximity to themselves and decreed their isolation. This did not prevent that same leadership from constantly employing the Rangers in the local area while their own soldiers stayed in town.

Part of the problem was the Rangers' own doing and the logical result of a self-fulfilling prophecy. Rangers were not good citizens. They would routinely wreck bars, refuse to pay legitimate bills and generally harass the population. They did this because the population disliked their ethnic makeup and refused to render them the minimal social benefits of their nation. Consequently, the Ranger families lived in the remains of wooden ammo box houses patched together with rain ponchos and stolen materials. Babies were born and old people died on the Ranger compound with no outside assistance or interest.

The majority of the battalion was composed of non-South Vietnamese groupings. The officers were predominately North Vietnamese Catholics with almost a messianic fervor to kill the communist forces. The soldiers were outcasts from the very rigid Vietnamese social structure. Most were Montagnards from the mountainous interiors with a history of domination and alienation. The majority of the remainder were traditional outcasts, Chams, Nungs, Laos, Khmers and the dregs of local society. Whatever problems and difficulties the individual encountered in the Ranger battalion, his life was considerably better than if he had chosen to remain independent. Even after the most horrible losses, the battalion could depend on a fresh influx of personnel escaping the grimmer realities of life outside the compound. For the first time in their lives, they could draw strength from their situation through collective experience.

The combined effect of social ostracism, close living and the shared emotion of combat created a great strength in the unit. Personnel were tightly bonded. They took great pride in the only thing that ever gave them social respectability to fight successfully. Their instincts for living alone and surviving made them great soldiers who instinctively understood the right way to destroy the enemy. They consistently met and defeated larger, better-equipped forces and had never experienced a surrender or desertion from their ranks. They lived for only two things—to kill people and live as well as they could when not deployed.

The Vietnamese leadership was at odds on how to handle such units. Politically and socially, they could not afford to give the Rangers much access to traditional society or the mainstream army. Militarily, they could not afford to ignore their qualities—especially in light of the pressure to demonstrate some valid Vietnamese military capability.

The solution was ideal. Rangers would be constantly employed in high-threat situations. This would keep them out of the towns and in constant contact with the VC and NVA. Casualties would not be a significant factor as the losses were not ethnic South Vietnamese. Their commander was equally an outcast.

8

The Commander

He was about 5 feet 4 inches tall. His skin was the color of a varnished paper lampshade. He had quick black eyes and fine, shaped fingers. There was a trace of black mustache on his upper lip. Other than that, his face was hairless. He walked very erect in highly spit-shined jungle boots. His uniform was always the same: starched jungle fatigues with sharp creases and a perfect fit. He wore a single black leather belt on which was attached a small leather holster holding a Walther 9mm. In his left hand, he always carried a highly polished ironwood swagger stick.

Whenever he spoke, it was direct and without equivocation. He had been immersed in this business for 25 years. His parents had been killed in North Vietnam by the new regime in 1954. He was commissioned originally by the French and had never served outside of a battalion. He was now a major in spite of many Vietnamese officers' attempts to prevent his progress. His training, his background and his personality all combined to produce an exceptionally effective killing machine. His development had progressed to this point as sure as if he emerged from a genetic experiment in a laboratory.

As a lieutenant, he had rescued a French platoon from destruction south of Saigon. Again as a lieutenant, he had saved his battalion commander from death by driving his truck directly into a VC ambush. He was promoted to captain then relegated to a staff job. Then as the only senior officer available when a convoy was ambushed, he commanded a battalion that relieved a U.S. 9th Infantry Division truck convoy. Shipped to another battalion as "too showy," he led it on the relief of Dong Xuai Special Forces Camp when his commander was too drunk to take the force. Promoted under pressure from grateful Americans (he personally led CMH winner Robert Q. Williams to safety), he was given command of a Ranger battalion and shipped to a location remote from Saigon.

In the manner of Vietnamese power politics, influence was in direct proportion to the proximity of the unit to the national capital. Within three months of assuming command, his battalion had saved the majority of an armored squadron of the 11th Cavalry that had been ambushed along Highway 20.

He organized and conducted a nighttime airmobile raid on top of the enemy under the light of artillery flares. As a result, the 11th Cavalry commander habitually used the Rangers, which further infuriated the local Vietnamese military. The arrangement was well-received by the Rangers, however. At last, they knew that if they got into trouble, they would get help.

Despite the best efforts and intentions of his superiors to deny him access to success, battalion commander Nguyen Hiep's destiny had arrived. The unit he was about to encounter was led by a communist cadre that had been raised in the same Red River village that he was born in North Vietnam. He knew the commander by name and person. Knowing that and the unit he was going to fight, he also knew that he would have to be as good as was humanly possible to survive.

Hiep's family home was Tan Hoa, a mid-size town in North Vietnam. His family had lived there for several generations. His father was a civil servant in the maze of bureaucracies at the local level the French had formed to create the facade of local control without true release of authority. In the fall of 1952, the French began to lose physical control of Tan Hoa and by Christmas, it was firmly in communist hands. Hiep's father was one of the first "reform" targets. One evening, the local cadre came to Hiep's house, dragged the entire family into the town square and shot his mother and father as an example. Shortly thereafter, an uncle took Hiep and his sister and fled south to Saigon. On his 18th birthday, Hiep joined the French Army in Saigon and was commissioned a second lieutenant.

From his parents' last moments in Tan Hoa Square, Hiep lived to kill and the army provided him an instrument. He had welded a diverse group of people into a very effective killing machine and he was about to have an opportunity to fulfill both his assigned mission and his personal proclivities. Twenty kilometers to the west, the object of his desire began to move toward its intended engagement.

9

The Assembly

Binh Tram 42 was located 13 kilometers from the Dong Nai River close against the Cambodian border. This was one of many way station systems located along the Ho Chi Minh Trail designed to support and throughput soldiers and material transiting to the war in the south. Each Binh Tram was a self-contained unit with security forces, engineers, mechanics, quartermasters, and a variety of support personnel.

Depending on location and threat, each Binh Tram could be adapted to local conditions. Those in the North had extensive anti-aircraft units and vehicle maintenance facilities. Their southern counterparts tended to be lightly equipped but well-organized into factory facilities, providing both repair of equipment from the North as well as original assembly—a reflection of their relative distance from the support source.

General Thanh had chosen Binh Tram 42 as the support element for his push into this part of South Vietnam due to its relative isolation from the probable attack and the ease of movement into the heart of the Allied area. From here, he could move toward Bien Hoa, reinforce War Zone C or shift toward the Central Highlands and Dalat. The heart of his plan rested on easy access to Xuan Loc and the notoriously weak 18th Vietnamese Army Division. The chance for a quick, stunning victory with great political overtones was a distinct probability. After reviewing the enemy order of battle at his North Vietnamese training center, he had ordered the newly formed 5th VC Division to begin its movement from the vicinity of Dien Bien Phu in the far western portion of North Vietnam into this designated Binh Tram specifically to seek battle with such a unit—poor enough to likely defeat while close enough to Saigon to garner excellent press coverage.

From here, the soldiers could acclimatize and train away from American air and ground attacks and spend some time developing the best assault targets using the extensive infrastructure that existed within the civilian population. This was a popular choice among the cadre as many had relatives and close friends in the Bien Hoa and Saigon areas and could visit during holiday periods.

In the morning following Hu's departure from the main camp, the Binh Tram had been aware of the results of his mission by the increased activity just to its east. They had heard and occasionally seen a small spotter aircraft as it worked the Dong Nai River with the attack fighters and bombers preparing the ground for the anticipated Ranger assault. Several soldiers had accompanied work parties to the new base camp under construction and heard the artillery as it fired on the Ranger landing zone. In the mid-afternoon, everyone had heard the persistent intermittent beating of the helicopters as they began to ferry the Rangers to the land nearby.

None of this was a surprise to Thanh. He had been informed by his intelligence that the 18th Division had been chosen to respond to the information provided by Comrade Hu. This was particularly important as it meant that maneuver options by the Southern forces would be limited. While the Americans might move the assault force anywhere in the area, once deposited, they were pinned to the ground. While he didn't expect the response to occur so quickly, he was quite certain what the objective of the operation would be. The circling of the L-19 spotter aircraft and artillery preparation confirmed his thought.

By mid-morning, he had directed that a reinforced battalion occupy the base camp and extend the trenches with all haste so that they tied in with both the Dong Nai and the Soui Long. This would create a complex that could not be flanked and would force the attackers to assault into the teeth of the pre-determined fire lanes of the automatic weapons.

Immediately behind the reinforcing battalion, he ordered a second battalion to follow along with the heart of his command group. Each of the regimental commanders was given specific instructions to be executed as the attacking force revealed its intentions.

The First Regiment was to occupy and hold the base camp. The Second was to reinforce the crossing site at the Dong Nai but not to expose itself to fire. The Third and smallest regiment was to remain in the Binh Tram until called forward. This unit would move necessary ammunition to the battle and act as the final fresh assault force at the proper moment. Thanh wanted the unit fresh and unharmed when finally committed. Thanh was well aware of the psychological effect of Western firepower and had seen disciplined units break under the combination of artillery, air strikes and concentrated automatic weapons. In so much as possible, he wanted this regiment to be untouched, physically or mentally, until he threw them into the fight where they had to be crushingly decisive.

By the time the Rangers landed, Thanh's dispositions were to be set. He sent the First Regiment commander across the river to insure that construction was moving with haste. He estimated that the Southerners would not move against the base camp until sometime the following day, choosing instead to move into the edge of the jungle and scout. Thanh ordered that all scouts remain well beyond the landing zone so as not to encourage pursuit should they be discovered.

The arrival of the First Regiment commander had the proper effect. He immediately ordered elements of a second battalion across the river to add more shovels and saws to the effort. The movement of this element was less than half accomplished due to American air activity when actions and decisions further east began to unfold.

10

A Proper Regiment

Following Tanh's announcement, the Rangers and the 48th were formally alerted. The Rangers were to move to a large open field to receive their helicopters and the regiment was to assemble further to the north within short marching distance of the Rangers' base camp objective. This came as an abrupt surprise for the regiment. This was a "Palace Guard" unit for the 18th ARVN Division responsible for the security of the province capital, Xuan Loc. Though there was little intention of actually employing it in the field, its alert status was established by the necessity to have a larger ARVN force committed than the Americans—at least on paper.

The regiment was a comfortable unit. Assignment guaranteed a relatively combat-free life. Battalions were posted on the large bend of the Saigon River north of Bien Hoa and at Xuan Loc. Units occasionally sortied out for minor field operations but only after a great deal of preparation and discussion. Secrets were very hard to keep if ever they were intended to be.

The unit wore clean and starched fatigues. Helmets were standard issue but were embellished with camouflage nets that looked very dramatic on parade. Vehicles were invariably clean and waxed and soldiers appeared happy—a countenance reinforced by the fact that the regiment always had the least casualties within the division. Operations orders were hallmarked with their attention to detail and adherence to American professional schooling. Advisors invariably liked this unit as preparation and order at the staff level eclipsed other like units.

The unit had the best equipment available to the army. Though the basic weapon was the M-1 rifle, they were clean and well-maintained. The artillery was new and well-provisioned. The APCs, unusual equipment for an infantry unit, were well painted and maintained. In all, the unit always shone on parade.

The commander, Colonel Trinh, was a short man with distinctly Chinese features. He had a Charlie Chan moustache and carried a well-polished mahogany swagger stick. Colonel Trinh spoke precise English and went to great lengths to accommodate his advisors. Often, he would take them to Saigon for extended weekends, particularly if a major operation was about to begin. He was recognized as a master at manipulating the Americans. He would ingratiate and flatter new advisors and spend extensive time explaining his rationale for avoiding operations or adjusting troop deployments to accommodate "local conditions." Invariably, the flattery and cajolery worked and the advisors soon became sycophants to the colonel's decisions.

His relationships with General Tanh, the division commander, were strained but correct. Trinh was a force unto himself and often overrode the division commander's decisions, but always behind the scene and through intermediaries. A call to Saigon, a visit to a friend, resulted in a call to the division commander and a shift in plans. Usually, this meant that another regiment would replace the 48th in the field. The previous day, at the operational briefing, General Tanh had chosen the Rangers to lead the attack, knowing full well that Trinh's unit would never move past their assembly areas despite the fact that the Rangers had been out of the field less than a week.

Trinh had been present at the briefing when the cavalry commander and the 18th Division commander conferred on Comrade Hu's seemingly invaluable intelligence. Here was the possibility of destroying a newly arrived VC regiment. Usually, the VC never organized above battalion level but this was an ominous indication of both strength and confidence that the division commander could not let pass. If he were able to make this an ARVN operation, supported by the Americans, instead of the opposite case, he would be well-rewarded by the high command.

The division had a poor reputation and needed a victory. Accordingly, he told the Cav commander that the division would make the primary assault, led by the Rangers, as part of a larger force from the 48th Regiment with the Americans providing support. For cosmetic purposes, Colonel Trinh at the direction of General Tanh, would take the regiment to the field to preserve the facade of full division involvement and commitment.

Colonel Trinh was very unhappy with this requirement but he recognized the political aspects of the decision. Reluctantly, he ordered the 1st Battalion of the 48th Regiment to move north and occupy the area designated as the pickup zone for the Rangers once the assault was concluded. He also sent a trusted agent in civilian clothes and in an old French-built Diane automobile to the Don Dien De Catachouces Rubber Plantation headquarters with the movement plan.

Assembling the First Battalion for a field deployment took considerable effort. Many of the officers had already departed for Saigon and Bien Hoa for the weekend to join their families. Xuan Loc was not considered a good posting. Consequently, many families stayed in the major cities and husbands commuted over holidays and weekends. Most officers did not have access to a telephone and consequently were unable to be recalled. This left junior officers or NCOs in charge of platoons, companies and staff.

The soldiers of the battalion, scattered across the province capital in the bays, shops and family dwellings, while relatively easy to recover, were somewhat bewildered at the requirement to prepare to move out. Usually, such orders were preceded by several days' notification and thorough preparation of the area to be occupied. This approach allowed the leadership to develop sufficient reasons not to participate and generally insured that the unit would not be attacked during its short sojourn to the field. Now, they were required to assemble and move out with less than a day to prepare.

Officers, as ignorant as the men to the intent and purpose of the operation, reacted with haste and irritation. As soon as sufficient troops had been assembled, regardless of unit integrity, they were packed on trucks and sent to an assembly area at the juncture of Highway One and Highway 20. This was an intermediate staging point preparatory to their moving to the area known as the Chinese Farm. Here, with the Americans, they would be assured initial security to protect their internally inept assembly procedures far from the critical eyes in Xuan Loc.

There, they dismounted and gathered in a confused passion under the shade of the rubber trees while the adjacent American cavalry units looked on in unconcealed amusement and contempt. Nonetheless, from an hour of the initial order, the regiment began to make a highly visible move out of the capitol.

It was important to the regimental commander to present an image of aggressive adherence to orders regardless of the inadequate state of the deploying forces. Units left without key officers and at half strength or less. Soldiers were mixed together regardless of unit integrity. Consequently, the assembly area resembled a collection of milling cattle as soldiers sought to reform themselves in their units and officers vainly searched for some coherent description of their mission.

Watching from the porch of the regimental headquarters, Trinh sipped a cold tea and idly tapped his spit-shined boots with the brass tip of his swagger stick. Next to him sat his American counterpart, a lieutenant colonel, in equally well-maintained clothing, drinking from a Coke can beaded with condensed moisture that rolled down the sides and dripped on his pants crease. On his right knee, a dark wet ring indicated where he had unconsciously rested the can. The crease was now flattened at that spot as the water dissolved the starch, exposing the short cotton uniform fibers. Tanh noted this out of the corner of his eye and kept his handkerchief firmly between his hand and the large tea glass.

By noon, the regiment had largely vacated the city and was busily organizing itself out of the sight of the division commander. The regimental commander took a leisurely lunch with his American counterpart. During the dessert, he excused himself to make a phone call. As he talked, he checked his watch and then hung up. After a few minutes, he made a broad gesture to the American and they both departed in the commander's highly waxed Japanese-manufactured jeep.

At the assault pickup zone, the Ranger communications NCO handed the battalion commander a note. In neat block letters, the NCO had written the numerical designation of the regiment and battalion that was to be in support of the Ranger assault. Hiep glanced at the note, crumpled it in his hand and threw it on the ground. He took an irritated pull on his Pall Mall and returned to his map study.

No less than the 48th Regiment, the Rangers were highly agitated at having to return to the field after such a short stand-down period. They had just returned from 19 days of extended operations with minimal logistics support and considerable casualties. The Rangers were exhausted and desperately in need of time for their bodies to recover so that they might effectively return to their lifetime career of killing and being killed.

Arriving in individual and small packets of trucks, the Rangers dismounted and moved to the edge of the pickup zone. There, in the available shade, they sought to reconstitute as units and await some form of specific information regarding their fate and purpose with the weary resigned detachment of all soldiers long used to such conditions.

Next to the Ranger commander, Comrade Hu sat quietly smoking. He had been delivered to the Rangers in the rubber plantation by the Americans as soon Hiep had appeared at their command post. Hiep had questioned Hu quietly but forcefully and had satisfied himself that Hu knew where the objective was located. Without time to properly interrogate the man and reach an independent conclusion, Hiep chose to take Hu with him. In this way he would either lead them to the objective or die with them. In either case, Hiep would be in charge of his destiny. Hu was acutely aware of this and began to chain-smoke the army cigarettes he had been offered in return for the pack of Camels provided by the Americans.

11

The 175 Artillery Battery

Upon his return from the 18th Division briefing, the Cav commander gathered his staff and issued quick precise instructions. Among the most important of those decisions was the establishment of artillery support for an operation that would take place in less than six hours. The commander believed that his elements would be fully involved in the fight and he wanted to insure that as much firepower as possible was in position. Not having operated in the target area for some time, his artillery was not in good position and would have to be hastily positioned before the Rangers initiated their assault.

He placed his finger on a spot on the map approximately 21 kilometers from the battlefield, designated Landing Zone Boxer, or Firing Position W03 as it was charted in the fire direction center of 1st Squadron, 11th Armored Cavalry Regiment. Orders were issued by radio for it to be occupied by Battery B, a composite heavy battery consisting of two 175mm guns and two 8-inch howitzers—hence the term "Heavy" designating large calibers.

The battery was designed to provide long-range fires for interdiction and destruction missions—not to provide direct support to combat elements. However, due to the extreme range that the combatants were operating at, only the 175mm guns could support the initial Ranger assault units.

This firing unit was not a formal part of the 11th ACR, but was a composite battery formed because of the unique requirements imposed by Vietnam. It was part of Corps Artillery but was farmed out to the 11th ACR area to provide long-range fires in the Xuan Loc area. Both the Cav and the Rangers had taken turns securing the battery at its isolated firing sites and all parties were very familiar with each other. In fact, a solid relationship had developed between the supporters and the supported.

The 175mm artillery piece was a unique weapon. It was mounted on a tank chassis and the crew rode on top of the gun carriage or on the side of the vehicle. The gun itself was the longest in the Army inventory, measuring just over 28 feet from breech to barrel tip. The length of the barrel provided a clue as to its greatest asset-range. The 175mm could heave a 150-lb high explosive shell over 32 kilometers—the longest range of any conventional tube artillery piece. However, as a gun, rather than a howitzer, it also fell prey to another characteristic of such ballistics, it had a great range probable error—it fired over or under the target somewhat indiscriminately though the farther the target was from the gun the more indiscriminant the range errors became. As if in compensation, its deflection error (deviation to left or right of the axis of the round) was virtually nil.

Its 8-inch sisters, howitzers, were the most accurate in the U.S. inventory and could place a 200-pound round literally within inches of the desired location. However, their range was limited and in this engagement they could play no part. Both artillery pieces relied on hydraulics and an extended fire-direction process and were accordingly slow-firing. Their great value to the user was that they fired large rounds with tremendous explosive effect and were particularly effective in deep jungle, being able to penetrate through dense foliage with killing force where smaller-caliber artillery was rapidly dissipated.

Alerted at mid-morning in its permanent position at the Xuan Loc airport, the battery had hastily packed itself for a noon move to be in position to fire by 1500, the designated H Hour of the Ranger assault. An escort of five armored personnel carriers, specially configured ACAVs (armored personnel carriers with additional machine guns) from the 11th Armored Cavalry Regiment arrived at 1130. Amidst a cloud of noise, dust and diesel exhaust, the contingent headed west on Highway One toward the other cavalry elements laagered at the junction between Highway One and Highway 20.

Leading the road march was a pair of ACAVs followed in order by a 40mm Duster (a twin-barreled anti-aircraft gun mounted on a tank chassis), two 8-inch howitzers, an ACAV, the two 175mm howitzers, another ACAV, the mess truck, a quad 50, two jeeps, another truck and the remaining Duster/ quad 50 all shepherded by the trailing ACAVs in the drag position. Overhead, cutting slow circles in the clear midday sun was an L-19 aircraft talking to the convoy commander and to the cavalry regimental headquarters monitoring the move.

If the unfolding action was a movie, the pilot would be the director and his plane the moveable chair. He alone could move from scene to scene, describe the action and relay instructions and information to the players. The commanders, restricted to the view from the ground and what the radio told them could do little but guess at the situation. The pilot, alone, could see the entire scene. On his eyes, experience and judgment, the story would unfold to its conclusion. The players recognized this despite the ego aspects and anxiously awaited his arrival on the scene and the inclusion of his voice on everyone's radio net. He, above all others, had the ability to exquisitely view the unfolding disintegration of life.

The pilot, a veteran of dozens of such missions, knew by heart the location of every supporting artillery unit and would automatically check into its net as the convoy crossed into its area of responsibility. Occasionally, he would nose the plane into an excursion toward points of interest along the route. The pilot was particularly fond of overflying the French rubber plantation compounds. Often, he would catch several white females lounging next to the pool. Recently, they had become wary of this tact and covered themselves with towels at the first hint of aircraft noise. This forced him to adopt the tactic of treetop flying a mile or so out and he often lost radio contact with the convoy. Accordingly, he now restricted his fly-bys to those portions of the road that fronted a fixed ARVN base camp.

Approaching the juncture of Highway One and Highway 20, midway between Xuan Loc and Bien Hoa, the convoy commander requested a sweep of the intersection and the grassy hills just to the north and east. Here, a month earlier, an entire squadron of the 11th ACR had been ambushed and fought through an afternoon and evening just to extricate itself. Later that night, assisted by the same Ranger battalion it was now racing to support, the unit finally extracted itself after killing more than 300 VC, many of whom were chained to rubber trees and their machine guns.

The pilot made an intentionally low and slow pass over the highway hoping to pick up any sign of human use or to attract a sucker shot from a scared guard. Nothing occurred and he reported all clear to the convoy which was just turning north at the junction. He saw the still very visible signs of the recent engagement but could discern no tracks in the exposed mud and wet grass that marked the previous stands of rubber trees. To a distance of a hundred yards from the road, the trees had been largely blasted by bombs and artillery. The Rome plows, brought up the day after the engagement, had insured the sterility of the scene. Water now stood in all the craters and the remains of trees were windrowed perpendicular to the road or shoved into the larger craters. The soil, laid bare, retained no secrets from the pilot's view.

Rome plows, large Caterpillar D8Hs with an angled blade and sharpened steel lance on the leading edge, had worked their way along Highway 20 almost to the battery firing sight. The pilot, aware of the original ambush force laager site, guided his plane further to the east, past the road, and scouted the low flat shrouded ground between the hills that previously had hidden a reinforced regiment. He could see nothing of interest and continued following the ridgeline keeping the road to the west and the high ground to the east.

Shortly, Firing Position W03 crossed his right wing and he climbed to gain altitude. At 8,000 feet and in a slow orbit over the position, he could see the rooster tail of dust marking the column as it slowly wound its way toward him. The pilot called into the Cav operations center and within two minutes a large white cloud suddenly burst over the position. Artillery was being adjusted by the pilot as a standard security measure. Because this position was so frequently used, the firing data was resident at the battery and quickly applied. As always, the pilot liked to make the first round white phosphorous fired at 400 meters in the air. This permitted him to get a firm fix on the initial round.

Seeing the accuracy of the first shot, he immediately shifted to the four cardinal points around the site and directed a battery registration on each one approximately 100 meters outside the perimeter. This could not be done once the position was occupied but now would insure accurate registered protective fire should the battery be attacked in that position.

Today, the firing was executed by a 155mm battery firing from Xuan Loc. These mobile pieces, manned by veteran crews, were firing at medium range and quickly responded to each command. In less than 20 minutes, the pilot had registered the entire position. He appreciated experienced units for their prompt and accurate capabilities. New units were especially difficult to deal with and consumed a great deal of time in safety checks and basic gunnery. Often, the pilot could over fly firing units and select his battery of choice based on observation. His standard of measure was that the more shirtless torsos, umbrellas and folding chairs to be seen, the more veteran the unit. Uniform discipline was usually in direct disproportion to combat efficiency.

The advisor to the Rangers, a newly arrived U.S. infantry lieutenant, now talking to the pilot from the landing zone, did not have much luxury of choice.

The lieutenant was very familiar with the various characteristics of the available artillery and had taken special pains before each field deployment to meet with the battery commander (BC) and obtain his firing position plots. As the habitual great ranges from the supporting artillery emphasized the inherent errors in the system, the Rangers found it essential to avoid walking along Gun Target line (GT line) if at all possible. He knew from experience that his unit would be out of range of other artillery and that he would have to rely upon the 175mm for whatever artillery support his unit would need. He had explained the nature of these guns in great detail to his counterpart, the Ranger battalion commander, who would be totally relying on him to bring the fruits of American participation to his traditionally under-supported and overburdened battalion.

The lieutenant described the GT line as a straight line from the barrel to the impact point. The farther out the 175mm fired, the greater the range probable error. In that the Rangers were always outside other shorter-ranged artillery, this meant that they would always be faced with 175mm guns firing at maximum range and with maximum error. However, if they could stay off of the GT line when shooting, the deflection error of nearly zero would give them safety. Accordingly, the Ranger commander would try and plan his route as close to perpendicular to the GT line as possible though it often was not—as was the situation at hand.

In the field, the lieutenant had devised a scheme for firing the 175mm that seemed to work. In the evening when the night defensive perimeter (NDP) had been formed, the lieutenant would mark the four corners of his perimeter on the map and then all in registration points for the artillery 200 meters from each point for nighttime defensive protection. He would then confirm these locations by firing.

The initial problem facing the lieutenant was in confirming where he was. In open or broken country where he could see some terrain features, this was not a problem. However in the thick canopy, special measures were needed. If normal artillery was available, he would begin registration with a white phosphorous (WP) shell fired 400 meters in the air at a specific grid location. This would keep both the soldiers safe if his map reading was off and would provide a confirmed location. He would then follow this by firing high-explosive rounds at his registration points. The 175mm, however, provided a unique challenges. It had no WP round and could not fire an air burst.

The lieutenant would fire a single round at a location at least 500 meters away from where he thought he was. The huge shell would crash through the canopy and explode, sending reverberating echoes throughout the jungle floor. The lieutenant would attempt to gauge the distance and direction of the sound and call in adjustments, creeping the rounds into his desired registration point. The 175mm had a very slow reaction time, two minutes per round normally, so this became a laborious process. After three or four shots, the outposts would begin to yell for a cease fire. After the fifth shot, when the OPs would threaten to withdraw, the lieutenant would instruct the firing battery to drop 100 meters from the last round, register that location but not fire. At the ranges they were firing, the artillery rounds could have an error of as much as 200 meters between rounds fired at the same location.

The lieutenant noted that as large as the explosion from the shell was, its energy was quickly dissipated by the soft earth and encompassing jungle material. In the deep canopy, the sound was more dramatic than the effect of the blast.

Making initial contact with the lieutenant, the pilot confirmed friendly locations and nosed back to the south to pick up his convoy. The unit was traveling in close march order past the old ambush site. Appreciating the tension, he made a fast low pass to get everyone's attention and break the anxiety. He succeeded admirably and responded to the convoy commander's critique of his flying discipline with a barrel roll and a 360 degree straight up stall and upside down recovery.

Before more conversation could ensue, the lead elements of the convoy broke around a curve in the road and headed toward their familiar position, now in view. It was in the northwest quadrant of an intersection connecting Suoi Cat village and Nam Hoa village, both since leveled but with dark charcoal outlines remaining on the hard-packed clay earth. The position quickly filled as drivers found their locations directly from march order. It was parade ground simple and executed numerous times by the battery.

The intersection area had been bulldozed over to a width of 500 meters all around to the edge of the jungle. The raw laterite had turned into a greasy red ochre where the tracks of the firing battery had previously cut the tamped earth surface. Around the battery, an earthen berm circled the position.

At each corner were Dusters projecting their barrels over the lip. The Duster unit consisted of two quad .50 caliber systems and two tracked vehicles, each with two rapid-fire 40mm Bofors guns. These systems had been pre-eminent anti-aircraft pieces in World War II and had been successfully converted to ground protection roles in both Korea and this conflict. In operation, they were awesome weapons against exposed infantry and could be guaranteed to raise the butcher's bill of assault beyond acceptable limits. When the Vietnam War began, the systems were found only in the New Mexico National Guard and had been federalized and sent to the theater, now to be manned by Regular Army soldiers. The VC took careful note of the presence of such weapons and avoided them if at all possible.

The battery had occupied this position before and automatically knew what areas within the circle to occupy without orders. Thor and Odin, the crew-named 175mm guns, took the two positions to the northwest while Geronimo and Crazy Horse, the 8-inch howitzers, took the two positions in the northeast. The aiming stakes and collimators, standard equipment to insure accuracy, were quickly placed out and wire communications laid. The hardest part of getting the battery in place, organizing and protecting the ammunition, took much longer. This involved digging bunkers for the ammo and spare powder and was always relegated to the new members or those troops who had irritated the chief of smoke (Battery NCOIC) recently.

Each gun crew erected a canvas shelter it had prefabricated over time directly behind the gun. They then placed duckboard under the shelter and stacked the ready ammunition on the duckboard. Further to the rear of each gun, a pit was dug to hold the powder charges not used from each firing.

As the tasks of occupation were accomplished, some of the niceties of home began to be revealed. An ice chest, a lounge chair, or a beach umbrella emerged to join the mud and khaki colors officially accepted by the army. The sounds of Saigon and home began to mix with the coughing of the engines and the shouts of the NCOs.

Within the square, the soldiers had arranged poncho shelters and cots along the wall of the perimeter as soldiers from time immemorial had done in other places with other equipment. The interior was filled with the four guns, their accompanying vehicles and the mess truck. Wires were strung between the Fire Direction Center (FDC), the guns and the Dusters. As the heat of the day began to drive the unit into a torpor, soldiers not required to be on the guns retreated to their shelters to lay in the shade and sweat the boredom away.

The position sloped slightly to the south. Those who had been there in previous weeks understood the pooling effect of tropical rains and worked to avoid that portion of the perimeter. Those that could not, spent some effort in acquiring spare duckboards and ditching the back of their shelters. The battery settled back into the quiet heat of the midday and awaited the call for fire.

By mid-afternoon, the initial registrations had been accomplished. Of the four batteries within range of the initial landing zone, the heavy battery was the last to have been fired. The spotter pilot, well aware of the slow firing times, had chosen to work the more responsive 155mm units first. These batteries would be the first to fire against any live targets and could put a considerable volume of fire on any target before the 175mm could be brought to bear. While no other gun had the range of the large caliber weapons, they would not be needed until well into the Rangers movement off the LZ. Plenty of time to adjust fire.

The battery personnel were able to monitor the flow of the movement through the fire direction net. The FDC had placed the radio on a small loudspeaker to insure that all necessary personnel heard the commands during a firing mission. This was particularly important during an actual mission as the combination of noise and excitement distracted people's attention from the request for what was wanted from the competing local sounds.

As the battery settled down into its position and completed its registrations, the L-19 pilot swung his aircraft in a wide arcing turn and headed toward the now filling Pickup Zone. From his seat, the pilot could see in a single sweep of vision the Pickup Zone, the Landing Zone, the artillery battery and the long winding curve of the Dong Nai River that would draw all the players.

Behind this scene, small swirls of dust arose from the blue-green lush vegetation marking the trace of columns advancing toward their various destinations. Mentally, as if presiding over the world's largest second-unit movie production, the pilot began to coordinate the pieces.

His counterpart director, General Thanh, had gathered his commanders and was also issuing precise instructions. Quickly, the saws and shovels of the sappers were dropped as they withdrew to the riverbank to be replaced by the fresh-faced infantry soldiers dressed in black clothing with light blue and green ammunition vests. The soldiers exchanged few words but moved directly into the improved positions and quietly awaited the human tide that lay behind the precursors of developing sounds.

12

The Mortar Gunners

In the most recessed area of General Thanh's Binh Tram base camp, where the combination of shade and proximity to fresh water combined to make an almost mountain coolness, the fire support element of the Viet Cong resided. These were veterans and the skilled pool of experts that lent strength to the immature manpower that was often flung against the technical superiority of the Americans.

Here, the communist maneuver commanders could draw upon engineers, heavy machine gun crews, and the elite of the group, the mortar gunners.

Crews materialized from a combination of attrition, experience, and lack of desire for leadership positions. In the ultra-democratic leadership selection process of the communist forces, experienced survivors normally achieved significant positions. However, if such a person found him or herself lacking in either talent or interest, he or she could usually select a combat position of choice. Often, this was a mortar crew.

The heavy machine guns, while fired in support of assaults and somewhat prestigious in the hierarchy of the tools of death, still required direct exposure. Often in difficult situations, the senior cadre would tie both gun and gunner to the tree—both to remain there until the ultimate resolution of the battle.

The engineers, skilled specialists in building things or blowing them up, often were required to take the lead in assaults against prepared positions. Regardless, even if not in combat, their skills often caused them to be engaged in hard labor in new base camp areas for extended periods. It was not a unit for old people or those seeking a sinecure.

The mortar crew positions were the best of all possible worlds. For many missions, mortars were never employed. Thus, the crew remained behind in the base camps and performed non-combat support. When their services were required, the crew positions were always well away from the direct line of fire, usually behind a terrain feature and changed quickly after initial engagement of the target. Over time and experience, the crews had learned to respect the ability of the Americans to respond to initial mortar fires and had learned to avoid such obvious locations as crossroads or the open fields on the forward slopes of hills overlooking U.S. installations.

Despite the somewhat selective nature of the mortar employment, the crews were not without great skill and capability. Skills that were thoroughly appreciated by the commanders. Often, a single crew and their ammo bearers would move out in support of an assault or ambush. Their mission would be to provide covering fire against an installation during the initial assault or to covey the withdrawal of forces after the last attack.

These missions were orchestrated by a senior assault commander who often dictated the firing position location and sequence of firing and movement. These missions were not particularly popular as they removed the freedom of action of the crews. This situation was particularly perilous if the targeted force had artillery already aligned on likely mortar or rocket firing sites or had launched night-flying equipped helicopters. With a weapon range of less than 3,000 meters, the crews were very limited in the choice of positions and the defending force was aware of all of them.

The most popular tasks were those involving random attacks against villages or installations without regard to other programs. These were usually done to accomplish some form of political objective or simply to make a statement. In these tasks, the crew would deploy, select the best position for effect, fire a number of rounds in rapid fashion and then withdraw back to the base camp.

Occasionally, crews would be sent against high-value targets such as airfields or headquarters. These too were dangerous as the targets were always located deep behind a belt of defending forces and population. The crews often had to infiltrate for several days to get within range, running the risk of compromise. On the positive side, such sojourns usually meant several days in the general population and a chance to visit friends and the benefits of a wartime fueled economy.

A mortar crew usually consisted of three people, a gunner, an assistant, and an NCO. The crews were typically supplemented by local labor or conscripts, often women, to carry the ammunition. For most operations, a single crew would be sufficient. For particularly large operations such as an assault against a border Special Forces outpost, all available mortars might be massed even though they would usually engage from separate firing positions.

The mortar was invariably a Chinese-built 82mm with small base plate and bipod. Only on the rarest of occasions was a sight or aiming stakes used—common practice in most organized armies. However, use of these instruments, though guaranteeing relative accuracy, required more people and time to properly employ. The guerrilla movement, necessitating rapid movement and husbanded human resources, pared its support elements to the barest necessities. Here is where the skill shown and the crews were able to demonstrate their worth and status.

The chief gunner had as his guides a compass, a map of its equivalent, and a charge card. The charge card told him how far the round would carry for each small plastic charge wafer he attached to the mortar's tail fins and the necessary angle for the tube to be held in relationship to the ground to achieve that range. The map delineated the range between the firing position and the target for reference to the necessary range. Often, the map simply consisted of a notation of the range and directional azimuth between the various potential firing sites and the target. Firing consisted of holding the tube at the proper angle, sitting across the top of the tube with a compass to achieve the correct azimuth, and correlating the firing charge to the firing table.

Ammunition was virtually all high explosive. Unlike the Americans, the guerillas rarely used illumination except in set-piece assaults against inferior forces. All assault forces were trained to remove enemy mortar ammunition when they withdrew.

Though smaller than Chinese mortar rounds, the U.S.-built 81mm ammo could be fired in 82mm tubes even though the range was somewhat shortened. Usually, captured ammunition was saved for mass assaults by fire where accuracy was not particularly important.

Prior to departing the base camp, the crew would determine the amount of rounds to be fired and would pre-affix the charges to the fins. Arriving at the firing site, a good crew could set up, fire its rounds, and depart the position in less than five minutes. The speed was judged essential for survival as the Americans could usually begin random reaction firings within five to eight minutes after initial engagement. There was some morbid truth to the joke that the Americans usually selected the good mortar crews—those that survived.

Since General Thanh had joined the Binh Tram camp, the mortar crews had been largely ignored. The three 120mm mortar crews had been told to deposit their weapons and join the sappers clearing the new base camp areas. The amount of work scheduled by the general well exceeded the ability of the available manpower to fulfill. The 82mm crews felt somewhat smug at this decision as it validated their position in the hierarchy. Intuitively, they knew with some anxiety that they were being saved for a major event in which they would be important but subordinate players.

The crews remained in their privileged area and spoke little to the new arrivals. On the initial occupation of the camp, the crews had paid scant attention to the newcomers. Their presence was common practice as newly drafted forces were shuttled south. Rarely did such a group stay more than a day or two at most.

The camp commander disliked long occupations, especially by raw soldiers, as their cooking fires and latrine trips increased the possibility of air detection and attack. Their continued presence after the Ranger insertion presaged important events.

This was reinforced near noon on the day of the assault when the camp commander approached the dozing mortar crews and talked to the ranking NCO. By itself it was unusual for the commander to visit. Usually, he dealt with issues remotely, relaying employment instructions through the evening or morning committee meetings with his direct subordinates. For him to actually visit and issue instructions was decidedly out of character.

The commander was clearly anxious and uncharacteristically nervous. He talked quickly with the senior NCO and without awaiting a response turned and walked back into the darker recesses of the central camp core.

The NCO thought a moment and then went to that portion of the position that was darkest and coolest. This spot was adjacent to a small creek and had been laboriously transformed into near-resort conditions, which was a consequence of having a large body of highly intelligent, experienced soldiers with time on their hands and few alternatives to spend it.

Several sleeping huts had been erected. Each was lined with split bamboo flooring raised off the ground by several inches. The roofs were made of thick split palm fronds that drooped well below the roof line. This kept the rain out during particularly violent storms. Interwoven split bamboo mats had been constructed as protection against wind and prying eyes. This feature was particularly prized by the group as an occasional opportunity presented itself to dally with visiting nurses or families brought in from the populated areas. The crews made a good deal of food money by renting out their rustic facilities.

The center of the sleeping complex was occupied by a large open shelter. Underneath was a table and chairs as well as a kitchen area. The stove was a mud-walled trench covered by a flat piece of aluminum sheeting from a downed American airplane. This arrangement permitted hot food to be served in relative comfort throughout the rainy season. The facility was so good that it was often used by the camp commander to entertain important visitors.

However, the best part of the mortar crew encampment was the shower. Located next to the creek, the initial impression was that of a standard sleeping hut. On closer examination, several things became apparent. The roof was a good two feet higher than standard and the bamboo wall matting encompassed all four sides. A small entrance door revealed a floor composed of the remains of a truck bed, rectangular, flat and at an angle toward the creek. Running along the creek side wall was a shallow rock-lined trench with an artery that coursed toward the creek, fewer than 20 feet away.

Inside, the reason for the unusual height became apparent. Slung along the middle of the roof, just above the lower reach of the roof fronds, was an expended USAF auxiliary fuel tank. It had been found in the jungle and brought to the camp. Fitted with a standard shower head and length of garden hose, it now served as the group bath. Underneath, a long shelf of flat aluminum, bent at the edges, ran the length of the tank. In the rainy season, the mortar crew filled the shelf with bamboo splinters and heated the water prior to showering.

As a matter of practice, the crews would provide invitations to other camp members they wished to ingratiate or to the nurses. The nurses usually resisted the temptation until the cold breath of the rainy season turned the camp into near-morgue conditions. Then, at first timidly, and then in collective strength, they would descend on the shower and for a brief moment be engulfed in the warm womb of water.

Like most Vietnamese, the nurses were extremely shy about public exposure and would always shower wearing short pants and a bra. Nevertheless, the crews encouraged the use of the shower by the nurses as an opportunity to have a short conversation and a warm smile. In sum, this portion of the camp was as close to paradise as anyone was likely to get.

Now, the NCO made it clear that it was to be vacated immediately. A mutter of complaints and indignation arose but he was hearing none of it. He spoke briefly to the group from the kitchen hut and then directed action. To those who didn't get the message, he simply flipped them out of their hammocks or pulled the draw strings that attached the hammocks to the support poles. Amidst grumblings and bitching, the personnel gathered their belongings and moved off to occupy the space vacated by the 120mm gunners, now working as sappers well to the east. The reason for all this was soon apparent.

Within 10 minutes, a small group of personnel stepped from the dancing dappled light of the central base camp trail to the cool encompassing shade of this complex. The base commander led the group to the NCO who saluted them, bowed and led them on a tour of the facility.

The group was dressed uniformly in loose cotton shirts and pants. No insignia or rank was evident. All wore canvas tennis shoe style boots similar to that used by the French in earlier campaigns. Two of the group, Caucasians, wore wide-brimmed straw hats. The other three, distinctly Oriental but taller and bulkier than their hosts, wore blue cotton Mao caps.

The Caucasians were clearly grumpy and tired. They resisted the proffered tour of the camp and headed straight for the darkest shade. Their shirts were stained from the armpit almost to the waist. Their pants were wet from the beltline down to the point where the seat meets the pant leg. Both kept a constant dabbing motion of the handkerchiefs in their hand to their foreheads and the backs of their waists in a futile attempt to dry their skin in the humid climate. They went immediately to the kitchen table and heavily deposited themselves and began to fan their faces with large notebooks.

The Orientals, culturally polite and deferential to the NCO, followed him around the camp as he explained the layout and their accommodations. Satisfied, they shook the NCO's hand and began chatting amicably by the side of the creek. Within a few minutes, several other personnel appeared carrying the personal baggage of the group. They were met by the NCO, shown the layout and directed to their places. Two immediately began to use the kitchen. Reacting to the burning bamboo fire, the Caucasians looked up and shuffled off to the creek edge to smoke and immerse their feet in the cool waters.

Their cooling reveries were interrupted by the distant but clearly discernible explosions on the Landing Zone. Initially uncertain as to the noises' source, they silently assessed its meaning. Quickly, drawing upon their experience, they recognized the artillery and looked toward Thanh's command post. Wordless, they snuffed their cigarettes, rose from the creek and moved to the center of the camp.

13

Movement to Contact

Earlier in the day, the population of Binh Tram 42 was quiet and at repose as the sun began to rise in the sky. The light reached through the canopy only in hesitant dashes and streaks as it reflected off of leaves and occasional openings in the green curtain above. The soldiers huddled around their rice-cooking fires in small groups, warming their bodies with the heat and the rising warmth that grew from the ground and misted upward.

From habit, the hammocks had been left erected as had the rain ponchos stretched over them. Mosquitoes huddled in the shrouds and occasionally ventured across the blue bamboo smoke to escape to the wet leaf cover closer to the ground. Soldiers smoked and quietly drank instant Nescafe coffee and heavily sweetened tea from small glasses as they waited for the rice to finish cooking.

General Thanh's orders to move forward came unexpectedly and created a stir of activity even though it was several hours until departure. Most of the soldiers were new to combat and hurriedly packed their equipment and then sat on the wet ground. The cadre, more experienced, packed their rain sheets and miscellaneous gear but sat on the hammocks, smoking and writing last letters.

As the rice finished steaming in the helmet cook pots, the new soldiers ate it with anxious abandonment. Their older leadership dipped several mouthfuls and packed the remainder in small cream brown containers that they placed in the packs for future use.

By 9 o'clock, the cadre began forming the units in small columns. Each formation slowly disappeared into the gloom toward the East and was lost to the jungle. By noon, Binh Tram 43 was a ghost town occupied only by the supporting personnel and the remnants of dying cook fires.

The Binh Tram soldiers desultorily moved around the vacated positions looking for valuables and food left behind. Satisfied that nothing of worth was unclaimed, they drifted back to their positions and awaited the next passage of transient soldiers to their lodging. To the east, the last columns could be seen disappearing into the cathedral of forest, their sounds of movement covered by the distant beat of a helicopter.

14

The Pickup Zone

The helicopter pickup zone and Ranger assembly area was a long red laterite mud slash on the side of a hill. The mud had dried to a rock-hard clay in the steadily beating sun of the dry season. The edges of the PZ were crumbled into small clods where numerous soldiers and vehicles had gathered for the routine ritual of modern warfare—waiting for the leadership to decide its course of action, waiting for the helicopters to arrive and then waiting for the signal to load.

Since noon, the trucks had been arriving with Rangers trailing great clouds of red dust as the tires pulverized the delicate road surface into powder. By the second convoy, the Rangers arrived covered in sweat and with a thin red coating on their light ivory skin. With few words, they descended from the American trucks and with heads down moved to the closest shade at the edge of the track.

The advance party from the cavalry aviation unit had already arrived and was marking the pickup zone. Bright orange flags marked the leading and trailing edge of the PZ. Every 50 feet, they had placed a green flag to mark a helicopter parking spot. By the time they had finished, more than 30 green flags were visible. This was going to be an unusually large operation.

The Rangers noted this and it added to their already strong forebodings having been hastily summoned and assembled in the midst of an expected rest from the field. The experienced knew that only a military situation of the gravest consequences would cause such an abrupt change of plans. This was reinforced when they arrived and saw the size of the PZ and the obvious energy and anxiety of the Americans, now sheltered at the leading edge and talking constantly to their headquarters.

The PZ was surrounded by vegetation that provided a degree of shade for the waiting troops—but not enough to be comfortable. Comfortable, cool shade would have required tall trees and that would have posed a problem for helicopter blade clearance. Hence, banana trees and scrub brush clumps had little dots of men assembled under them escaping the harsh direct sunlight.

The men slowly rotated around the scarce shade like meat on a spit as the sun revolved across the sky.

Looking up, it appeared that the sun was always directly overhead and close enough to touch. Sweat popped off of brows and exposed skin with no physical exertion required. Uniforms quickly became soaked as the water leached through to the outer clothing. The officers had little information and seemed as ignorant of basic information as everyone else. Rumors as to their recall and operational objectives circulated wildly but quietly as the sun grew hotter and more and more troops filled the land looking for shade.

The second convoy load of Rangers were more fortunate. They were able to rest in the decidedly cooler atmosphere of the rubber plantation less than 500 meters from the PZ. The troops on the PZ could plainly see their brethren relaxing in the deep dappled shade of the tall smooth-skinned latex grove. The trees were over a hundred feet tall and planted in precise surveyed lanes. There were 20 feet between rows and 10 feet between trees. The undergrowth was a broad-leafed grass with no brush and the canopy of the trees did not begin for two thirds of the trunk length. The overall effect was cool, antiseptic and calm.

The relaxing troops had stretched hammocks between trees or matted the grass into resting beds, much like cattle. The hot Asian sun shown only feebly through the canopy and gave a sparkling diffused light with occasional flashes of hot color. Overall, the plantation was quiet and relaxed. Soldiers dozed, read papers or magazines and smoked in quiet conversation. Some would watch the rubber workers as they quietly and precisely worked their way down each row.

The worker had a long scythe-like blade on a short dark wooden handle. The blade and handle were covered in a grayish putty-like coating from the raw latex. Only that portion of the blade that routinely cut and the portion of the handle that was held in the hand was free of dried rubber. The worker would carefully cut away a half inch slice of tree bark at the base of previous slashes and readjust the drip bowl to the level of the new cut. He would empty the bowl into a large tin bucket slung over his shoulder and then move onto the next tree. The raw latex, snow white and with a milky consistency, would immediately spring from the new wound and pour slowly into the now empty cup.

Some soldiers would take the cup of latex, heat it over the fire until it boiled and became quite thick and then pull the taffy substance out of the cup, mold it in their hands and then play catch with the now grayish yellow partly cured rubber. The rubber workers would notice this, but to avoid conflict would say nothing and move on to the thousands of trees that awaited their service that day. Like the birds, they had learned to fly from the dangers that advanced upon them.

Between convoys, the helicopters arrived. From several angles, they quickly slid into view responding to the smoke from the ground control party and touched down next to the neatly staked flags. The engines were shut down with the blades coming to a slow and languorous halt. The crew chiefs roped the rotor blades and swung them perpendicular to the fuselage where they let them droop in the sun like the first line of Rangers standing just outside the sweep of its reach. The pilots and crew relaxed in their fuselage and tried to capture what little shade the aluminum offered. Seeing this, the Rangers crowded next to the body and settled under the hull like so many remoras on a shark.

On the PZ, the helicopter crews, mixed Australian and American, were resting listlessly in their crafts. Their legs were dangling over the shaded side of the troop compartment. Not quite able to touch the skids, the legs slowly waved back and forth under the helicopters as the crews idly talked, smoked, read and waited. While smoking was officially prohibited on armed and fueled helicopters, no one but new arrivals noticed or cared. Everyone was in a state of torpor hoping to catch some cool air as it coursed through the troop compartment.

Gazing at the scene down the long axis of the runway, there was the impression of dozens of masts, blades, strobe lights and engine cowlings all compressed together in the viewer's vision like a long telephoto shot of a multitude of ship's masts. Constantly rising above the scene were the wavering shimmers of density currents as the air reflected and rose off the metal hulls in the primary heat of the day. In the lead helicopter, the pilot listened to his radio, turned around to his crew and motioned with a rotating upraised finger.

As if in unison, the legs, moving aimlessly back and forth stirring the air underneath the aluminum skeletons, stopped and then began to respond to a larger impetus. Crew members stepped outside the helicopters and began in unison to go through a practiced ritual like so many ballet dancers at the bar.

One crewman stood to the left of the helicopter with a fire extinguisher seemingly too inadequate for the conflagration that such a container of fuel and explosives could generate. On the other side of the aircraft, another crew member unhooked the long tie down that held the blade parallel to the aircraft and swung it out to a 90-degree position. He then unhooked the lanyard and held the red cloth at its end in his hand. He went to each pilot position, slid the shrapnel shield forward and closed the pilot door.

The pilots and door gunners grasped their helmets on the earpieces and spread them apart as they donned the helmets from the rear of their heads and pulled them over the front until they sat reasonably comfortably. The earpieces immediately began to cause sweat to pour forth. Even with terry cloth covers over the plastic earpieces, the sweat began to form in drops and then in small rivulets at the bottom of the earpieces. Movements to adjust the helmet fit, tighten straps or release air pressure would release the sweat which would cascade down the juncture of the neck and the face and collect in a wet line on the Nomex collar.

On the more profusely sweating, the facial water would fall down the front of the chest and join the small rushes from the armpits and collect in larger streams that flowed into the folds and ridges of the stomach, waist line and belly button. Sweating is a personal thing and everyone had their own way of dealing with it until something of greater import diverted attention.

The door gunners laid out their belts of ammo and adjusted the rows of smoke grenades lined up behind each of them. Each gunner had arranged a commo wire line behind his head along which he had strung various smoke grenades. Red for injuries or enemy sighted, white to mark enemy positions, and purple or yellow to mark friendly positions. Green was universally rejected as being unusable in the jungle.

Some carried CS gas grenades and glass jars to pitch at villages. The technique was to remove the safety pin and place the grenade in the jar. On impact with the ground, the glass would break and activate the grenade. In this manner, the grenades could be reasonably safely tossed from a thousand feet or better without risk to the crew. It was against safety regulations to have CS grenades in helicopters but no one seemed to care, least of all the crews who planned to die anyway. Some crew members, invariably the youngest, took great pride in exhibiting the demented skills necessary to climb on the struts and fire weapons alongside the pilot or to wipe the Plexiglas from the outside from several thousand feet in the air.

Each machine gun had a C-ration fruit can attached to the feed tray cover. This kept the belted ammo feeding evenly into the gun and was the sort of modification that a stateside contractor would spend a year developing and testing. Next to the gun, jammed next to the interior engine wall, usually rested a large oil can and heavy rag. This was used to cool the gun during prolonged firing and to keep it well-finished after the heat of the bullets would convert the barrel into a whitish blue flat glaze.

Whatever message had caused the helicopter crews to react had the same effect on the troops. This time, however, the physical reaction was wavelike, beginning with the command group and then preceding to subordinate commanders followed by the subordinate units themselves. In this way, the message traveled from higher to lower, eliciting the same physical response but delayed from layer to layer, like oblique waves lapping at a beach.

One soldier in the group would hear the message over the radio, he would say something to his immediate companions and then shout the message to his left and right. Each group would stir itself. Soldiers would put their reading material into their rucksacks, close their canteens and place them in the case, snuff out cigarettes and slowly rise from the ground.

Most would look at the sun then hastily avert their eyes—taking a cotton "drive on" rag from their pocket and wiping their faces. Though not part of formal drill, almost every soldier seemed to go through this ritual. Each would then grasp his rucksack by the straps, right-handed soldiers running both straps through their right forearm, left-handed their left forearm, etc. A companion would then hold the bottom of the ruck while the owner swung the assisted load onto his back. He would then reverse roles with his partner. In a short time, the first lift stood as one in file by each helicopter, heads bent forward under the weight of the helmets and the rucksacks that weighed only slightly less than the people carrying them.

The recoilless rifle gunners, arguably the most burdened next to the radio operators, swung their weapons to a balance point on their shoulders and staggered to a position of loose attention. The machine gunners held their weapon cradled in their arms and the rifleman universally held their weapons by the front hand guard. Quickly, the sweat began to form and run down the length of everyone's arms where it fell drop by drop on the grooved wood channel on top of the rifle barrel and then rushed down to the barrel itself and disappeared under the hand guard like a lost desert stream.

A crew member would signal each file to advance to the aircraft and like trained horses, each group of six soldiers would move forward. Three would split away and move to the other side of the helicopter passing the front but oblivious to the pilots who were going over their last few pre-flight checkpoints. The soldiers would face away from the aircraft and then make a short hop sliding themselves into the troop compartment as far as their rucksacks would permit. Each soldier would have about six inches of his upper thigh over the lip of the aluminum floor and his boots would be an inch or two above the skids. Arms would then fold across waists and heads would turn to follow crew members as each soldier tried to anticipate the coming commands and anxieties.

From the edge of the woods, the Ranger command group converged on two helicopters in mid-line, numbers eighteen and nineteen respectively. The battalion commander, his radio operators and Comrade Hu settled in the first, while the lieutenant and his NCO along with the commander's bodyguards filled the second. As if their loading was a cue, the large body began its mechanical awakening.

In the front, the aircraft commander began the startup procedures. He would begin the second hand on the clock, depress the cyclic, and with his gloved forefinger, press the starter button and look at his instrument panel. Initially, the fuel would splash wet and cold on the engine gloplug with minimal heat exchanged. The engine turbines would emit a whine as the battery discharged at 100 percent and the blades began an almost imperceptible movement.

Quickly, within 10 seconds of the clock being started, the compression chamber began to ignite on its own generated heat, but still not enough to trigger the combustive process. The blades began to revolve faster and faster and the entire frame began to buck and jerk in rhythmic response to the released forces of torque and exhaust.

The soldiers could see each blade as it passed before their eyes and feel the kicking of the engine and power train as its vibrations passed through the beaded aluminum floor. The pilot's eyes remained fixed on the instrument panel and at a certain point, a point that had been drilled into his head from almost the first day of flight school, he made a quick flick of his wrist turning the cyclic full to the left and then sharply twisting it back to its original position. Coincidental with this motion, the engine gave a sharp cough and began to ignite itself without aid of the battery.

The temperature of the exhaust gas had reached hundreds of degrees centigrade and was pouring out through the exhaust flange after passing over the turbine blades which rapidly turned in reaction to the pressure exerted against them. In turn, the transmission revolved faster than the eye could track and the blades became a swift blur until all that could be perceived was a steady shadow of diffused light and the cooling downdrafts that evaporated the accumulated sweat on the outer surface of the fatigues. With the aircraft reaching 100 percent RPM, the hull settled into a smooth vibration and the soldiers eyes turned instinctively to the pilots to watch the left arm of the command pilot as it grasped the cyclic—the clue to lift off.

The pilot on the lead aircraft depressed the "press to talk" switch on his collective, made a short acknowledgement of the message, flicked his radio to another band, passed the same message to the other aircraft, alerted his own crew by pressing the other half of the button, and then more firmly grasped the collective. As he deliberately raised the collective, his feet made slight adjustments with the pedals as his eyes alternately watched the scene to his front and the instrument panel. Slowly the percentage of torque crept toward the yellow marker on the instrument and all could feel a slight nudge as the ship stretched itself on the struts to where they were fully extended but still touching the strip.

As the gauge reached the yellow slash, the aircraft broke contact with the ground and began to creep forward—slowly at first and then with greater acceleration. The pilot moved his collective slightly forward depressing the pitch of the rotating blade. This caused the helicopter to move forward faster, take a slight dip and then quickly accelerate along the open ground. At a point in flight, the craft reached translational lift, broke its bonds to earth and reached skyward toward the billowy cumulus to the front.

Within the aircraft, the soldiers had tensed as they saw the pilot's left arm slowly rise toward the ceiling as he increased the power setting. As the aircraft blade pitch changed to take a bigger bite of the air, it began to generate a larger downdraft, which raised the surface of the strip from the ground in gouts of granular columns. At first, the dust was fine small particles that merely irritated the eyes. Quickly, as the blade pitch became more pronounced as the aircraft struggled for sufficient power, it began to pick up the larger heavier grit and drive it against exposed skin and into any opening the body or clothing offered. As a result, the soldiers did not see the moment the helicopter left the earth but opened their eyes when the wind blowing across their face dominated the wind coming up from below. Behind the lead helicopter, each of the 29 remaining helicopters underwent the same experience.

Some pilots, more proficient or hasty than the ship to their front, would break contact with the earth early. This would cause them to hover and wait until the lead helicopter had cleared the strip before they too could push their noses forward and gain altitude. With so many helicopters lifting and moving and shifting to avoid collision, it a seemed like the beginning of a country stakes race with horses bucking and churning for position while the riders waited for the split second when an opening was presented and then they would surge for the brief moment that open sky revealed itself. Within the span of a minute, all 30 helicopters had left the strip and nothing remained except a towering red cloud of dust swirling itself about the remaining eddies and down drafts left behind.

The soldiers designated for the second lift watched in unison as the last aircraft cleared the PZ and hurried onward in the settling dust and debris to catch the thin pencil line of their companions as they lost distinction and definition in the clear cobalt blue sky. The soldiers moved in unison toward the red slash and occupied the positions so recently vacated.

To the west, slowly circling the Dong Nai, the L-19 pilot maintained radio contact with the helicopters and adjusted the artillery fires and tactical air strikes now pulverizing the landing zone. From his cockpit, he could see the artillery battery firing, the rounds impacting, the assault force converging and the small pencil streaks of the F-4 Phantoms as they delivered their last load of napalm on the elephant grass that composed the LZ.

Underneath his circles, several hundred soldiers waited quietly in the newly dug trenches as the jets screamed overhead, neatly bisecting their camp. Further to the West, General Thanh quietly sipped a cup of tea and drew deep puffs from his Pall Mall as he composed a message. To his rear, the large red-faced Caucasians talked excitedly and craned to see the jets through the small openings in the jungle canopy.

15

Airborne

The helicopters reached flight altitude, about 2,000 feet above ground and headed steadily on a course of 240 degrees and an airspeed of 95 knots. The 30 helicopters spread out in groups of five in staggered intervals in trail. From the ground, it looked like several flocks of ducks. All were going in the same direction but under the control of several leaders.

To provide sufficient time for the LZ preparation, the L-19 pilot directed the force considerably east so that its arrival on the ground would coincide with the last rounds exploding just on the flanks of the helicopters as they touched down. It was an act of delicate timing but with practice, the L-19 pilot and his helicopter crews had achieved excellent orchestration. The helicopter pilots knew to turn and follow the last bombing run and, barely out of the remnants of the trailing black exhaust, touch down as the white phosphorous from the last artillery rounds marked the edges of the LZ.

Within the helicopters, as the sensation of height registered, the soldiers looked around and instinctively drew inward. Noticing that there was no apparent impetus to fall, each relaxed and watched the flat checkerboard rich green country unfold underneath as the wind brought a welcome evaporative effect. The tiny red powder dust that had saturated everything was blown off and the only trace that remained was the dark brown mud streak where the dirt had joined the sweat as it progressed from the upper to the lower body.

The engine and transmission passed its powerful vibrating throb through the metal floor and across the buttocks of each man. The steady vibration messaged itself through the viscera of each man until it terminated along the headband of the helmet. The collective throb massaged anxiety and allowed each man to view the scene below him with detachment and remove the immediate future from his mind.

Below, the quilted pattern of land management was in obvious contrast to the non-geometric shapes and monochromatic schemes laid down by nature with the jungle copses and meandering streams and rivers. The tiny red and silver slashes of city roofs shown out against the brown and green earth slashes where the thatch roofs of the villages faded into the brown of the cultivated land. The water collected in the paddies and canals shimmered as the soldiers eyes passed the parallax created by the sunlight as the helicopters coursed across the sky. The scenes below began to change rapidly as the route of the helicopters passed from city to village to town to jungle. Soon, nothing shown below except the unbroken green carpet of War Zone D bisected by the Dong Nai River and its tributaries. Looking out of the right side of his helicopter, the lieutenant could see the small brown speck of the L-19 as it circled the black and white smoke columns rising from the ground below.

The pilots began to depress their collectives' cyclics causing the helicopters to steadily lose altitude and nosed toward the orbit point where they would wait for the last pass by the Air Force. Upon hearing it, the pilots would pull out of the circle and snake toward the exhaust trails pointing toward the burning ground.

Above the helicopters circled several F-4 Phantom jets from Bien Hoa Airbase. They were heavily laden with a full bomb load and were taking their turns prepping the LZ under the control of a small L-19 that was circling over the target less than 500 feet off the ground. The aircraft were loaded with mixed munitions. One had a load of napalm, "wall to wall nape," on his six wing stations and a cluster bomb unit (CBU) on his fuselage anchor point. He could not drop the CBUs on the LZ due to the high dud rate and made a mental note to drop it on the river's edge. The other jets had a mix of 250-, 500-, and 750-pound bombs. All the aircraft carried a 20mm Gatling gun and 2,000 rounds of ammo. The different weighted bombs were alternately fixed on the anchor points so that the heaviest would be dropped first working toward the lightest. Experience showed that the heavier bombs on initial passes would clear away a lot of the brush and mines and the lighter bombs could then be used to hit more precise targets as they were exposed.

The L-19 pilot was also adjusting some ground artillery and several helicopter gunships. The pilot had noted the gun target line of the artillery and bisected the programmed LZ using that base direction. He had called the artillery to the left of the line and the helicopters to the right. In that manner, both could be used simultaneously with minimal danger. In between helicopter passes, he brought in the F-4s to work the edges of the LZ. Since they flew above the maximum ordinate of the artillery, they could make their runs while the artillery was shooting. The result was that something was exploding on the LZ all the time. The soldiers in the orbiting helicopters could see this and it gave them a sense of satisfaction and greater confidence.

The Rangers could see the individual puffs of each of the explosions as they impacted with the LZ. The bombs made large black columns of smoke that rose immediately in the air. The artillery made smaller grayish white puffs that quickly dissipated. The helicopter rockets made a smoky yellow white trail as they impacted with a flash and white or gray-black cloud. In between, the soldiers could see intermittent streams of red tracers as the gunship pilots covered the flanks of their aircraft's traverse across the LZ. All around on the LZ, small fires were ignited that gained in intensity and added their smoke to the billowing TNT, steam, and burning organic matter.

In a coordinated ballet, the F-4s made their last pass, emptying their 20mm, the artillery shifted from the center of the LZ to 500 meters out on all sides, and the troop transport helicopters neatly bisected the LZ as they flashed over the tree tops with the gunships dancing ahead raking the flanks of the LZ where the jungle met the open ground. Disrupted by the unexpected assault on their nesting grounds, hundreds of birds flew up and around the haze seeking to escape the heat and noise of the concentrated fires. They flew into rotor blades, dove into the jungle canopy and circled above the scene in no order or direction. Sucked into the wake of rapidly passing aircraft, some were pulled along in the vortex to be ejected from the air-stream, tumbling to the earth in the period between helplessness and when their instincts and wings again regained control.

Above the scene, and safely out of the path of both aircraft and artillery, the L-19 slowly circled observing the unfolding scene. From his vantage point, the pilot could see the growing column of smoke rising from the ground in the heavy afternoon air. Each impact of artillery rounds or air force ordnance showed as a sharp bright flash and gray-black puff against the blue haze of the burning land. In one scene, he could see the friendly artillery positions firing, their impacts on the ground, the orbiting fighter aircraft and the inbound stream of helicopters fixed on the steadily rising column of smoke.

Like a single stream of geese, the helicopters stretched back from the pick-up zone to the initial landing spot on the LZ. As the first helicopter's rotor wash kicked up a cloud of ash and burning embers, the L-19 pilot could clearly see the waning rotor wash of the last helicopters as they departed the PZ.

The helicopters passed over the jungle canopy and crossed into the open LZ at full speed. The pilots, now all in trail, sped toward the intended touchdown points at the far end of the open field. Just prior to reaching that point, the pilots depressed the collective, pulled back on the cyclic and made quick pedal adjustments. These sharp movements dropped the helicopter from 85 knots to almost zero in fewer than five seconds and deposited the skids firmly on the ground as they slid like a sleigh across the moist, newly churned earth.

The helicopter came to an abrupt halt as the troopers were spilled flat on their faces into the dirt while the door gunners steadily raked the foliage searching for an unseen target. The transportation spent no more than five seconds on the ground before they began to rapidly ascend into the sky behind a huge trail of dust, flying brush and smoke that engulfed the soldiers—much faster than they took off at the strip.

With a mixture of curiosity and anxiety, the soldiers, poised on the struts of the helicopters, leaped off just slightly before touchdown and moved away from the rotorwash which kicked up angry swirls of dirt, smoke and burning embers. As the initial helicopter lift faded into the distance, the soldiers picked themselves up and moved toward the tree line. Very suddenly, as the noise of their transport faded into silence, the soldiers were utterly alone.

16

The Movement

The Rangers rapidly picked themselves off the dirt and began to aggressively move toward their assembly points on the edge of the LZ. The LZ had more brush and reeds than anticipated and most of the vegetation was aflame. The beating wind of the helicopter blades had breathed a fire and fury into the smoldering grass that had now joined with other burns to make a series of loud and obscuring obstacles.

The soldiers fought to orient themselves in the swirl and rushes of smoke and seek comfort with visual and voice contact with their buddies. The leaders had the radio earpieces next to their heads and were talking intently into the mouthpieces, looking down toward the ground and moving rapidly in the direction their radio operators were leading them. Above them, slicing slow circles above the LZ, the L-19 pilot continued to radio artillery adjustments and take reports from the advisors on the ground.

The Rangers began to organize themselves and initially moved slowly, then more rapidly toward the tree line where they collected into company perimeters to await the second and final lift into the LZ. Quickly, the Rangers placed forward security positions deeper into the jungle and sent small patrols to sweep the LZ in the opposite direction. The leaders began to coalesce around their maps and compare the actual with the anticipated.

Within the command group, Major Hiep placed himself between his radio operator and Comrade Hu. He wanted to refer to both means of intelligence with minimal waiting time. The lieutenant contacted the L-19 and relayed the coordinates of the route for artillery registration. At this extreme range, the lieutenant hoped he would not have to use the 175mm battery as he could see his route was exactly parallel to the GT line.

Four and a half kilometers south and slightly west, other people heard the helicopters and the explosions. Fires were quickly started and extra rice was cooked. Hasty letters were written and placed with the regimental courier. The rice, still hot from the helmet cook pots, was stuffed in socks and placed in small packs or an empty grenade pocket.

As the last artillery marking rounds exploded on the LZ, the second battalion of Viet Cong extinguished its cook fires and began to send its personnel across the river. The movement took some time as the craft could not be launched until the L-19's route could be timed to where it was out of sight of the river bend. The rotation was such that more than four hours were required to transport the additional 350 personnel to the fortified camp. As the last launch reached the eastern bank, elements of the Second Regiment began to depart the cool shade of the Binh Tram and move slowly to the just-vacated positions just inside the edge of the western shore.

The Rangers formed into two columns at the edge of the LZ. Initially moving through the heat, smoke and dense obscuring atmosphere of the burning ground, they loosely coalesced at the first sanctuary that offered shade and clean air. As officers joined the assembly, organizational order began to assert itself. By the time the final assault lift departed, the battalion had begun its slow movement to the west.

Initially within a few yards of each other, the columns spread apart to a distance of more than a hundred yards, just beyond the point of visibility but still within range of hearing if one stopped to listen. Through time and hard experience, the unit had learned that such a formation minimized the chance of an ambush and provided maximum flexibility and firepower should a force be encountered on the march.

Each column was of roughly equal size and firepower. Each was led by a rifle company and point platoon. The battalion commander, the American lieutenant and Comrade Hu followed just to the rear of the point platoon. In the opposite column, the battalion executive officer and the American sergeant with their radios trailed the sister lead platoon. Movement continued in this manner for approximately an hour when a halt was ordered.

Here, about two in the afternoon and approximately three kilometers from the map objective, the twin columns rested. The jungle, once thick and tangled at the edge of the harsh light that marked the open ground, was now deep, silent and open underneath. The vegetation of the canopy began 50 feet or higher on the smooth barked columns that held the green cathedral in place. Small patches of scrub or newly sprung trees grew on the smooth brown peat floor where stabs of light had penetrated. Shafts of light played and sparkled across the dark background in a blue-white haze that obscured all but the closest objects.

The soldiers, responding to experience, took the cue to halt by silently dropping to the soft floor and looking out toward the dark wall that trailed invisibly beyond their sight. The Montagnard machine gunners silently extended the bipods on the front of the barrels and lit their pipes as they lay behind their guns. The command groups spoke quietly on their radios confirming the comforting proximity of each to the other. The lieutenant spoke to the pilot, whose presence could only now be ascertained by occasional sound bites that escaped into the green-roofed amphitheater. Below him, the pilot could detect almost nothing of interest. Trails of smoke still wisped from the LZ. The road columns had reached their destinations and the air was clear for the length of his vision. To west, on the river, the streaks of chocolate silt stirred by the long props of the boats were quickly rendered invisible by its fast-flowing coffee-black waters.

The battalion commander and Comrade Hu, accompanied by Hiep's bodyguards, moved quietly to the lead platoon and sat down in a small circle with the point squad. Hiep took a lit Pall Mall from his bodyguard and gave it to Hu. A second cigarette was offered to the group and Hiep took this and placed it in his mouth. He began a soft interrogation of Hu and looked toward the obscured light to their front. Hu, at first submissive, pointed in the same direction and animatedly began gesturing as he described the configuration of the base camp.

Hiep gave a short order to the platoon leader who immediately moved forward with a squad. In the absence of the small unit, Hiep and Hu rested and talked quietly, the smoke from their cigarettes slowly climbing upward unimpeded by competing breezes to be lost in the obscurity of the green above. Shortly, the group returned with the platoon leader excitedly confirming what he was asked to find. Less than a half kilometer to their front, a low depression marked the spot where the ancient alluvial riverbed began. As Hu had described it, the base camp lay less than two kilometers away. It was now three o'clock. The objective could easily be reached within an hour.

Hiep stood up, gave short quiet instructions to the group and stepped aside from the main column. The soldiers began to rise as so many legs on a millipede and quietly move forward. Hiep, Hu, and their party waited patiently as the soldier stream passed by and then joined at their usual position.

Off to the side of the columns, just beyond view, a dozen other people observed this movement. On General Thanh's specific orders, the VC regiment had sent its best scouts to the LZ once it was firmly identified by preparatory fires. Their instructions were to fix the soldiers, report their nationality and strength, and then trail them to their destination. It was important to Thanh's plan that he know as soon as possible who he was fighting, where they were coming from and in what strength. Depending upon the answers to those questions, he would choose the nature of the battle.

He had taken the unusual step of personally briefing the scouts and instructing them on the necessity of remaining hidden. On his orders, they stripped to the waist and took no weapons. With this arrangement Thanh felt an individual would be much less willing to chance an encounter or defend rather than retreat. It was critical to his strategy that the assault force be fully committed at his time and place before they were aware of the circumstances.

The scouts had moved to the base camp under the leadership of a senior engineer. He had picked the best men in his unit and briefed them intently. A scout would cover each point and trail element as well as the flanks of the unit as it moved. In such a manner, the scouts would act much like cowboys securing a moving herd of cattle. Comfortable but not obtrusive.

Thanh had determined that the base camp could only be approached from two directions—either the open ground to the east or the low but trafficable route from the south through the hills the French had taken years past. Only Americans would venture on the southern route. Any helicopter force would have to land on the open ground to the east and Thanh believed that the haste of effort would dictate such an approach. When the rubber workers reported that no armored columns moved north from the Highway One road junction, he ordered the scouts to move east. As the initial artillery fires impacted on the ground, the chief scout sent his party forward.

The group consisted of 24 personnel, more than twice what would be needed at any one time. However, to insure that Thanh and the defending soldiers had sufficient early information, the chief scout planned on a system of couriers along the route. The group reached the LZ and rested several hundred yards within the wood line while the predatory fires rained on the open ground. As soon as the white smoke arose, the scouts moved to the western corners of the ground and awaited the helicopters.

As the troops offloaded and slipped into the jungle, the scouts adjusted their distance by sound and quietly slid around the force. As the Rangers moved, the scouts moved with them, shadowing the flanks. Ebbing and flowing as the Rangers twisted their way west, the scouts, like polar magnets kept just far enough to avoid contact but close enough to confirm presence. Periodically, a courier would be sent quickly to report progress. A soft intelligence collar had been slipped on the unsuspecting force.

Drained by the sun while waiting, and exhausted by the large loads carried in a steaming green oven, the Rangers were unaware of their pilot fish companions. Dropping down the brown depression that was the jungle floor, they moved steadily onward into the dark mottled air and rapidly dwindling afternoon light. After some period of time, the point man on the southern column surprised a VC bathing in a small creek less than a hundred meters from the base camp. The VC scouts, surprised by the rapidity of the Ranger advance, had not been able to pass a final alert before the first encounter occurred.

17

The Decision

At the sound of the first hesitant shots, the battalion commander called his forward element and requested a situation report. He knew that he was within a kilometer of the objective and that the lead elements may have triggered a scout or guard. As the fire picked up, his instincts overrode his initial assumption. He knew he was moving into something serious and wanted to quickly move forward where he could actually see and feel the action. Comrade Hu dropped to the ground and diverted his eyes as everyone's energy swirled around him.

With 22 years of almost constant combat experience, Hiep had learned that reports were usually worthless and that there was no substitute for the finely tuned instincts gained from physical presence to the action and close proximity to the soldiers engaged. He needed to judge the nature of the combat, the spirit of enemy resistance and the attitude of his own troops. He would subliminally process this data and make rapid, lifesaving decisions. Usually, he knew he was in a deficit strength situation. Here he was unsure as to the balance of forces and needed to make a clear personal judgment.

He steadily passed his own column of troops moving slowly forward. They were still fairly far to the rear of the action and not physically engaged in the fighting. As soldiers weary from extended combat exposure, they appeared somewhat emotionally uninvolved with the noise to the front. They pressed forward with heads down and heavy breath, their eyes and instincts becoming more tuned to the primordial senses that lay latent within.

As veterans, their ears were sharply tuned and their instinctual juices had begun to flow. Their eyes followed his back as he rapidly passed them with his radio operators pressing toward the rising and falling sharp sounds of the engagement as they filtered through the dwindling light and haze.

As he moved forward, he noted the changing degrees of awareness and reaction on the part of his soldiers. From his initial location in the column, soldiers continued to plod forward. Closer to the sounds of action, the column slowed down and begun to spread out—rifles were held at the ready and anxious eyes screened forward and toward the flanks as they moved toward the now distinct sharp fire to the front.

Closer still, the commander could feel the vegetation part and rend itself against metal as the column dissolved into the ground and forward motion stopped. At this point, the soldiers were flat on the ground or moving on all fours to take whatever meager protection the terrain provided. Leaves were falling in small flurries as automatic weapons from both sides began to chew and dissolve nature's patient work.

Hiep inched his way through the jungle until he had reached the rear of the lead platoon. At this point, he found himself in an open clearing looking directly into a fortified base camp. Even on the quickest of glimpses, he knew this was a far larger and more developed complex than he had expected. For the first time since the initial shots were fired, he knew his battalion was in serious trouble.

The base camp was laid out in a linear fashion stretching from one creek to another and apparently in great depth. It was composed of a series of zigzag trenches interspersed with block houses at ground level that were constructed at a 45-degree angle to the front. Each of the angled bunkers had two machine guns stitching overlapping fires and chewing the delicate woody vegetation at a uniform height less than 12 inches from the jungle floor. The overall effect of this design was an awesome array of dug-in positions laterally and in depth with withering cross fires. The battalion's lead elements were frozen to the ground and any initiative had been lost.

As Hiep dropped behind a large tree, he quickly noted that the positions and logs were brand new. The earth was still bright red and hadn't been assimilated into the soil cover by the rains. The thatch covering the cook houses and sleeping huts was still green. He guessed that the complex was only partially manned. He also estimated that it was built for at least a regiment and was fully ready. He wondered how many people occupied the camp and where the main force resided.

He found the forward platoon leader and company commander and rapidly assessed the situation. They believed that a reinforced company occupied the camp and had been caught half alert. They reported a great deal of noise in the rear of the camp and guessed that the company was requesting and receiving reinforcements from whatever sources were nearby.

At this point, Hiep believed he had two options. He could pull back and attack later with artillery support from the 175mm battery or he could assault with what he had and hope to take the camp before a decent defense could be mounted. His instincts told him that a much larger force was across the river and would make an all-out effort to annihilate him if they could get across. His experience told him that he had a much better chance for survival if he held the camp rather than offer them the chance to trap him in the jungle with no hope of rapid reinforcements.

Accordingly, he quickly issued orders, stood up on a knee and blew his whistle signaling an assault into the camp. Less than two minutes had elapsed between the commander's first view of the base camp and his order to move—such is the power of instinct and experience.

From this moment, soldiers would win or die in this position but no one could freely chose his options. The issues would be decided by brute force, will, skill and luck.

18

Closure

The initial shots alerted both forces—the Rangers moving toward the river and the VC already occupying the base camp. The Rangers picked up their heads, moved their hands nervously up and down the handgrips on their rifles and pressed forward. The VC, having assumed at least an hour of leisure before engagement, scrambled for the leading trenches from the heavily shaded growth next to the riverbank.

Though both forces intended to meet at this point, neither was fully prepared and the initial fight was more of an engagement than a deliberate assault and defense. This was not how he intended the action to be fought but he resolved to make the best out of what his scouts had presented him.

Hiep yelled at his column to move forward and directed that his southern column do likewise. His plan was to assault the camp as quickly as possible and even though outnumbered, gain as much of the fortification as possible and then use it to his advantage for defense—trapping the superior force between their own fortifications and the river. Given some time and good work by the L-19 pilot, the Americans would reinforce, more than balancing the odds. Retreat was not an option as the greater portion of the lead units were already in the initial trench line. The rapidly building firestorm would quickly have destroyed most of them should they have attempted to rise and withdraw.

At the sound of the first shots, the lieutenant had notified the L-19 pilot of contact and had requested artillery. This was immediately relayed by the pilot as he broke out of his orbiting reverie in the waning sunlight. The 155 batteries, normally the first to fire, were just beyond the range of where the lieutenant believed the base camp to be. The pilot switched his instructions to the heavy battery south and east of the engaged forces.

The battery personnel had been monitoring the flow of the initial Ranger movement through the fire direction net. The FDC had placed the radio on a small loudspeaker ostensibly to insure that all necessary personnel heard the commands during a firing mission. This was particularly important during an actual mission as the combination of noise and excitement distracted people's attention from the request for what was wanted from the sounds of what had been. Still, through the actual landing, no fires were requested. In truth, the radio served as entertainment as well as strengthened the growing kinship between the heavy battery and the orphan battalion that so frequently needed them.

The lieutenant checked his map as the battalion column hurriedly closed onto the leading edge of the base camp and the trenches that stretched past their eyeshot. He threw a yellow smoke grenade into the only cleared portion of ground he could see as he protected himself behind a large tree that was shedding bark and branches above him. Quickly, the sergeant joined him and began firing to the front as other Rangers quickly passed by in a low crouch and filled the available trench lines.

Unsure of his exact position on the ground as well as the dangers of using a 175mm gun at maximum range, he asked the pilot to adjust against a target well away from the map objective. The pilot selected a small bump in the canopy south of the bend in the river and began the adjustment process.

Several minutes after the initial request, the lieutenant could hear the deep rolling boom of the first round even as it overrode the more immediate crack and thump that surrounded him. Several seconds later, a deeper shorter crash was heard as the sound exploded. Both forces took a momentary pause in the action as they were transfixed by this new sound. Above the men, several birds broke into flight and called excitedly. The noise of the explosion rolled slowly across them and disappeared into the dappled half-light of the deepening afternoon.

At the battery position, the request for fire had stirred everyone into action. The 8-inch guns, though there, were unable to fire due to the extended range. Nonetheless, the two crews moved to their guns and sat on the tracks watching their brother crewmen and mentally participating.

The crews, though helmeted, were without exception naked from the waist up. Sweat wore small trails down each body coursing through the thin microscopic red dust layers that had accumulated through the afternoon. The officers, more formal, wore shirts though those in the FOC had no headgear.

The ammo handlers stood well behind the gun, holding the long aluminum barrel swabs. The gunners hunched over the optical sights on the tracked carrier aligning the crosshairs with the split between the aiming stakes that ran to the front of the gun.

The rightmost gun was the registration piece. Its crew executed a well-rehearsed drill. The FDC called the range and elevation for the gunner to place on the sight. The charge and fuse setting was then relayed to the ammo handlers. Each recipient, in turn, shouted the instructions back for the gunnery sergeant to confirm.

The ammo handlers tore off the unneeded powder bags and slung them into a deep hole that was excavated well to the rear of the position and toward the center of the battery. They then placed the shell on an aluminum cradle and attached it to a hydraulic lift at the rear of the barrel.

The gunner would push a small red-knobbed black post and the cradle would swing up and lower the shell on the open breech port. A second handle would be tilted and a mechanical ram pushed the shell well into the maw of the breech.

The powder bag was handed up to the gunner, who pushed it up the breech. When the breech was closed, the gunner placed an ignition primer in the center of the breech, closed the opening and indicated all was ready. His assistant stood aside the barrel and to the year with a lanyard in hand. On command, he gave a quick short jerk to the rope and the gun fired with a loud violent buck.

The combination of charge, backpressure, and barrel length caused the entire carriage to heave upward and backward from the front. The great weight of the system would drive the bulldozer-like spade at the back into the dirt at the rear. The gun would recover its gravity and then transmit an equal thrust back into the front portion as the gun achieved equilibrium.

To the front, the explosive energy released at the lip of the barrel traveled faster than the speed of sound in a perfect circle and impacted on the ground beneath it. The earth threw up its smaller particles, which hovered in the air just below the barrel. The smoke and gasses spread from the opening and propelled themselves forward. Looking up from his position, the gunner could follow the trace of the shell as it arced out and beyond his sight.

During the time consumed by the artillery process, both sides had made dramatic adjustments to their respective conditions. The Rangers, responding to nervous energy and Hiep's very physical presence, had occupied approximately two-thirds of the trench line. Though now better protected and with the advantage of initiative, the fixed and sinuous nature of their entrenched positions acted to dissipate and weaken their firepower. Once flowing from a small point, they now found themselves spread across a relatively wide front facing an enemy with far greater firepower and superior numbers.

The VC, initially surprised, were now strongly occupying the remaining trenches. The regimental commander had ordered all of the First Battalion into the remaining trenches and sent the newly arrived Second Battalion to the Ranger flanks. This unit was carefully instructed to refrain from attacking until both flanks were identified and then to close from the rear first. As Thanh had instructed him, the assault force was to be pulled into the camp, cut from the rear and pinned against Soui Long Creek.

During the time elapsed between the initial request for fire and the round actually landing, Thanh's plan was largely achieved though neither side yet realized it. The momentum of the Ranger assault carried it to a high water mark in camp but left them bare of forces to their rear. In this vacuum, a company of the Second Battalion began to surge. Already, sister companies had hit against the Ranger flanks and locked the southern position against the creek. The southern company, having secured the other side of the creek, slid two of its platoons to the Ranger rear to reinforce its partner as the artillery impacted.

The initial round was noted by the pilot who adjusted its burst against his best reference point, the bend in the Dong Nai. In what seemed an eternity of time to the lieutenant, the second round was sent on its way. This exploded with tremendous force less than a hundred feet in front of him and brought great torrents of splinters and metal raining down. Hiep grinned widely and made a broad thumbs-up sign. The lieutenant blew wood and dirt from his handset and requested four rounds.

At the second adjustment, both guns were now loaded and set. On command, they detonated with a great surge and wash of smoke, dust, and overpressure. Immediately, the barrels were cleared by an air blast and the breeches opened. As quickly as hydraulics permitted, the charges and warheads were inserted, the breeches closed, and the crew awaited the next command. The crews had moved with great energy and purposefulness as all realized that the unit was in direct contact and only they could help. The 8-inch howitzer crews had initially hesitatingly and then with speed, moved behind the 175mm crews, and doubled their capacity.

The two rounds, though fired simultaneously, landed in considerably different locations. One landed on the leading edge of the foremost Ranger trench and the second well to the rear. This round landed directly on top of the VC company forming to the rear and virtually destroyed all but the outer squads. However, what registered to the lieutenant was that two rounds landed with devastating effect on his position. He ordered a cease fire as Hiep withdrew his now dazed forward elements to a closer trench line.

The result of the artillery had several effects. The VC regimental commander, surprised at the effect of the artillery on his own forces and unaware of the mistaken trajectory, ordered the assaults to halt. He wanted time to define the boundaries and to reconstitute his elements. Hiep was forced to withdraw his lead elements and upon the discovery of the force to his rear, withdraw his flanks to provide sufficient forces to cover that area. The net effect was that the Rangers now held a smaller and more effective perimeter and received a breathing spell. It was now about 5 o'clock and light was giving away to darkness. Even in the newly opened canopy, more obscuration than illumination showed itself.

19

Aid to Brothers

Farther east, the 48th Regiment was still moving itself to the Chinese Farm along Highway 20 to the north of the 175mm artillery location. The operation had taken the entire day to complete. Remnants were still trickling in when the initial contacts were heard through the distance. It was a cool area, shaded on its edges by the remains of an abandoned rubber plantation. By map distance, fewer than 10 kilometers separated the regiment from the Rangers. Without trying, the soldiers could distinctly hear the competing precise short flat sounding vintage American weapons and the much quicker and sharper communist AK-47s. Overarching them both was the deep distinctive throaty bursts from the heavy machine guns. Hearing the sounds, the soldiers glanced anxiously at the officers and into the jungle toward the battle.

The regimental commander had established his command post in a farmhouse overlooking the road. The family was engaged in cooking the evening meal for the group and the children peered inquisitively from behind the pig shed. The father had sent his daughter and oldest boy further up the road to a relative when the troops had first arrived.

In another hut, the regimental radios in the operations room had been established. Jeeps and a small truck were parked outside. A long wire cable ran from a series of batteries in the truck bed to the radios now resting on a table inside the hut. From here, the operations officer listened to a radio and marked dispositions on the map. The American advisor listened anxiously to the radio and referred often to his own map. Occasionally, he would move to his own jeep and talk to the senior American headquarters in Xuan Loc.

Trinh, avoiding the heat of the house and the small mosquitoes that hid in the darker recesses of the corners, sat on the front seat of his jeep. The vehicle had been pulled under the shade of the brush arbor attached to the hut. Normally, this area, with its hard-pounded dirt base, was the principal family living area. Only when it rained would the area be vacated in favor of the cover of the tightly woven thatch roof. Here, the fire was kept to cook, the pigs were fed, the baby rested in a small hammock strung between thin support poles, and the father smoked his locally grown harsh pipe tobacco.

Today, the family had hastily vacated it in favor of the regimental command group. Trinh's aide had tried to persuade the family to remain and tend the fires but the father had politely declined. Instead, he sat under the arbor and made tea for the group as a mollifying gesture. Under this brushy canopy, Trinh had driven the jeep and sat in it listening to reports of his troops assembling. The seat was a custom item of vinyl covered with thick cotton quilting. It was soft and comfortable and Trinh began to doze in the warm afternoon breeze.

Around him, the open rolling fields and isolated huts began to fill with his soldiers as they arrived from their abrupt departure from town. The trucks halted at the center line trail amidst clouds of dust. Troops would then dismount and occupy the best huts and shaded wood lines available. In this manner and with minimum direction, the bulk of the regiment found itself largely assembled. This information was duly reported to Xuan Loc by both Trinh and his American advisor.

Trinh rose from his seat, turned around and saw the remains of the artillery mission dissipate in the darkening sky. He turned and entered the house. At the side of the single room, a flat pallet bed rested next to the wall. It was constructed of ironwood and was polished shiny black with use. Over it, a white mosquito net hung suspended from the ceiling poles. Trinh lay down on the pallet, rested his head on the wooden Chinese pillow and fell fast asleep.

20

Division of Responsibility

The lieutenant and the sergeant had thrown themselves behind the nearest large tree when the first VC had exploded out of the brush to their front. They had lain parallel to the ground and continuously worked the radio throughout the artillery adjustment. The lieutenant took the handset from the NCO's rucksack and called the Ranger executive officer at the other end of the perimeter. He provided a brief sketch of the situation in his area and the actions he had undertaken. The XO was clearly excited but in control. Due to the nature of the VC flank attack, he had found himself at the point of a continuous firefight and was trying to seek shelter in the center of the two wavering columns.

Hiep quickly briefed the lieutenant. The plan was simple. It was written by the VC. The Rangers had to hold exactly where they were because they could do nothing else. The Rangers had attacked the new base camp and physically occupied about half of it. However, in so doing, they had placed their flanks against the S curve of the river and the reinforcing VC had infiltrated to their rear. Night was about an hour away and there was no communication with the outside world. The concept was to hold until daylight and either attack or withdraw depending on the VC initiative.

The lieutenant quickly briefed the sergeant on the concept and began to study the immediate area for a good defensive position. The sergeant was a veteran of Korea and a very good hunter at home. He had a natural eye for ground and its strengths and weaknesses and rapidly spotted the solution to their immediate need. Without explanation, he grabbed the lieutenant's equipment harness from behind and in a rapid low-slung gait moved toward his selected spot. The lieutenant, trained by now in the need for reflexive mutual action said nothing but allowed himself to be pulled to the sergeant's destination.

The sergeant had selected a very large banyan tree to terminate his rush. The tree was fully five feet broad at the trunk but was given another five feet of girth at the base by the wide-spreading but shallow root structure that anchored the tree into the ground. Like enveloping hands, the trunk buttresses held the two soldiers in its grasp and provided cover from the incoming bullets.

The rounds began to chip away at the tree trunk and root structure above their heads, but the thickness of the trunk absorbed everything that impacted to the front. The two dropped their rucksacks between them and propped the radio so that the antenna was upright resting parallel with the trunk. They then reached into their rucksacks and stacked the spare ammunition magazines and grenades.

The sergeant cautioned the lieutenant not to use the ammunition in the web gear carrier ammo except as a last resort. They might have to leave in a hurry and they would need all the bullets they could hastily carry away.

The pair adjusted their rucksacks in front of them, rested the front hand guards of the rifles across the frames and watched their front. Almost immediately, as if in the space of a breath, black lines began to appear to their front. Initially engaging the objects in the black lines with a mixture of anxiety and fear, repetitiveness quickly reduced their emotions to rote execution. The black lines would waver but never disappear.

21

The Black Lines

At first, the lines were not particularly discernible. Glimpses of people in black or blue shirts could be seen moving forward through the base camp and from the flanks. Later, as small arms fire trimmed the leaves and branches and artillery, mortars and rocket-propelled grenades (RPGs) shattered the trees themselves, the lines became more visible. The lines became people, people aligning themselves, facing the Rangers, and moving forward with weapons at the ready. As bullets impacted, the first lines would fall and those in the rear would move forward to maintain the momentum. Throughout the afternoon and early evening this dance of death continued in its rhythmic pattern little changed from the grim reality of Gettysburg and Verdun.

The VC would move quietly out of the trees by the river bank and occupy the closest unengaged fighting trench. Trenches to the rear would be filled by further reinforcements. Cadre would filter small groups of men to replace those killed in the fixed positions along the flanks or to vacated mortar positions in the rear.

On signal, usually a whistle, the most advanced line would crawl out of its trench toward the Rangers. Concurrently, two lines in the rear would rise on one knee. All three lines would move forward simultaneously. The first would open fire on full automatic and attempt to gain the next line to its front under a cloud of grenades and supporting machine-gun fire. The two lines to its rear would hasten forward to the just emptied trench and from there provide covering fire for their comrades to the front. Bodies from previous efforts would have to be scaled and avoided or occasionally utilized for cover as individuals and small groups failed to gain the sweet cover of protective earth when the Rangers gained momentary superiority of fire. Assaulting soldiers were impacted by rounds from both friend and foe. In the charnel ground of close-quarter life and death, bullets took no sides and selected the flesh geometry and chance ordained.

In this manner, over the afternoon and into the mid-evening period, the VC were able to wrest back all but two of the most forward trench lines. But they did this at a frightful cost.

The Ranger machine gunners had learned to key themselves on the whistle. They were now close enough together to intuitively establish mutually supporting fire. Instead of firing straight ahead, each gun swung on a cross-front axis providing the greatest possible killing potential. The Montagnard gunners, knowing that a long night was in store, fired in three-round bursts except when they had clearly defined targets. As it got darker, and the lines shorter, these opportunities were more and more prevalent.

The guns were laid across fallen trunks and could be swung across the front at almost ground level. The gunners did not have to raise themselves above the logs but simply guided their fire based on the noise and direction of the incoming small arms. From experience, they could judge the combination of air pressure created by closely passing rounds, the snap of passing bullets, and the sense of human pressure as direct assaults on them. Direct being a personal judgment of response or sure death.

When a line arose to charge forward, it was met by a stitching of machine-gun bullets interspersed with the bursts from grenade launchers and rifles. Invariably, the leading VC line was chopped in the torsos and heads as it rose above the scant cover of the trench. The technique of death visited on the Rangers initially was now turned full on the attacker. The scope of the battlefield was now so compressed that any bullet from any gun could range across the entire area and kill without discrimination. Fratricide and homicide were impossible to differentiate.

The trenches became full of dead and wounded to the point where succeeding lines of attackers had to pause to remove the contents of the previous charge. Bodies became stacked to the rear or front of trenches in such profusion that reinforcements had to jump over them to advance, thereby increasing their own casualties.

Despite the casualties, the weight of numbers began to slowly tell. With every charge and butcher's bill, the Ranger lines became smaller and the VC hold on their perimeter greater. Slowly, but at great cost, the Rangers became surrounded and knitted together in the tight bounds of their original assault position. While they grew closer together, there were less Rangers to share the space. Less ground to move upon. Less ammunition to share. No backdoors to open. No help to hold on for.

Each attacking event took on a grim similarity. A whistle blew, fire erupted from both directions. A crescendo of sound and movement was achieved and then an abrupt trailing off of both as each side readjusted to the new realities. Wounded crawled back to their last position or lay quietly awaiting help or death. Leaves, separated from the trees, would slowly shimmy down from the sky as so many snowflakes and rest equally upon the dead and alive to quietly camouflage the scene. The air would lessen its reek of cordite and blood and filter itself in the newly turned earth and just-revealed sky.

The organizational dynamics and efforts of supporting forces were lost to the combatants on the ground. Their life focus was on the very small but active center stage in which they dwelt. Each man was surrounded by a cacophony of fire, explosions, yells, falling branches, impacting earth, tree splinters, bright flashes and alternating waves of pressure and heat intermixed with sweat, blood and life matter spattered across individual consciousness. Soon, all this was mentally dulled to permit a fixed focus of survival effort on each soldier's immediate front.

A few seconds took on a life's importance as men on both sides struggled within the whole for his and his unit's survival. Each side experienced the same sensations, only the direction of effort varied. Life revolved around finding the lowest portion of the ground and the most protective tree limb while still maintaining the minimum of fighting effort to retain bonding within the group and survival of the whole.

Each man could feel more than see the effect of the unfolding action. He could discern explicitly the rounds inbound and outbound. The volume of discrimination soon became so great as to overwhelm the senses and to relegate them to a lesser place in the mind. Instinctively, each could judge the ebb and flow of the action.

No individual action took place other than the most basic. Initially, soldiers reached for their ammunition and mechanically loaded, fired, and reloaded magazines. A sense of supply soon overcame each soldier as the conflict wore on and firing became more discriminating. The soldiers in the bunkers, reasonably well protected and with good reserves, fired on automatic the longest.

The Rangers, mindful of the desperateness of their situation and their complete isolation, switched almost immediately to semiautomatic fire and husbanded each shot to a sure thing—of which there were many. At a mutual point, as if informed by some unseen messenger, both sides switched roles and assumed the other's tactics.

This gave the VC a sense of strength and they renewed their assaults with great intensity. However, the Ranger machine guns coupled with focused fire from a narrow front amassed sufficient casualties to dampen emotions to the point of rational self-protection. Soon, both perimeters settled into desultory fire from distances of less than 20 yards. Only the machine guns, sheltered and resourced, kept up a constant deep-throated beating chunk-chunk-chunk as they swept across the front cementing their targets to the jungle floor and raining bits of leaf and bark on the huddled defenders.

Light gave way to deepening darkness. Soon, the sharp chattering of the day gave way to the quiet blanketing obscurity of night. Unlike other nights, though, no animal or bird noises broke the silence and eyes with fixed and staring pupils looked into the inky darkness. On both sides, adrenalin overcame exhaustion as each soldier was reduced to hearing his own heart and lungs and to drawing upon his sense of unit to maintain his equilibrium and alertness. Every sound became intensified. Every sense magnified. Every man felt truly alone.

These short lulls would ensue, to be broken later by a reenactment of the previous event. This went on through the late afternoon and well past darkness. Then, as if on some command from the heavens or a mutual recognition of organizational exhaustion, the battlefield became totally quiet save for the low cries of the wounded and the anxious beating of each soldier's adrenalin-charged heart.

In the quiet solitude of pure aloneness, the lieutenant began to reflect on his recent past. In the mind's dark eye, he revisited the crucible experiences of death and killing.

The first was blind reaction. The column was moving slowly through the canopy in a single file. They knew they were close to the designated base camp location and were moving cautiously—smelling, hearing, feeling and sensing. Sensing with that sixth sense that people acquire who routinely deal with death.

It was an inbred visceral acquisition that controls the reflexes and nerve endings of humans and comes from somewhere deep within their primordial past that is subjugated deep within each person. These soldiers, like the other animals that lived in their environment, were on the leading edge of survival and had honed this visceral sense to a fine edge. That was why they were walking erect at this moment as they had first done several million years ago—ears attuned to slight anomalies and eyes peering beyond the mind's vision to see.

The lieutenant was walking behind the fifth man in the column. He had acquired the habit of moving gradually to the front as each day wore on. He would begin in the center of his column and through a combination of curiosity, boredom and energy, always manage to be with the lead element as the march terminated. At the moment, he sensed but could not register that something was different. He slipped his right hand across the pistol grip of the M-16 and placed his thumb on the selector switch as he swung the barrel further to his right to clear the back of the man in front of him. None of these actions mentally registered but were done nonetheless. Almost at the same time as his barrel swung toward the brush, the unmistakable sharp report of an AK-47 sounded toward his front.

The soldiers immediately took a half crouch and returned fire in the direction of the noise. The lieutenant quickly shifted his gaze from the point man to half right where his ears had registered the sound direction.

Approximately 50 feet in front of his gaze, there appeared an indistinct figure shrouded by the low bamboo bushes. Entangling vines descending from the trees and a maze of small trunks sprang up from the jungle floor. He could not clearly define the target but in a single involuntary motion moved his thumb rearward which shifted the safety to semiautomatic and depressed the trigger. The rifle remained at his hip as his eyes focused on the muzzle flash from the AK-47. The M-16 fired three shots, reflecting three sharp pulls on the half-inch crescent-shaped trigger. The steel-jacketed 5.56mm impacted on the indistinct shape and caused a large explosion that disintegrated the VC. The exploded form was wearing a light powder blue canvas jacket especially made to hold a dozen stick grenades. One of the bullets had struck a grenade and the VC exploded in a series of sympathetic detonations that took less than a millisecond to run their course. The only thing the lieutenant could register in his consciousness was the AK-47 flash and the blinding bright light and dirty gray smoke as the shadowy figure disappeared.

The second was a slow-motion rerun. The man was one of two that appeared from the dense undergrowth to the lieutenant's front. The lieutenant had been laying behind a large tree root and dividing his defensive sector with the NCO. Together, their fire had kept the VC from risking frontal attacks—instead, the VC had slipped to the right or left where they had a better chance against more inferior weapons. The M-16s and disciplined fire had earned a quickly found respect.

Now, however, the VC had received reinforcements and the pressure all along the line indicated a major assault was underway. The precursors began to move steadily forward sending a steady stream of bullets to their front as they cautiously advanced toward the Rangers.

Suddenly, two appeared in the lieutenant's sector to his immediate front—approximately 15 meters away. This was the first time that more than one man had appeared. The lieutenant rolled half over to warn the NCO for help but was immediately aware that the NCO was fully occupied and rolled back in time to see and shoot the first man as he crossed a fallen branch five meters to his front. No aim was taken and none was needed.

The bullet, fired from the M-16 held in the lieutenant's wrist, otherwise unsupported and certainly not in keeping with basic marksmanship techniques, was nonetheless effective. The lieutenant clearly felt the weapon jerk in his wrist and saw a small hole appear on the lower right cheek of the victim. Most noticeable to the lieutenant, however, was the way the body reversed itself. While the body was moving deliberately forward, the head suddenly acted as if it changed its mind and violently urged a movement to the rear. The hair, long and black, shot out behind the head as if pointing toward the desired direction.

Very quickly the head lost and the body prostrated itself straight forward, falling almost at attention across the tree root the lieutenant was peering over. The head actually crossed over the root with the neck resting on the jagged edge of the root top next to the M-16 barrel. The back of the assailant's head was opened like a ripe honeydew melon and the lieutenant could clearly see the ridges of the brain and the grayish, brown lining of the skull's interior.

Registered in the lieutenant's mind was a slowly moving body fighting itself that slowly, ever so slowly, became larger and larger as it moved in a direct path from its point of emergence in the jungle to its resting place next to the triangle shape of his front sight. It seemed almost unreal until the lieutenant simultaneously sensed the fountain of brain matter that coursed through the air from the back of the skull in a long arc that impacted on his helmet and drew a fatty bloody line from the helmet rim across his left eye and ended on his collar.

It reminded him of a photo of a girl with long black hair emerging from a pool and swinging her hair out of the water, causing a water trail to arc over her. The lieutenant knew better but sensed the similarity.

The third was very quick and much more reactive. The companion of the first VC followed directly behind his fallen partner and actually stepped on the pant cuffs of his fellow. At this point, the lieutenant clearly saw the rubber sandal and dirty feet with widespread toes as they covered the frayed black pant cuff and ground it into the dirt. The lieutenant could see the rise and fall of the metatarsals as the attacker shifted weight in his stride. The lieutenant had now taken a half squat behind the tree in a burst of energy caused by the falling VC and the image of the second man following closely behind.

His view of the attacker's foot was unimpeded though he could not see the rest of his body nor could the attacker see him. With the image also came the realization that the M-16 was out of ammunition. The lieutenant had a full magazine in his left hand and the empty magazine in his right palm, the rifle resting in a crook in his arm. The VC came over the root and looked behind the tree as his momentum carried him forward past the tree itself and past the lieutenant.

In a reflexive action, the lieutenant dropped the load from both hands and reached across his body with his left hand extracting his large Buffalo Skinner knife that was held by a leather sheath perpendicular to the ground. Almost before the M-16 hit the ground, the knife, aided by the energy of the lieutenant and the momentum of the victim, was buried to its hilt in the attacker's rib cage. The lieutenant had expended a tremendous amount of adrenalin energy and the power and torque of his left arm—even while fighting the momentum and weight of the VC—and picked up his victim like a feather and swung him against the inside of the tree where he was stuck bolt upright between the lieutenant and the NCO—the lieutenant and the dead man now at eye level with each other.

The lieutenant looked for a split second into the surprised eyes of the dead man and then reached to the ground to recover his M-16. Not until he reloaded and was behind the shelter of the root mass did he look up and back toward the trunk and notice that the VC was still perfectly erect with bent head and feet flat on the ground. The lieutenant remembered this image and returned to the tasks at hand.

As darkness fell, the jungle began to reassert itself. The permanent inhabitants of the area emerged as if to reassert their primacy.

22

The Bug

The lieutenant had spent the remainder of the daylight behind the tree roots and beside the log. Minding the sergeant's advice and example, he had fired on semiautomatic throughout the daylight period. Even so, he was astounded, and scared, when he inventoried his remaining ammunition magazines. Beginning with over 600 rounds, he now had fewer than 300 and he knew the greater requirements lay ahead.

Never had he raised his head more than a foot off the ground, and then only to engage the targets as they presented themselves in his area of responsibility. When the snap and impact of the incoming bullets had overcome the sense of confidence his own firing had provided, the lieutenant would drop his head and rifle across his rucksack and wait to regain his mental balance. During these brief escapist respites, he had found himself focusing on each detail of the world within range of his eyes.

He had noted the rough patches along the log where nature and small animals had made courses and scratches across its surface. He saw the fine cilia-like green hairs that marked the initial stages of the fungus attack that would eventually consume the log. He guessed the length of time it would take to destroy the log and compared it with an estimate of his own longevity. He observed the many small insects that traveled across the earth floor within a foot of his eyes—insects that he had never seen before.

At one point, he could no longer resist the urge to relieve himself. However, the enemy fire was so heavy that rather than move behind the tree and leave the sergeant, he simply rolled sideways and irrigated the ground between the log and where it met the earth. In a strange way, this gave him a feeling of security and he felt mentally refreshed. He watched the new liquid work its way through the leaves and detritus of the soil and become absorbed by the whole. Small insects worked their way from under the newly refreshed leaves and tested the air and water with their antennas. Without thought, the lieutenant absorbed this in his mind and went back to the task at hand.

Night quickly captured the scene but the action never ceased. Between loading his weapon and ducking from close fire, the lieutenant continued to drop to earth level and watch the world unfold six inches in front of his eyes. As the night claimed his vision, the lieutenant began to be aware of various phosphors and shimmering lights that replaced recognizable objects. Once, when he dropped an empty magazine and reached out to recover it, he scrapped the edge against the earth and was rewarded with a yellow-green glowing streak where he had disturbed the leafy cover.

After a while, the firing died down and both partners rolled inside the grasp of the banyan roots, back to back taking comfort from the warmth of their physical proximity and breathing as if united. Now, both had renewed the primordial nerves of animals and lay fully awake listening to each sound and judging with newly renewed long dormant instincts.

The lieutenant had no thought of sleeping but quickly calculated the meaning of what he heard and his planned reaction. After a while, the night became totally silent save for the occasional clicking of the bamboo batons held by the VC patrols as they marked their limits of advance to each other.

The lieutenant continued to watch the world within his vision and to draw analogies between the world he saw and the world he had previously known. At this point, a large beetle entered his view from directly underneath the log.

The insect was quite large. It measured almost two inches by the lieutenant's judgment. It was the largest non-human thing he had seen all day. It had large hook-shaped mandibles that had small barbs about halfway down the outreaching arms. Over these moving scythes waved two long silky antennas that moved rapidly from side to side in paired rhythm as it tested the path it had chosen. The bug was raised off the earth a good quarter inch by stiff black legs that broke halfway up into sharp turned knee joints that resembled two thirds of an equilateral triangle. Its body was hard and shiny and reflected the occasional green glows of the local phosphors. Carefully, but with deliberation, he made his way directly toward the lieutenant's waistline. It would move several inches, stop, wave its antennas, cross its mandibles and then proceed on. It did this several times as the lieutenant carefully watched this intrusion.

The bug finally made its way to the edge of the lieutenant's shirt at the belt line, tested the cloth surface and made an initial move across the material. The lieutenant had watched the entire movement carefully and was transfixed by its progress. By the time the insect reached his shirt, the lieutenant had reached deep within himself for mental comfort. For an instance, he reached for an empty magazine that he normally would have used to swat the life out of the intruder. Instead, he took comfort in observing another living thing also trying to survive the night. Without a trace of movement, the lieutenant relaxed his hand and watched it traverse his waist and move on into the darkness toward the sergeant. Once the vision of the bug was lost, the lieutenant returned to concentrate on listening, living and praying for the sunlight.

23

Command Decision

Like all military organizations since time immemorial, each combatant had a command location where information was processed and decisions made that affected the players present. On the western side of the Dong Nai, the Viet Cong command post was being used for its historical purpose. However, unlike most VC command posts in the South, this one was markedly different.

While it bore a complete similarity in physical outlay to the myriad of base camps that proliferated in the jungles of the South, the members present were unlike those found anywhere else in the communist structure in South Vietnam. Huddled around the thatch roof structure in the center of the camp were eight figures. All were seated in a circle around a large table under the roof of the hut. In the center of the table was a map. The table was built over the roof of the command bunker so that two of the participants were sitting over the floor-level entrance to the bunker with their feet dangling into the air. The rest were resting their toes on the earth or had wrapped their legs under the bench seats.

The central figure, General Thanh, was very neatly dressed in long-sleeve khaki shirts and pants. He wore no badge or rank but had a brightly shined NVA belt buckle directly centered on the seam of his pants and shirt. His hair was closely but professionally cut, unlike that of most of the participants at the table. He had brilliant white teeth with two large gold caps over the bicuspids and piercing dark brown eyes. He talked in a low but urgent tone and looked directly into each man's eyes as he spoke and pointed at a spot on the map with a gold Cross pen. This was the Commanding General of the Central Office of South Vietnam, COSVN, the man who ran the entire war for Hanoi in the South.

Seated around him were members of his staff and the commander of the VC unit that was presently in contact. The intelligence appraisal had been made with additional input from the scouts who had watched the initial insertion and counted the helicopters. Also present was the battalion commander that initially stood the brunt of the Ranger attack. He had left the base camp on direct orders of the COSVN commander to provide a personal assessment of the enemy encountered.

Seated at the table but separated from the rest by body language was a pair of heavy-set Caucasians. They were dressed in light cotton civilian clothes and even in the relative coolness of the evening had large sweat pools staining their shirts almost to the belt line. Both had blue eyes and close-cut hair with large florid cheeks and broad noses set over fleshy mouths. They resembled a piece of newly carved meat still exuding lymph fluid where the butcher had cleaved the flesh. Neither said anything but followed each speaker with pig-like eyes that carefully judged the sincerity and intent in the voice.

The commander had two broad courses of action available. He could withdraw the committed forces and retire to seek a better advantage. This would minimize his losses but it would also risk losing the opportunity he had so long planned even if it occurred in much more rapid fashion than he had envisioned. It was one of the rare instances where his forces could engage in combat with both numerical and technical superiority.

His intelligence officer indicated that the Rangers, though aggressive, were badly outgunned and understrength. The lack of artillery other than occasional 175mm fire was indicative of the fact that no other artillery units were close by. This also meant that no U.S. units were close enough for quick commitment. All were aware of the existence of the 11th Armored Cavalry, the Blackhorses, but discounted its ability to effectively reinforce by nightfall. Regardless, that contingency had to be considered.

The second option was to attack. The ground was favorable in that the Rangers were basically trapped in an unfriendly and unfamiliar base camp with the river flanking two sides and VC firmly entrenched in the rear of the position. The strength available was almost disproportionate to the task. Fewer than 300 Rangers were facing more than 1,100 main force Viet Cong with another 1,000 irregulars available within a day's march. The VC commander had heard very few automatic weapons and fewer than four machine guns had been counted in the last light probes. The landing zone was covered by scouts who indicated that no new forces had landed. Scouts to the south on the trail leading from Highway 20 to the base camp area reported no movement of U.S. units or helicopter sightings. The ARVN reinforcements, though within a short march from the Rangers, were discounted.

Once the facts were presented to the assembly, the conversation turned to the subjective aspects of the situation. The unexpected attack had caught the VC off guard and could damage their initiative to activate the larger plan if not broken off. However, the lack of immediate reinforcements to the Rangers provided a rare opportunity to strike quickly with great strength and destroy an elite unit—in effect, successfully executing the strategy.

Such an act would result in major positive publicity for the cause. This was also an opportunity to display the results of the training and arming of the unit that had taken place in North Vietnam for the past six months at significant cost and personal risk to the senior commanders. The unit had been handpicked and then as carefully trained as time could be made available. This was seen by many as a test of competing strategies within the Hanoi policy-making apparatus—slow attrition or highly visible direct combat encounters.

Thanh had intended this force to be the base unit within this area of III Corps. It would gain great prestige among the populace if its initial exposure was with a great victory. The COSVN commander had personally accompanied this unit to Binh Tram 42 and intended to accompany it to its base area and insure its complete understanding of its role within the overall program. He prided himself on personal exposure with maneuver elements and his ability to successfully transition from low-level tactics to national strategy and back.

The COSVN commander was also aware that time was an important factor. By his estimation, the Rangers would have informed their headquarters in Xuan Loc of the predicament. This had caused the initial spotter plane to appear in mid-afternoon and to stay until it was replaced by the AC-47 Spooky gunship at last light.

His senses told him that if ground reinforcement arrived, it would take until daylight for a plan to be developed, orders issued and troops moved from either Xuan Loc or Blackhorse Base camp. He knew the enemy would never run an airmobile insertion at night on the only LZ in the area. Lack of 155mm artillery also told him that no U.S. reinforcing units had forward deployed. He estimated that he had about 12 hours to conclude the battle or he must break off to insure freedom from reinforcing units. If he broke off now, the escape of his force would be relatively easy but he would lose a rare opportunity.

The general sipped hot tea in a large half-quart glass and listened silently while his companions argued the details of an attack or withdrawal. The heat through the glass felt warm on his fingers and he rolled the glass in his hands and rested it occasionally against his cheeks while looking at one or another of the speakers with piercing black eyes.

At last, he placed the glass in the center of the map, directly over the base camp in question and began to speak without waiting for silence.

They would reinforce the base camp with all available forces and annihilate the unit at first light. They would get additional forces to occupy this position to reinforce or counter-ambush any pursuing forces. They could not afford to lose such an opportunity for a politically significant victory even if it meant throwing off their basic timetable. With no reinforcements available until mid-morning, the Rangers probably could not hold out much beyond dawn if the VC pressed their attack from all sides. Luck smiles only once.

The table immediately disbanded with members going in various directions. The general rested his head on his elbows and looked directly at the Caucasians and the group of Orientals that had remained quietly in the background. He then outlined the plan using a mixture of French and English. The audience listened intently and slowly pulled on their cigarettes.

As he talked, he gestured toward a map with a small circle. This small spot would be critical to the outcome of his strategy and the probability of either side's survival as viable combat units. The group leaned forward and studied his words.

24

The Spot

The circles on General Thanh's map, the spot the visitors intently examined, lay south of the engagement, approximately five kilometers away—a natural passage point for American ground reinforcement between the open hills that protected the populated areas of Long Kanh Province and the deeper jungle recesses of War Zone D. Or more specifically, the natural route for the cavalry moving to the base camp battleground. Both sides had traversed this spot in their comings and goings since the French occupation after World War II. Where the U.S. forces could pinpoint the obvious movement route by maps unaided by experience, the VC were intimately familiar with through long association. Any unit attempting to enter the conflict area would have to pass through this terrain, an area of swampy low ground, a creek with limited fording sites and patches of dense impenetrable vegetation. These were conditions the maps did not well indicate.

General Thanh issued quick but clear commands. A group of sappers, augmented by infantry, assembled in the darkening obscurity of the base camp and gathered their equipment. The sappers brought axes and saws as well as considerable mines manufactured from dud U.S. artillery and air force cluster bomb units (CBUs). The infantry elements carried several large claymore-type mines.

Handmade in the camp, they were either 12 or 24 inches in diameter. Each was round like a large apple pie and had a raised cone in the center. Under the tin crust was a densely packed mass of explosive, the top of which was covered with either small ball bearings or cut segments of common nails.

Each mine was accompanied by a long length of coiled electric wire and an electric generator or clapper acquired from U.S. base camps or Vietnamese positions. These allowed the mine to be placed in trees along the likeliest path of movement while the initiator could hide some distance away from the approach path itself.

The infantry elements were in distinct contrast to the sappers. They were quite young and fresh faced and had clean light blue uniforms and short-cut hair. Recently arrived from the North, they had just refitted in the local Binh

Tram and were as of yet unexposed to the jungle and its toll of time. The sappers were a rude contrast. They were older in the face and hands though chronologically probably about the same. They wore black shorts cut quite high on the thigh and light beige cotton shirts. Several wore no shirt at all. Their feet were almost as black as the earth, reflecting constant exposure to the mud through well-worn sandals. They had a tough tired expression while their fresher escorts wore looks of curiosity and excitement, not yet tempered by the reality of the environment. Quickly, the mixed force gathered up under the command of a captain and moved off into the increasing dark.

Moving swiftly, in single file, the group covered the three kilometers from its base camp to the ford site south of the battlefield. Arriving there, the captain conducted a hasty reconnaissance with several sappers and infantry and relayed short instructions. Both groups began to execute his guidance.

The infantry fanned out along the relatively clear area leading from Highway 20 to the creek and assumed ambush positions along the ford site. However, rather than ambush the near side as they normally would have done, they developed their positions to engage the Americans at the far side crossing point. The infantry commander also sent two scouts toward Highway 20 to provide early warning of the Americans' arrival.

The sappers began to improve the banks of the creek to make a more inviting entrance. Large claymores were hung in the trees on the far side about 20 feet from the bank and behind the first row of trees at bank side. Smaller claymores were placed at ground level on the near side, facing toward the axis of advance the Americans would have to take to cross the creek. Further up and down stream, claymores were mixed with trees hastily felled parallel to the creek.

The trees were cut about three feet from the ground and dropped without cutting through the stump. This created the effect of a fence blocking access to the creek. The construction could not be seen from the ford site. Beyond the tree fall, both south and north of the ford, the ground was low and swampy. As a last measure, the sappers concluded their work by hasty diversions of water from the creek into these areas to reinforce the effect and reduce what little purchase would be available for tracked vehicles.

The work went on steadily through the evening. The sounds of the battle added purpose to the collective efforts. The captain had taken some pains to explain the significance of the work and the necessity to complete the work before the Americans could arrive at the site.

He emphasized that there was an opportunity to destroy a major ARVN force and win a significant political victory. He reviewed the great pain and deprivation all had suffered to arrive at this point in time. Finally, he reminded them of the awesome firepower of the Americans and the Cav in particular. At this spot, the firepower would be negated and hope lost for the trapped forces to the north. Here, a small group of low-ranking soldiers could achieve truly heroic results.

The discussion had a marked effect on the soldiers as they returned to their tasks. During work breaks for cigarettes or water, the soldiers would discuss the captain's remarks and relate them to personal experiences. This seemed to provide added vigor to the effort and both time and exhaustion were lost in the work.

By mid-afternoon, most of the key work had been accomplished. The captain ordered most of the soldiers into the center of the work area to prepare meals. Normally, in situations such as this, the routine would have been for each small group of deployed soldiers to prepare their food by themselves on their own schedule. This insured that everyone was where they needed to be in case of attack and somewhat compensated for the lack of effective communications equipment.

There were several aspects to the captain's decision. He wanted to provide a sense of security and assurance to the very new soldiers, most of whom had never been in direct combat. Their co-mingling with the veteran sappers and scouts would renew their confidence and enthusiasm. The break would also provide sufficient time for the captain to walk the entire ambush area with the chief sapper and review the work.

With all the laborers at a central point, he could quickly shift priorities and effort with minimal disruption and wasted time. He also made a point of having a quantity of extra rice prepared, which he had the new soldiers carry to the scout positions. The net effect was exactly as the captain had hoped. The new soldiers returned to work with enthusiasm and strength and work progressed at a fast pace.

During the course of the day, the group heard the artillery fire from the highway position to the battlefield. The noise of the guns seemed far away and reached their ears after long audio erosion through the canopy. It seemed less like artillery and more like a recurring undercurrent of jungle sounds reflecting off the leafy roof. Most of the rounds went well to the north but an occasional searching round would land nearby and cause all to momentarily halt their work and reflect on what lay just ahead. With minimal interruptions, the force completed the bulk of its labors by late afternoon and continued general improvements into the night. The captain sent a courier to report this to General Thanh and settled his personnel into position while the scouts moved to Highway 20 and the rubber plantation to the south.

During the course of the labors, the L-19, unseen but heard, would pass over the worksite. Though unable to ascertain what was happening below, the pilot could judge the steadily descending sun as well as the long-term aspects of the Ranger engagement. He flipped his radio switch to the regional air control net and requested that a Spooky gunship be launched to his location.

(Then) Lt Nightingale returning to Suoi Long the day after the engagement.

11th Cav laager position after Suoi Long.

Wounded Rangers.

52nd Rangers awaiting pickup after Suoi Long.

Dead VC.

Ranger tending to wounded comrade.

VC POW captured by Rangers.

UH-1H landing at Suoi Long pickup zone.

Rangers carrying wounded under fire near Cu Chi.

52nd Ranger Battalion commander receiving U.S. Presidential Unit Citation for Suoi Long.

52nd Ranger Bn advisory team 1967. (Then) Lt Nightingale is fourth from the left.

(Then) Cpt Nightingale the morning of 1 February 1968, Tet Offensive.

25

The Spooky

At the end of the Tan Son Nhut airfield, adjacent to the Vietnamese Air Force maintenance facility, eight large aircraft and a dozen smaller ones were arranged in rows. The smaller aircraft, Korean War vintage Skyraider prop A-1E fighter-bombers, were on the front row. Behind them were the draft horses of the Vietnam War, the AC-47 Spooky gunships. Together, the collection resembled more of an air museum than the leading edge of ground support.

Time had demonstrated the worth of these overage and undervalued assets. Flown by Vietnamese, the A-1E aircraft were exceptionally good close-support aircraft. They could carry as large a bomb load as the American jets but could stay on station more than six hours compared to the 20-minute average for American missions. More importantly, the aircraft could fly very slowly and consequently were very accurate. With four 20mm cannon, the shiny aluminum-skinned aircraft could provide the difference between a base camp or unit's defense or defeat. Now, in the waning hours of daylight, the pilots had closed their canopies and were off to the VNAF Officers Club for some in-depth crew rest.

Warming up behind the last A-1E was a solitary AC-47. It was bathed in the blue-white exhaust gas of the just-ignited gasoline engines. The base commander had placed both types of aircraft at this isolated location as a safety measure. Using gasoline rather than less volatile diesel, these aircraft were a distinct danger to themselves and others with the large amount of aviation gas that was always resident in the wings. The philosophy among the jet jockeys was that if a stray mortar round or satchel charge hit them, only the antiques would be harmed. This arrangement was generally OK with the isolated crews as they didn't have to worry too much about appearances and were rarely visited by anyone of consequence. Regardless, the crews on both aircraft routinely logged double the sortie rate of the jet pilots. This despite the far shorter turnaround time for the faster aircraft.

The Spooky, as it was commonly called, was a World War II-era C-47 outfitted with mini-guns and flare dispensers. The data plate on the airframe and accompanying logbook indicated that it had been built in El Segundo,

California in 1943. It first served at Normandy, participated in the Berlin airlift, dropped troops in Korea, transported goods to the remains of Chiang Kai-Shek's army in China and served as a photography plane at Edwards Air Force Base until 1963. It then deployed to the Philippines where it was armed for the first time. This considered an experiment by the U.S. Air Force and was not well-regarded by the traditional afterburner-oriented leadership.

As a consequence of its ancient past and dubious future, the aircraft were manned by crews accumulated through disciplinary infractions, love of mission, or lack of interest in fighting what was considered a less than choice assignment. As if to highlight their outcast status, the crews wore non-regulation clothing, floppy Aussie hats, and an air of scorn for the formal aspects of military life. However, in compensation, they took great pride in their work and routinely spent much more time in the air than crew safety regulations permitted. The crews and their aircraft were much loved by both the American and Vietnamese soldiers, who they serviced equally without distinction.

Flying a thousand feet above the battle, the crews could clearly see most of the antagonists and could immediately judge the impact of their involvement. Unpressurized, each plane had several large openings cut into its fuselage to accommodate the weapons and flare dispensers. During engagements, the crew could lean out of the aircraft and follow each round as it impacted on the small human forms moving below. The crews had rigged speakers in the rear that broadcast the ground-to-air frequency. This permitted them to become directly and emotionally involved in the engagement as they could clearly ascertain the situation on the ground and the effect of their presence.

In particularly tense situations, it was not unusual for a crewmember to lean out of the slowly circling aircraft and fire his rifle or pistol at pockets of enemy soldiers seeking cover from the heavy airborne weapons. Some crews carried grenade launchers as a last-ditch support asset when their conventional ammunition ran out. Not unexpectedly, this engendered a strong sense of purpose and independent dedication within the crews who invariably led the unit reenlistment statistics. This was a fact not well understood or appreciated by those used to fighting at several thousand feet in an air-conditioned cocoon responding to the professional monotone of bored spotter pilots.

The crew of the warming AC-47 had been enjoying itself at the Vietnamese Officers Club prior to assuming alert status at 2200. Drinking was strictly prohibited within eight hours of a mission but this was a nicety routinely ignored by the crews and their immediate leadership. It was not unusual for a crew to add a cooler of beer to the load plan prior to a particularly long or boring mission. If challenged by a far-ranging dedicated base duty officer, they would reply that it was for a Special Forces camp and would be parachuted in. This response was generally accepted as the AC-47s were often called upon to resupply isolated camps under siege in addition to the more traditional fire support missions.

The command pilot was a Puerto Rican born three years after the plane was built. He had been commissioned after serving two years in the Air Force as an enlisted man. He freely admitted that his primary motivation for joining the Air Force was for the benefits of a steady income and the better aspects of crew rest as he now enjoyed them. He had surrounded himself with the crew as well as several hostesses in flowing red, saffron and blue national dresses.

His copilot was 22 years old and had just graduated from the Air Force Academy and seemed quite unsure about the captain's social integration techniques. Seated next to him, engrossed in deep conversation with one of the ladies, was the crew chief. He was almost 50 years old and had been in the Air Force when it was part of the Army. He had no wife and enjoyed what he knew to be his last tour in uniform. He had spent five consecutive years in-country, arriving with one of the first field advisory groups.

The remaining members of the crew, gunners, loaders, navigator, flight engineer, and ground personnel were engaged in a game of combat volleyball with the A-1E pilots outside the bar. Though taller than their competition, the Americans were decidedly slower and less prone to teamwork than their Vietnamese counterparts. Games were always close and split fairly evenly. Around them, the waitresses and hangers-on laughed and made side bets on every play as the warm afternoon sun began to slant and tinge the scene with a golden orange light.

Suddenly, the bell over the bay rang and a voice called for the command pilot of the AC-47. He excused himself from the table, talked briefly to the bar tender who handed him a telephone. The pilot listened briefly, hung up and motioned to his crew chief by twirling his finger in the air and pointing out the door to their jeeps.

It was quickly becoming dark as the crew arrived at the briefing room—a renovated Quonset hut next to their flight line. The crew assembled in an irritated mood with bitching and griping as they settled into the school desks with the writing board across the right side. They had conducted night operations against the Ho Chi Minh Trail for the last two weeks and had spent most of last night supporting a besieged Special Forces camp at the Seven Sisters Mountains on the Cambodian border. Tonight was supposed to be a relief. Consequently, several had partied hard and arrived in sweat soaked T-shirts reeking of bourbon and beer.

The intelligence officer briefed them on the events that had transpired less than sixty kilometers from them on a straight line. He pointed to the map and indicated the initial assault insertion point, the probable Ranger location, the Cav column location en route to relieve the Rangers, and the assessment of the L-19 pilot. He also mentioned that the 18th ARVN probably could not relieve the unit and that the 11th Cavalry was going to try a linkup in the morning. Key to the briefing was the fact that no artillery was available. If the Spooky couldn't support, there wouldn't be any.

On this note, the room grew quiet. They had conducted dozens of missions in support of soldiers in trouble. In the vast majority, they were used as bit players to a greater effort. While admittedly important bit players during their scene, they nonetheless took subordinate precedence to the more expensive hardware that was invariably present. Here, they were the only show. That appealed to their independent spirit and they trailed out of the room charged with a degree of personal responsibility they rarely felt. The only disconcerting note was that the weather prediction was poor, promising mixed rain and thunder. The crew hated thunder as any electrical strike against the aircraft invariably triggered the flares and the Gatling guns—sometimes when they were being loaded. From experience, they avoided any bad weather if at all possible.

The old aircraft lurched into life with a cloud of blue aviation gas exhaust fumes and flame bursts spewing from behind the engine cowlings. The crew sorted itself out in an informal atmosphere within the fuselage. The gunners rotated the elevation gears on the banks of mini-guns—.30 caliber Gatling guns—that protruded out the left side of the aircraft. These guns consumed huge quantities of ammunition and the loaders sweated and scraped the large now open feed boxes across the floor as the aircraft lurched to the takeoff point.

Others in the crew wrestled the flare dispensers out the open rear door and attached the electrodes to the connecting wire cables. Once aloft, the dispensers could not be adjusted due to the wind pressure. As a safety precaution, the dispensers were never loaded until after takeoff. While this was regarded by the officers as a safety issue, the crew believed that the wind resistance against a loaded dispenser would prevent the plane from achieving sufficient speed to take off. Tonight, it might have been almost true as the NCOIC had filled all available floor space with flares and ammunition. He didn't want to break off an engagement due to lack of ammunition if no one could replace them on station.

The pilot called back for a final crew check at the end of the runway. The crew sat on the floor resting on their flak jackets as the pilot stood on the brakes, revved the engines to their maximum shaking and wavering capacity and then suddenly released his foothold.

Usually, the plane took a slight hopping lurch forward and then surged down the runway. This time, there was only the briefest hint of release as the aircraft began its roll. The copilot held the throttle arms full forward as the now-bright runway lights began to course past. The crew noticed the unusually slow passage and looked anxiously out of the open left-side ports. At the final point of decision on the runway, a parked fire truck, the pilot pulled back on the wheel and the airplane slowly wobbled off the ground as the tin shacks of the abutting airfield housing passed a bare six feet underneath.

The pilot maintained his initial course for some distance. Normally, he would have initiated an immediate left bank and headed toward his destination. Now, aware of the over-grossed nature of the load, he was concerned that a turn at marginal speed would stall the aircraft. A mile after takeoff, he took a slow turn over the new Y bridge that spanned the Saigon River and headed for the last vestiges of the sinking Asian sun.

Within 30 minutes he reached an area to the east of the Rangers roughly over the Highway One and Highway 20 intersection. Here, he connected with the L-19, now circling below him. The pilot described the target area and warned that a major storm line was moving from the south.

The weapons officer had tweaked his systems as soon as the aircraft departed the populated areas. The low-light TV camera and infrared sensors were all functioning well. From his screen, he was able to pinpoint features on the ground and mock-engage them by placing the small red cursor over them, locking in the gyroscopic controls and then selecting the burst feature.

Personally, he liked the one-second burst as he could make quick adjustments to the impact. The new crew members invariably suggested the five-second burst for its evocative effect—spiraling tetrahedrons of red coiling to the ground as the plane executed a tight continuous left turn with its left wing rotating over the target as if to point at the bullseye. Once experienced, they quickly tired of it as such a maneuver expended large quantities of ammunition and they had to feed the guns' insatiable appetites while fighting gravity to get to the restrained ammo boxes on the upper right side of the fuselage.

The pilot selected a course from the intersection that would carry him directly over the bend in the river where the base camp was thought to be. He switched to the ground operational frequency and immediately made contact with the American lieutenant.

The lieutenant barely heard the aircraft through the trees and suggested an azimuth of travel based on what he could discern penetrating the canopy above. The pilot made the adjustment and his track was distinctly more audible. The lieutenant then asked that the track be repeated and he would order a flare drop at the highest pitch. The discussion was not well understood by the pilot as the lieutenant had to speak very softly and was hard to hear over the noise in the cockpit. Usually, the plane was supporting troops in clearly recognizable base camps or facilities, finding a spot in the vast blackness above and below him was a new and anxious experience. He made a mental note to watch for vertigo and blackout.

The flare was dropped as requested just as the pilot saw lightning flashes to his front. The flare ignited several hundred yards from the Rangers but was readily visible. The light was not distinct but played and flickered through the foliage with dancing flashes and glows. Despite its relative ineffectiveness, it represented the first outside help the perimeter had experienced and they welcomed its presence like the sun.

A second pass was made to refine the perimeter location for the weapons officer before he fired his guns. As that flare was dropped, lightning struck the aircraft firing the remaining four flares. They simultaneously left the dispenser searing the loader and gunners with their collective tail streams. The pilot veered to the east to escape the cloud line now immediately overhead.

Under the canopy, the perimeter was bathed in an intense greenish yellow glow that lasted for more than a minute. The lieutenant made another correction and was notified by the L-19 pilot that the Spooky had departed to wait out the storm. As the first rain drops began to announce their presence on the green canopy overhead, the glowing light faded and the creatures underneath were left to themselves and silence. Muffled by the beating of the rain on the leafy overhead, the Spooky's departure went unheard. At the choice of the L-19 pilot, the lieutenant was equally unaware of another failure to his south.

26

The Ambush

Throughout the day, reports of the Ranger contact had filtered into the 11th Armored Cavalry Blackhorse base camp. The organization, captured by the intensity of its own operations in the area, paid scant attention to spot reports as it wrestled with the management of its own problems. Two squadrons were spread throughout the area of operations and required constant attention.

The cavalry operations were generated in the same haste as the Ranger insertion and for the same purpose—to take advantage of immediate information that indicated an opportunity to catch and crush a major communist unit before it was positioned to react. Two squadrons were dispatched to the west and north with great haste, sweeping the flank areas of War Zone D hoping to entrap support elements and add strength to the Ranger direct strike.

The squadron that normally operated in the Xuan Loc area was spread to the north and east of the Ranger area in locations long familiar to it. Troops, cross-attached into tank and ACAV packages, rolled into familiar working areas and began sweeping the open farmland and occupying villages along the lines of drift leading into War Zone D.

A second squadron, transiting from the southern portion of III Corps back to its home base had been halted at the juncture of Highway One and Highway 20. It rested in several laager positions among the dappled shade of Don Dien de Catachoucs, the largest single rubber plantation in Vietnam. Though unfamiliar with the operational area, the squadron commander had organized his forces to work north along the highway and to act as a pincher force should the Rangers establish significant contact.

The elements of this squadron were separated into four packages. One was conducting road sweep operations between Xuan Loc and Bien Hoa. A second was still moving through Bien Hoa to join the main force to the east. The third and fourth elements were spread across the road junction between Highway One and Highway 20 seeking shade from the increasingly tortuous sun. One of these shaded units, K Troop, occupied the northwest quadrant of the road junction and was closest to the Rangers.

For most of the morning, K Troop had established itself in the cool dappled cover of the towering rubber trees. ACAVs had spread themselves between the trees arcing their vehicles between each major highway. The tanks had interspersed themselves between the ACAVs. A maintenance crew had occupied the clearing at the road junction and spent the morning fixing vehicles. The key tasks were in replacing broken main gun hydraulic units in the tanks and broken torsion bars on the ACAVs.

Directly across the road to the east of K Troop, a 155mm battery had emplaced itself. It occupied an area that had been cleared of trees by the Rome plows in anticipation of establishing an ARVN military outpost. The plows had windrowed the fallen rubber trees perpendicular to Highway 20 to a height over a man's head. Mixed throughout the debris were chunks of concrete and barbed wire, remnants of a parallel French strategy.

The artillery battery had fired all morning in support of the movement and insertion of the 175mm battery and later in support of the Ranger assault. Now, by 1500, the guns were still and the crews lay dozing either inside their tracks or in the artificial shade erected next to the windrowed trees.

Though quiescent in the field, the exertions of the field operations had taxed the headquarters at Blackhorse. The demands of an American organization, even when not in contact, were immense. Feeding, watering, fueling and gathering information consumed large quantities of time and attention. Initially, the diversion of helicopters and gunships to support the hasty Ranger insertion was managed as a necessary distraction. Upon completion of the insertion, the assets had reverted to supporting the cavalry elements now spread throughout the province.

By 1700, the requests for support from the U.S. liaisons at Xuan Loc had taken on a desperate tone. The Blackhorse command operations center was buried underground and crowned with large creosote-soaked timbers that supported 10 feet of dirt and steel planking. As the day wore on, the interior became heavy and laden with the smell of the timbers as the humidity and sweat of human bodies combined to suck the smells out of the building materials. By noon, the CP had a heavy oily atmosphere that could not be dissipated by the best efforts of the large floor fans. Issues of time soon became lost to the occupants who lived by the call on the radio and the necessary reactions trained by countless repetitions and previous instructions.

Here, the interior was bright with the glare of neon fixtures and buzzed with the drone of radios and watch personnel. On a floodlit wall, a huge Plexiglas-covered map of III and IV Corps areas reflected unit dispositions and the blue arrows that indicated the commander's intent for his subordinate elements.

On top of those marks, a series of small red dots began to appear. These were number-coded and reflected each spot report of enemy action as transmitted by the L-19 pilot. The Second Squadron positions at the road junction to the west were marked with a black prancing horse and a smaller number two.

The watch officers, as a matter of routine, had placed command frequencies of the three cavalry squadrons on loudspeakers. Though it created a cacophony to the newly initiated, over time, the practice insured that everyone was aware of what all the elements were doing and call signs alternately activated or depressed attention appropriate to the individual listener's responsibilities. By 1600, the operations officer had reduced the volume on the cavalry speakers and introduced the lone but controlled voice of the L-19 pilot circling slowly over the Rangers and requesting any form of assistance with increased anxiety. Soon, those soldiers not directly involved with needed tasks, drifted toward the speaker and quietly absorbed the situation.

The regimental commander, upon returning from a helicopter visit to his field elements in the late afternoon, stopped by the CP to review the reports. Inbound from Bien Hoa, he had been alerted by the Xuan Loc Control of a major firefight underway. He learned that the 175mm battery had been firing constantly but had been ordered to cease fire due to close proximity. He was also notified that his gunships had been expending over the scene of action but could get no definitive description of the actual situation.

He landed outside the CP and strode down the long shaded ramp that led through a 90-degree blast door into the CP. His eyes dilated in the light as the room was brought to attention by the Operations Officer. By the time the commander's eyes had adjusted, he was in front of the map and peering intently at the block of red dots that had been accumulating all afternoon.

The intelligence officer described the various spot reports but could provide no sense as to what was occurring other than a steadily growing action. At this point, the voice of the L-19 pilot cut through the air and relayed a request for a Spooky gunship. The commander abruptly cut off the discussion and moved toward the speaker. He took the handset from the operator and talked directly to the L-19 pilot.

The pilot described the unfolding action and his assessment of the situation. His voice became increasingly intense and emphatic as he traded questions and answers with the commander. Though outwardly calm, the pilot's anxiety and concern were clearly captured by the interrogator. As a veteran of two wars, the cavalry commander could accurately judge the demeanor of men overwhelmed by events. The L-19 pilot was well regarded for his calmness and experience and this carried significant weight in the commander's decision-making process.

After talking to the pilot, he phoned the U.S. compound in Xuan Loc and asked for an assessment. Little was known beyond that which the pilot had already relayed. What was known was that the Rangers had run into something very big that was rapidly growing beyond its capability to handle, if indeed that point had not already been reached. He was able to gain no commitment from either the 18th ARVN Division commander or his American counterpart to reinforce the Rangers. He reminded the American advisor that the 48th Regiment was to be the reinforcing force and that he was prepared to assist them in any way. Receiving a non-committal answer, he broke off the conversation.

After consulting the map and comparing his unit's positions with the red dots, he issued quick, clear orders. The unit engaged was the unit that had been decisive in saving one of his units from ambush in the same area less than ninety days ago and the cavalry was going to repay the favor.

The Second Squadron, at the road junction, was to send a relief column up Highway 20 to the south of the battle and swing up the eastern bank of the Dong Nai sweeping in from the rear of the VC force. He then moved to the radio and passed this information to the pilot and asked that it be transmitted to the Rangers. As a veteran of many actions, he recognized the psychological need to the engaged elements to provide support when no tangible assets were immediately available.

The requirement quickly filtered to the road junction. K Troop was not unprepared for the order to move out. Since 1400, the troop commander had placed the L-19 pilot on the command speaker. Throughout the afternoon, the soldiers had listened at first as a diversion and later with mounting intensity as the battle unfolded through the pilot's transmissions. When the order came through by 1600, the soldiers knew with some certitude where they were heading. The troop commander quickly briefed his platoon leaders to the extent that he could. Move north. Cut in at French Fort. Find the river. Swing north. Kill what you find. Rescue the Rangers. Move out. A good cavalry order.

The large beach umbrellas and hammocks were quickly stowed and engines revved. Boxes of machine-gun ammo were opened up and placed inside the splatter shields of the side gun systems. On the floor of the ACAVs, ammo box lids were sprung open in anticipation of need. The vehicles began to line themselves on the road in awaiting the formal order to move out.

Monitoring the command net, each track was aware of the unfolding events to its north and the role they were all about to play. The radio carried the firing and explosions of the Ranger battlefield as background noise to the quick and anxious support requests relayed to the pilot. Even in war, jaded as these soldiers were by experience, the primordial desire of the cavalry to close with the enemy welled inside the unit.

Gunning the engines, each vehicle seemed to nervously anticipate the order to move out as so many bulls awaiting the Sunday parade at the Plaza de Toros. The vehicles were organized in a standard march column with ACAVs leading, interspersed with M-48 tanks. In the intense unshaded sun, the blue-black exhaust smoke rose in small columns directly skyward. Absent a breath of wind, the soldiers, now exposed to the direct rays of the sun, began to break out in beads of sweat that quickly coursed down their bodies, visible through the arm holes of their flak jackets, and steamed across the barrels of their weapons from the small rivulets that had formed on their chins. In the center of the column, the troop commander sat in the hatch of a tank and checked attendance. Once he confirmed that all his responsibilities were on the road and that the L-19 pilot was overhead, he ordered the unit to move north in the hot midday afternoon.

Deep within the shade of the rubber trees, the actions of K Troop were observed by two scouts from the ambush element. They had filtered into the plantation maintenance compound and discussed their requirements with the local foreman. He had tasked several children to guide them to the road intersection. They, in turn, had led the scouts to a position to the west of the troop and slightly above it. Hiding in the piles of underbrush recently cut by the workers to clear lanes for the rubber tappers, the scouts were able to observe the soldiers as the children made their initial introductions into the perimeter.

For most of the afternoon, the scouts saw nothing of particular interest. Then, with the near-simultaneous starting of engines and subsequent move to the road, the scouts began to retreat. They carefully observed the formation of the unit into a march column on the road. As soon as the senior scout ascertained that a movement was about to take place, he took his partner and began a slow but steady trot to the north. He did not slow until he had covered several kilometers on a direct route to the ambush site. Occasionally, he stopped to catch his breath and fix the convoy location by listening to the L-19 as it orbited overhead.

The column moved out in greater than normal acceleration. The wind cooled the soldiers and the overwhelming combination of noise and movement seemed to provide a comfortable mental blanket for the participants. The grass by the cleared roadside waved and snapped with each passage and white birds wheeled and called from the jungle edge as they disturbed themselves in response to the shock waves generated by the new predators. Soon, the troop passed from a state of anxious anticipation to one of monotonous languor as the combination of noise, vibration and heat worked its mental toll.

The troop commander, riding in the cupola of the second tank in column, monitored both his own internal net and that of the fight ahead. He advised his personnel on the status of the movement as reported by the pilot and provided updates on the Ranger fight. It was increasingly apparent to him that his unit would either duplicate the classic Hollywood rescue or the unit he was tasked to save would cease to exist. Though on his second combat tour and thoroughly experienced in such scenarios, his demeanor became increasingly anxious as he spurred his people with a tension in his voice they had not heard before.

Despite the conditions, the captain truly loved this situation. Riding in the commander's hatch on top of the tank with its immense exuding strength barreling down the road, he could find kinship with the cavalry commanders in the books he had read and the movies he had seen as a boy.

With the blue-black exhaust venting its rooster tail to the rear, the noise shrouding him in a world of speed, strength and motion and the world fast passing by so small and inconsequential below him, he was in a personal dream warp. The Ying in him was exhilarated with the prospect of meeting the enemy with his steel extension that responded so well to his direction while the Yang recognized the blood and penalties that would be paid for such an engagement. In his mind's eye, he saw both sides and pressed himself and his people forward, anxious to resolve the conflict.

The L-19 pilot could not devote full attention to the movement. He had opted to remain aloft for a second shift rather than relinquish his duties to a new pilot. He could visualize the forces at work and the convergence of energy that he was directing. Having set the stage, he had no desire to exit at the climactic scene. He was very much aware of the emotional bond that had built between himself and the Rangers and felt a sense of loyalty and connection that both filled him with pride and foreboding.

His voice had become an emotional umbilical cord and he viscerally desired to retain that God-like connection. On a rational plane, he had justified his continuance to his commander as being the necessity of the situation. Changes meant loss of information and hesitant reaction. The situation was too critical. He could provide the best support until the situation resolved. Everything seemed to be converging to the ultimate scene in the drama and he was the only director capable of managing the unfolding script.

He had followed the Rangers from their initial insertion and now felt a kinship to the unit as it found itself in the deepest of peril. He made occasional passes over the cavalry column but spent most of his time over the troops engaged. If nothing else, he felt the noise of his presence would add some comfort to the troops below.

The column took approximately an hour to reach the 175mm artillery fire support base. Just beyond that location was a spot commonly known as French Fort. This was a cleared area to the left of the road and slightly beyond the artillery that was a common reference point for units operating in the area.

Next to the cleared ground, astride a ditch, were the remnants of an old French armored car, now rusting and covered with grass but still clearly discernible for what it once was. Before the Rome plows had done their work, this area was the only spot along the entire highway that provided an open laager area. Accordingly, a history of its occupation could be read in the chopped grasses and crushed C-ration tins and machine-gun links that intermittently sprung from the depressions partially driven into the soil by past occupations. At this point, the troop commander's finger paralleled the previous movement of another commander's finger as it followed the trace of the land as it flowed from the road.

The French Fort marked the entry way into a small valley between two low hills that traced its way to the Dong Nai River more than 10 kilometers to the west. From either a map or the air, this point seemed the most logical location to establish a juncture with the Rangers. The troop commander had indicated this spot would be the turn-in point from the road as another commander had believed he would.

The lead armored element broke past the fire support base and continued its race up the road toward the location where it would disappear into the jungle. The pilot conferred briefly with the point platoon leader and reduced his speed and altitude to where he could clearly see the juxtaposition of the French Fort, the 175mm artillery base and the Dong Nai River. He conducted a slow recon of the route beginning at the fort and traced his way across the low ground toward the river drawing an aerial trace of the route he assumed the cavalry element would take. He saw nothing of interest below and confirmed the road exit to the troop commander.

Had the Cav commander known the local history, he would have noted that his French predecessor, 15 years before, had the same concept. Now, a more contemporary reinforced armored cavalry troop was about to reenact the event that created the rusting signpost by the road.

The lead platoon leader spotted the remains of the French armored car at the exit point. It had rested there since its destruction. Some time ago, all items of value had been stripped and the empty, wheel-less carcass lay between the road and jungle, grass growing through the holes in the hull floor and empty wheel wells.

Behind a large tree north of the artillery base, the VC scout sergeant had spotted the column long before it made the turn at the fort. The two junior scouts closest to the road had retreated to the ambush site as soon as they heard the vehicles well to the south. They had reported this to the captain and joined their platoon at the ambush site.

The second pair of scouts remained near the fort to confirm the turn-in point of the American unit. As soon as the lead platoon diverted off the road, they too quickly moved to the ambush site and reported that the Americans were moving in relative haste down the old French trail.

The French Fort clearing encompassed several acres of grassland that abutted the jungle. On the lowest portion of land, a trail beckoned into the jungle. At first, the terrain was relatively open with new growth trees. The lead platoon leader chose to separate his force into three columns moving abreast approximately 50 meters apart.

Initially this was relatively easy. The basic trail was clearly discernible as it threaded its way deeper into the jungle. Leading the center unit was a tank with its main gun depressed and swung to one side to permit easy destruction of the small trees that had grown along the trail. The flank columns moved in single file and were somewhat slowly having to thread their way around the larger growth trees.

The soldiers welcomed the newly acquired shade and stood full up in the center hatch or sat on the side of the hulls as the vehicles weaved and swung among the trees. Their eyes alerted to the flanks and front of their new environment, the troops soon were lost to themselves as they rode the bucking swaying tracks west to the river.

The lead platoon leader had advanced less than three kilometers when it was apparent that the flank elements were having great difficulty in maintaining the pace. The far larger trees demanded more circuitous routing and the tank-led column was often forced to halt.

It became increasingly difficult for him to gauge movement of his elements as they were obscured in the darkening shadows and distances. This movement and separation was also noted by the watchful scouts who walked just beyond the vision of the Americans and kept pace with the sound of the rising and falling exhausts.

Less than five kilometers from the river, the platoon leader halted his tracks and moved ahead on the thin barely discernible trace. By his map, he was less than a kilometer from the creek that marked the turning point to the north. Ahead of his unit, he was able to lose the sound of the exhausts and begin to discern the muffled sounds from his intended direction.

The sounds of that battle were relatively clear. Muffled explosions and occasional cracks and whines were heard as stray bullets escaped the battle and returned spent through the canopy. Registering these sounds, the platoon leader returned to his track and conferred briefly with his senior.

The troop commander, monitoring the conversation between the Rangers and the L-19, was increasingly conscious of the need to make all haste to the battle. He ordered the flank units to fall in on the trail and moved the tank to the front. He instructed the lead platoon leader to move as fast as possible to the ford site. All this was reported by a chain of scouts who fell back as the column moved forward.

The troop commander ordered the entire column to close from the flanks and guide on the center element. Now, haste was a necessary factor in the decision process as darkness and desperation became apparent to the command.

Aware of the shifting movement by the Americans, the ambush commander reviewed the plan with his subordinates. Both groups were now separated by less than a kilometer and the battle was about to be joined. Success depended on the Americans advancing to the creek on a narrow front and in closing up so as to make the shortest possible column.

Success also depended on his soldiers not acting until the Americans were so far into the boggy ground that they lost freedom of maneuver. Then, the Americans would have to fight for their survival. Hopefully, this would consume the remaining daylight and buy sufficient time to insure the annihilation of the trapped soldiers to the north.

In less than 30 minutes after closing into a single march unit, the element reached the ford site. The lead vehicle, the M-48, had lost the hydraulics on the gun tube from innumerable impacts with trees. Its tube lay drooped across the front with the blast deflector twisted sideways. The driver halted the tank on the near side and awaited instruction.

The platoon leader halted just behind the tank and the vehicles to his rear quickly halted in column in a herringbone pattern. The platoon leader dismounted and moved to the front of the tank to inspect the bank. He ordered several infantry to dismount and wade across to the other side.

Normally, he would have reconned by fire before sending them, but the troop commander believed their approach from the rear was still undetected and wanted to achieve maximum surprise. Accordingly he ordered that no weapons be fired.

The infantry, clad in flak jackets and bulging fatigue pants dropped into the creek and waded slowly and cautiously across. Thanks to the efforts of the sappers, the water level had dropped almost a foot, so the depth of the stream never exceeded the beltline of the infantrymen. They crossed without incident and moved in a semicircle beyond the far bank until they were lost from view. Fewer than 10 feet from the flank American, the VC captain held his breath and relaxed the grip on the electric detonator in his hand.

The American platoon leader was satisfied with the site. The banks were shallow and the water was low. The stream bed was solid when he probed it with a stick and the vegetation was relatively open. Occasionally, he caught a glimpse of the L-19 against the patches of blue in the canopy and that gave him a sense of renewed confidence.

Behind him, the tracks continued to belch blue smoke and vibrate with anticipation of the coming movement. Most of the sappers and infantry could not see the Americans but they could feel that the ground no longer vibrated and the exhausts were now a steady drone, signaling a halt to the movement. They turned their eyes from the column and awaited the next act.

After a short conversation on the radio, the platoon leader motioned to the tank driver to move forward. Simultaneously, he climbed onto the top of his ACAV and plunged into the stream immediately behind the tank. The column, activated by the signal, charged their accelerators and with a multitude of blue-black exhaust plumes, jerked forward in close column. The VC captain curled his fingers around the detonator.

The tank drove down the shallow bank and slid into the water. The chalk gray water was immediately awash in a dark black and chocolate brown swirl as the bottom mud was hurled through the treads and across the bow. The driver gunned the engine and lunged across the creek, less than 20 feet in width at this point.

The tank threw up a bow wave that crashed back on the driver who momentarily lost his foot on the accelerator. This brought the tank to a momentary halt in the middle of the creek until the driver regained control and accelerated up the far bank.

The tank ground up the bank streaming cream-colored water and slammed on the high ground as gravity overcame acceleration. Stopping momentarily, the tank then began to move forward closely followed by the platoon leader's track which was just behind it. To the rear, the column of APCs moved almost bumper to bumper as they focused in on the now well-identified crossing site. As the platoon leader's track cleared the far side bank, a third APC was in mid-stream and a fourth waited poised at the near side bank, now worn smooth and sticky by the preceding treads.

The tank passed across a small water-filled hole. As it did, the captain squeezed the detonator. Immediately, the remains of a dud 250 pound bomb and 155mm artillery shell went off. The duds, buried in a deep narrow hole, exploded directly upward and channeled their gasses and energy at the point where the left front portion of the tread met the hull.

The explosion sent the driver and tank commander hurtling skyward along with the front portion of the left tread. The tank, still powered by the last draught of diesel, spun to the right and ran the rest of the left tread off the guides and then swung to a halt in the dissipating smoke.

The platoon leader's ACAV had just cleared the stream when the mine went off. Immediately, a dozen RPGs were fired from the flanks striking it and the vehicle in the stream. Several of the larger claymores rigged in the trees and pointing toward the crossing site also exploded. The steel nail slugs, imbedded in the melted explosive were driven down into the openings on the armored vehicles reducing the crews to dead pieces of flailed red meat. Several of the RPGs penetrated the diesel fuel cells and they began to leak and burn with an inky black smoke. After this short sudden cacophony of death, the VC remained silent and unfiring in their positions, awaiting the Americans to plunge deeper into the trap.

A dozen tracks to the rear, the troop commander heard the explosions but could see nothing. Those vehicles unengaged by the RPGs immediately began to fire to the flanks and front while attempting to move off of the trail and into the flanking jungle. The commander could not raise the platoon leader on the radio and directed his driver to move immediately forward.

Far to the rear of the column, a VC sergeant listening to the explosions to the front, selected the APC with the most antennas, and detonated a second mine. This mine, facing only the soft aluminum of the APC's belly, surged through the floor and created a gaping hole that previously held three men and most of the interior stores. Concurrently, a flurry of RPGs were fired stopping the rearmost elements and blocking the trail.

The troop commander was unaware of this as he was now fully engaged by the noise and events to his immediate front. The ACAVs around him were all firing into the increasing smoke and haze at no apparent target. Tree limbs and leaves were being shorn off as the deep coughing trip hammer of the .50 calibers mixed with the short sharp burst of the light machine guns.

The grenade launchers, supplementing their fires, exploded with crumps and crashes sending splinters flying back.

Above the gunners, red ants, angered by the concussions and blasts, fell on the gunners and immediately attached themselves to the exposed skin with long hypodermic mandibles. Some gunners ceased firing to spray themselves and their companions with mosquito repellent while others, emotionally blank and running on adrenalin, ignored the pain and intently continued firing. There was no return fire.

The troop commander, unable to talk to his advance elements, dismounted and ran forward to the near shore. Squatting behind the most forward ACAV on the creek bank, he could make out a stalled vehicle in the creek and the burning track of the platoon leader on the other side. He could not see the tank but he could distinguish its deep-throated idling engine sounding through the smoke.

He returned to his track and talked immediately to the L-19 pilot. The pilot had been orbiting over the Rangers when he looked south and saw the canopy separate at the approximate location of the crossing site. An upward draft of green canopy was immediately replaced by a whitish orange flash followed by an oily dark cloud boiling skyward. This was shortly succeeded by a similar and even more spectacular blast at a point approximate to the rear of the column.

The pilot immediately increased airspeed and began calling to the troop commander. Unable to raise the ground unit, he called to the Cav headquarters and notified it of the explosions and alerted the artillery unit at the crossroads. As he approached the smoke column, he noticed red tracers climbing skyward all along the trail and quickly gained altitude to avoid collision with them.

Switching down to the Cav unit's internal net, he heard the breathless shouting and cursing between stations and attempted to interject several times. Finally, he was able to talk with a platoon leader and asked him to mark the unit locations with smoke. He had a general appreciation for the unit's dispositions based on the tracer fire, but it was very easy to lose orientation against the flat featureless canopy. He wanted the smoke as a reference point for the artillery that was about to be fired and the helicopter gunships that were already moving toward him.

In the VC regimental base camp, one of the communications operators bent over his captured American radio and began to signal his partner with a football-throwing motion. His partner ground the handle on a dark yellow field phone and spoke rapidly into the mouthpiece. Very soon, the pilot saw soft columns of colored smoke wafting through the canopy all around the ambush site.

The pilot flew over each smoke column but could not clearly identify the forces below. The clearest object was the grouping of the tank and ACAV on the far side of the creek. The ACAV was now consumed in flame and the tank was fully exposed in the newly created opening in the canopy roof. He spoke quickly to the heavy battery artillery base which was now a flurry of activity.

With the shout from the FDC of "Troops in contact," all four gun crews raced to their pieces strewing sun shades and hammocks across the ground. Shouts and commands resounded in the shadowing afternoon light as the crews, some yet incomplete, manually assisted the shells into the breech. For what seemed like an eternity to the pilot, the ponderous actions of the heavy artillery mechanisms went through their sequences. Finally, in a millennium that took three minutes, a round was on the way.

The pilot could see the gunfire as he heard the command on the FDC net and followed the invisible flight to its anticipated strike point. The first round landed well on the western side of the creek and boiled up through the canopy. The pilot gave a correction placing the next rounds on the eastern side and just north of where he believed the most extended Cav elements were. Through the drifting smoke, he could see the occasional red and green tracer course through the sky and increased his altitude to avoid accidental impact. The next rounds, fired by all four guns, impacted on the northern edge of the ACAVs at the point where the level ground began to taper toward the swampy bottomland.

Under the canopy, the heavy artillery landed at ponderous intervals. Each round announced itself with a huge crash that sent large chunks of mud flying through the canopy impacting on the inhabitants and tree trunks. Leaves and limbs shattered and scattered about the newly opened exits to the sky. The ambushed Cav crews bent low over their weapons and fired randomly into the jungle. To this point, other than the initial onslaught of RPGs, no return fire could be discerned.

The ambush forces, scattered at the edge of the swamp, were able to avoid the small-arms fire simply by laying low. The bullets passed harmlessly several feet above them. The artillery, loud and shocking as it was, was largely dissipated by the wet earth and vegetation. Some soldiers, wakening from the depths of concussive unconsciousness, observed that the large impact craters were rapidly filling with water.

Both commanders now began their respective tactical Kabuki dances. The troop commander, buoyed by the combined sound of artillery and friendly outgoing fire, gave orders to attack through the flanks. The VC commander, anticipating such traditional tactics, ordered his southern unit to commence firing.

The sappers, bolstering the thin infantry detonated their remaining claymores and retreated to the creek. The infantry opened up a steady fire at the tracks to their front. The scouts, now withdrawn, began to fire at the rear of the column which was completely halted along the trail.

The flank platoon leader, responding to the incoming rounds, executed a full left turn of his column and crashed toward the infantry firing along the creek bank. Quickly, one track struck a mine and the remaining tracks swung inside and continued toward the creek, firing as they came. Within a hundred feet, the lead tracks struck the boggy ground created by the sappers' earlier damming. Pressing forward in the soft purchase, two carriers assaulted at full throttle directly toward the infantry along the creek, some of whom exposed themselves to the gunners as they ducked along the creek bank.

Plunging forward, the ACAVs lost sight of the creek bank amongst the brush, debris and floodplain. The lead track abruptly nosed forward over the creek bank and drove itself half into the main stream. VC on the other side, to this point silent, fired a salvo of RPGs and assault fire into the now exposed top of the vehicle, bringing it to an abrupt halt. The second track, nosed against the rear of the first and went into reverse. Before it could regain distance from its companion, it was hit in the rear door by an RPG and a satchel charge was thrown against its side. The charge broke the track and left the crew momentarily senseless. The VC now swung away from the front and filtered to the northern flank and rear while the troop commander assessed his situation.

The troop commander, in less than five minutes, had lost approximately one third of his force and still could not ascertain the strength or direction of enemy forces. The pilot was able to give little additional assistance. Two of his platoon leaders were down and the third was fully engaged to the rear. Unsuccessful on the thrust to the south, the troop commander ordered all remaining units to swing north and flank the attack from that direction. As he gave the order, he ordered his tank to swing around and press toward the gently tilting earth.

The VC commander, essentially unengaged at the center, was able to observe this shift and sent quick messages to his forces. The scouts continued to snipe and interdict the rear successfully engaging the only viable reserve left to the troop. Remaining scouts and sappers were sent across a small log fall bridge that spanned the creek.

The VC infantry immediately opened a high volume of fire on the advancing tank and ACAVs. This accelerated the American attack and focused it on a thin front led by the troop commander's tank—now plunging forward and firing main gun canister into the gloom.

Quickly, the tank arrived at the artillery impact craters, now filled with water. The reinforcing VC infantry slid into positions behind the craters and fired a rain of RPGs. These exploded into trees and vehicle sides and forced the crews to button up, significantly reducing their vision.

At this point, the VC began to crawl forward and expose themselves for short bursts across the upturned earth. Moving toward what they could see, the Americans plunged into the craters miring their tracks and spinning for purchase. As the vehicles wheeled and wormed their way to solid earth, satchel charges were flung through the air bringing trees crashing across the tracks and obscuring the battlefield.

Unable to move effectively forward, the troop commander ordered his forces back toward the main trail. Overhead, the pilot maneuvered the first cavalry helicopter gunships overhead but could not get a firm direction from the preoccupied troop commander. Accordingly, he directed the helicopter pilots to trace an attack parallel to the creek. Their initial run with rockets and machine guns was largely lost amongst the din of the closely engaged forces. However, the VC commander noted the new players and ordered his remaining forces to the eastern bank where they could hide among the deadfall and hug the American forces.

At the cavalry headquarters, all ears were tuned to the anxious transmissions on the troop internal frequency. Both the L-19 pilot and the squadron commander had given up trying to raise the troop commander on the squadron net. At the first notice of contact, the cavalry commander had taken his helicopter to the battle scene. Now overhead, he could see the burning tank on the western bank and the destroyed ACAVs on the southern flank. Through open portions of the canopy, he could see intermittent views of maneuvering vehicles and the scattered threads of exchanging red and green tracers as they bounced off of metal sides or were deflected through tree limbs.

Well to the north, the increasing din of this battle overwhelmed the larger action. Between pauses in the attacks, both sides could hear sounds of combat other than their own. Now, the L-19 was not a familiar presence and the occasional crack and zing of a long-range rifle shot plunged through the canopy. The distant rumble of this engagement took greater precedence as the heavy artillery crumped in support with a deep resonance and echo denied the closely engaged forces to the north.

The American Ranger lieutenant, alternately adjusting to actions at his front and to the insistent conversation of the pilot, judged a major action underway. He was aware that a variety of forces were attempting to reinforce but was to that point, unaware of their direction or success. In his stomach, he began to realize that his unit was increasingly dependent on its own devices. The isolation of the jungle, the deepening gloom of the receding day and the sound of intense conflict to the south combined to make a mantle of isolation and intense loneliness... Slowly, the lieutenant turned away from the radio and faced around to his portion of the front and awaited the next shadowy black suspicion to appear over the top of his front sight. For short periods, eyes fixed on the area just ahead of the spreading flange of the front sight, he could damp his worst fears and concentrate on the immediate task at hand.

In the primary communist base camp, General Thanh followed the southern actions with great interest. Success there would mean success for the greater plan. Accordingly, he dispatched an additional force of sappers and infantry to his captain. These soldiers had specific instructions to engage the cavalry from the southeastern side of the creek and to prevent their forcing a crossing. Aware of the American tactics, he knew that he only had to delay for an hour or less before all maneuver options by the Americans would be exhausted by the curtain of night.

His orchestrating counterpart, the cavalry commander, now airborne in the darkening afternoon, was concerned with consolidating his forces and preserving the command. He ordered the remainder of the squadron to march order to the French Fort to be preceded by the 155mm battery. He directed the troop commander to laager where the trail met the creek and to recover his forces. Upon consolidation with the squadron, a full force maneuver would be undertaken. But, this could not happen until daylight and General Thanh was now free to execute the heart of his plan.

Within the shrinking Ranger perimeter, realization of the American failure struck home. Now, survival largely depended on the ability of the Vietnamese 48th Regiment to come to their assistance. The Rangers, fully occupied by the needs of their own survival, faced to the front and repeated the rote process of killing and being killed as darkness and the din of a tropical rainstorm began to shroud the bodies and their minds.

27

The Rain

It started about 2200 and was coincidental with the lull in firing. The firing and the rain worked a counterpoise with each other. As the firing reached a peak of noise and seemed to surround everything, the rain began to drop slowly on the assailants. It was very gentle and almost unnoticeable at first. Then the combatants individually became aware of its presence and it seemed to lessen their volume of fire.

It diverted their attention from the task at hand and caused everyone to react at a slower and more deliberate pace. As the rain increased, the firing decreased. Soon, the rain, in concert with the darkness, brought the jungle to a standstill. Where moments before the crash and chaos of noise was so great that nothing individually could be perceived by the soldiers, only the ceaseless and all-encompassing sound of rain and running water could be heard.

The jungle took on a uniform stillness and sound as if to cleanse itself of the violations it had experienced. The sound of rain blotted out all other sensations. Both sides ceased activity for several moments once the rain began to course down. Each man lay in his position drinking in the sounds of life and relaxing from the sounds of death. The rain, like a giant fetal heartbeat, consumed everyone into its sphere and brought a uniform calm to the scene.

Slowly, the unwounded and undead began to react to the respite created by the rain. Both sides shifted their positions. At first individuals moved to better locations—locations thought better to survive the next onslaught or seek protection from the endless streams of water.

Then the leadership took charge, moving people to positions of better tactical advantage. Not necessarily better from either the viewpoint of survival or comfort. The soldiers of both sides knew this but assumed their directed location with the stoicism of disciplined experienced veterans. They looked anxiously to their front with their faces flush on the ground, their weapons under their arms and the rain pouring steadily from their head to their face to their hard metal rifles as they waited. Waited for a lull in the rain or the peaceful natural noise that seemed to encompass and overshadow everything else and wash their memories clear.

The wounded of both sides lay in the wet and waited. Many took scarce notice of the rain, other pains or no pain at all overpowering the faint impression that rain made on skin or dry clothing. Some, those with stomach or chest wounds, welcomed the rain. They lapped eagerly with their tongues to catch the flecks that dropped directly into their mouths or rolled off their cheeks and lips.

The rain began to beat hard on exposed faces. Some tried feebly to cover their eyes with hands or arms but the pain was too great or the interest was not sufficiently strong enough. They simply closed their eyes and waited for either death or assistance—either form a relief.

The medical personnel from both sides began to make their way forward between the lines of combatants, now fewer than 20 meters apart. Each side began to recover its charges. The distinction between friend and enemy was nonexistent to this group as they impassively but with intensity practiced their trade.

The crashing rain provided a covering sound for the medics and they felt safe in venturing forward from their respective log or tree protection. Here and there they would find a living soldier and pull him back to their lines for treatment. Other times they would find a dead soldier. The rain made diagnosis of death easy. Half-open eyes would be pooled with water and would cause a sparkling reflection of false life that drained immediately when the medic placed his hand on the throat to check for pulse. If the eyes didn't blink when the medic touched the face, he moved on.

The rain and fear made the medics work at true ground level. They pushed their faces sideways into the dirt and moved slowly ahead, their bodies flush with the dirt. Their actions would stir the covering of dead leaves, limbs and organic matter that matted the jungle floor and activated a trail of phosphors behind them like the wake of a ship. The rain would quickly activate the grayish green glows and just as quickly extinguish them into the nothingness of the black earth. The boots acted as propellers in the sea, taking a bite, exposing the photons, and then moving on with only the slightest green trace remaining after the initial pass of the blade on the virgin water.

The medics moved forward and sideways, reaching into the darkness, feeling for their charges. The medics on both sides had to rely totally on feel and past reflections. One side's soldiers had hard canvas grenade bags across their chests, the other had equipment straps. If a medic could not feel friendly gear, he removed his hand quickly to the nose and felt for some breath of life while his other gripped a pistol even tighter.

After a moment's hesitation, he would feel the body for the wound area and speak softly and comfortingly. In some cases, the medic would reach out and feel a warm wet sensation on his fingertips but no clothing identifier. He would then move his hands slowly up the body until he could feel the face and scalp. One side had short hair and the other long. Regardless of identification, the wounded received whatever attention was appropriate.

Occasionally, there would be nothing to feel beyond the torso or the rented clothing would reveal cold wet skin and he would move on. Each man was careful to remember the distance from his sanctuary position and would move in a circular motion, the outer periphery of his journey no more than he imagined would be halfway to the enemy side. This technique was not taught at any school, but it was instinctual as medics from both sides used it. In the early glimmer of dawn, the space between the two assailants was covered with circular patterns broken only by lifeless bodies and the drag marks of the still living recovered to their own lines.

The lieutenant noticed the rain only after it began to pop and smoke off the barrel of his rifle. The increasing fury of the rain then took precedence over his other senses as the sound of the beating water washed out the last few hours' sensations. The water, coursing down his neck and pouring off the helmet lip onto his nose and chin seemed to cleanse him of emotions and his mind drifted to the point where he could focus solely on the rain and nothing else. He turned sideways, his back resting against the back of the sergeant and his face resting on the rifle that lay on the wet leafy floor.

The two enjoyed the warmth of each other and allowed their minds to concentrate on the sound of the rain alone. Slowly, they were able to repress the deep visceral instincts that had shielded them throughout the afternoon and to regain their more common human feelings. As the rain beat down, each man began to think, reflect and once more become aware of matters of personal comfort.

28

The Fog

The rain halted as abruptly as it started about midnight. Soon, it was replaced by a heavy shrouding fog. The fog began at the river. It rose slowly with the passing of the rain and collected over the Dong Ngai. Initially, the tall jungle on the river banks held the fog in check and collected it in with increasing density. By 0100, the fog had broken its walls and began to drift through the trunks and foliage of its prison and over the top of the canopy. Freed of its bonds, the gray cloud roiled and poured its way through the canopy top toward the jungle floor and met its reinforcing vapors that had slowly worked their way through the foliage. Together, they quickly shrouded everything in a thick, wet womb.

Both sides detected this conversion and each was apprehensive as to its effect. The difference between attacker and defender was moot and each side concerned itself with how the other could use the situation to advantage. As is usually the case, soldiers attest greater capability to their opposition than reality would dictate. However, this evening, one side would be able to validate this shibboleth.

On the western bank of the river, the VC had waited and prepared for this moment. Throughout the day and into the evening hours, they had been prevented from revealing their positions on the west bank. The low-flying spotter aircraft quickly brought artillery down on anything that moved. The pilot of the L-19 aircraft was very watchful of the entire area surrounding the conflict zone, especially the river edge because it stood out in such contrast with the rest of the jungle cover.

Several times during the day, the VC had taken surprise casualties from single 175mm rounds the pilot had called in on likely gathering points. Now, with the fog covering the river and the jungle roof to where it was impossible for an airborne observer to see anything other than the fog cloud, the VC felt safe to implement their plan.

Both antagonists could hear the steady drone of the aircraft overhead. To the Rangers, the comforting noise represented their only tenuous link with support and a hope for future life. For the VC, it represented that link to firepower that they recognized could not be overcome with the best of planning and foresight. Now, both sides realized the aircraft could see nothing below the thick, gray wet mass that shrouded everything in a blanket of anonymity.

The first people to expose themselves on the river bank were the boat haulers. There were twelve of them. Six to a side. They were dressed in black pajama pants that were rolled up to their thighs. Barefoot to gain better purchase of the slippery clay riverbank surface, they wore no shirts and were bareheaded. They held a long sampan between them and carefully lowered it into the water. One man held it by a rope to the bank while another two men stood in the water holding it at the prow from the swift current.

Two more men emerged from the shadows of the bankside trees and roiling fog and carried an engine with an extra-long propeller shaft. The engine was carefully lowered onto the stern and the screw locks tightly closed down. Hands emerged from the foliage to pass a section of rope to the engine operator.

The operator, kneeling in the boat, took the free rope end and lay it in the floor of the craft. He quickly began feeding the rope in long strands the entire length of the boat as it was fed to him from unseen bodies beyond the range of his vision. Something was said to him and he stopped feeding the coils and lowered the long shaft into the water.

The boat was now parallel with the river bank and the almost submerged crew anchors were straining against the current as they steadied the boat against the pilot's exertions.

The pilot quickly started the engine with a rope pull and throttled it. The noise reverberated with a dull consistent throb that quickly dissipated against the combined weight of the fog and river's roil. He made a motion with his free hand and two figures emerged from the shadows and stepped carefully into the boat and made their way to the prow where they took a kneeling position.

They were undressed and unarmed except for rolled pants. The pilot gave a signal and the prow anchors swung the boat abreast of the current and passed it along their hands giving the boat both direction and speed against the river until the propellers were able to influence the sampan against the rushing water.

The pilot placed his boat in a quartering direction against the river current and headed toward the opposite shore. Fewer than 20 feet from his start point, he lost sight of the bank in the fog and from then on relied solely on his ability to run contrary to the river to carry him to the other side. His forward passengers anxiously looked into the black, amorphous atmosphere for signs of the far bank.

Abruptly, too abruptly to reduce speed, the sampan crashed into the soft earth of the eastern bank and began to swiftly nose upcurrent as the weighted stern carried the craft downstream. The forward crew quickly jumped out and grabbed some overhanging roots and anchored their boat to them by holding on with their arms while their bodies lay sandwiched between the hull and the mud of the bank.

One of the two passed over the other and scrambled ashore, rested for a moment, and then disappeared in the murk. The engine cut off and all remained silent save for the sound of water rushing across the side of the hull and the anxious breathing of the waiting crew.

Minutes later, the crew member returned with two uniformed soldiers. Together, they grasped the free running rope end and moved several dozen feet up river. They tied the rope end to a large tree whose root mass was being steadily undercut by the rushing river. The soldiers then returned to the sampan and pulled it upstream to where the remaining crewman could grasp the rope that now spanned both river banks.

Hand over hand, the forward crew member pulled the sampan slowly along the rope until the long propeller shaft was free from the bank. The pilot then started the engine, lowered the prop into the water and sped along the line outlined by the rope, now securely fastened to both banks.

As the first crossing, the boat impacted abruptly into the far bank throwing the forward crew member almost out of the boat. The sampan was quickly anchored with a small rope and both remaining crewmen stood on the shore and began an anxious conference with a man dressed in long pants, long-sleeved tan shirt and Sam Browne belt. He listened carefully to their conversation and then disappeared into the jungle.

In less than five minutes, the fruits of the plan began to emerge from the inner recesses of the jungle. First to be seen was the nose of a large raft. It was about 12 feet wide and made of logs 8 to 10 inches thick. Due to the weight, the raft was not carried but instead was rolled across a ribbing of six-inch logs placed perpendicular to the trail, skinned of bark and greased with soft, wet clay. By every log rib, there were two soldiers who alternately pulled the raft and lifted it across their rib. The rafts were about 20 feet in length and took some time to pass.

The combination of darkness and fog prevented the laborers from seeing each other. Instead, they simply began their tasks by feel and regreased the log ribs when nothing was within their hand's grasp. In this manner, three rafts were placed in the water within 30 minutes and were anchored to the shore.

Meanwhile, the sampan had made two more trips. Using the first rope as a guide, it had laid two more crossings further upriver, each about 100 meters apart and quartered against the current.

Once the rafts were in the water and manipulated by hand to their respective tow ropes and held in place fore and aft, the cargo began to emerge. Soldiers, four abreast, followed the rafts and stood quietly by the bank debarkation sites waiting for the rafts to settle in the water. On command, they began to load the rafts.

Two at a time, they dropped onto the raft from the bank and made their way to the front where they knelt down equidistant apart across the width of the raft itself. Following soldiers filled the gap between the initial two and then began to fill the raft in depth from the front to the rear. Quickly, each raft was filled with 40 soldiers who reflected the exhaustive rehearsals they had just completed.

As soon as each raft was filled, a leader gave a silent signal. The 10 soldiers along the up-current side of the raft grasped the rope and began to pull in unison. The raft, slowly and then with increasing speed, nosed out into the river and began to make its way across the current.

Each raft was quickly seized by the current and swung downstream as it crossed the water. The exertions of the rope pullers were uniform which caused a jerky motion to the craft as it steadily propelled itself into the nether fog and gloom.

The combination of speed and current caused the logs on the up-current side to submerge and flood the passengers with water up to the point where their upper leg rested on their calves. The soldiers silently pulled on the rope and stared straight ahead into the darkness. Their teeth clenched tightly together and their lips pursed almost into their mouths, the soldiers breathed rhythmically and heaved their bodies against the silent strength of the river.

Slowly, the soldiers could make out the far bank and the rope anchor points. Half exposed in the water to their front was another line of soldiers between themselves and the bank. This line stopped the forward motion of the raft, held it to the shore as the raft swung with the current and served as a stepping stone for the passengers.

Each soldier disembarked by stepping on the shoulder of one of the immersed personnel and placing another foot on the slightly higher bank. Once ashore, the soldiers were directed by a party of guide personnel to an assembly area at the rear of the base camp where they awaited the remainder of the force.

The raft, now devoid of most of its load, was pulled to the other shore by the same 10 men that pulled it across. Once returned, it quickly filled with 30 more men and proceeded across the river. This process continued throughout the early morning hours without letup except to switch tow crews.

By 0400, two and one half additional battalions were ferried across to be committed in the creeping dawn of the new day. General Thanh's reinforcement had gone decidedly better than that attempted on behalf of his antagonists.

29

Reinforcement

After his nap and throughout the remainder of the day, Colonel Trinh had closely monitored the radio. He insured that the division commander and his American counterpart were advised when each of his units had assembled and occupied their field positions. He personally visited each one in his jeep and spent some time touring their positions. He had felt safe in napping as everyone would understand that units were in transit and nothing significant would happen. Once the Ranger insertions began, he wanted to insure that he was not readily available to the higher headquarters but on a plausible professional task.

The troops, irritated by their sudden departure from Xuan Loc and uncertain as to their future, said little to Trinh but gathered quietly in groups in whatever shade they could find. Occasionally, as the report from the heavy artillery registered or one of the cavalry helicopters passed overhead, they would look west with anxiety and with downcast eyes, return to their conversations. Should Trinh be with them during one of these interruptions, he would tense internally and make an effort to be gregarious and involved as if to mask the reality of what was occurring less than four kilometers away.

By late afternoon, it was impossible to hide the intensity of the conflict. The air droned with the monotonous rumble of the engagement and invaded every conversation. Birds and small animals, chased from the jungle by the intensity of the fight, swirled in the air overhead or raced across the open fields seeking shelter. The soldiers noted this and looked with increasing anxiety at their leaders and the radios.

Orderlies occasionally would find Trinh and pass messages from the division. He would provide them a short response and they would return to the thatch hut headquarters. After a while, Trinh turned off the jeep radio that netted with Xuan Loc and satisfied himself with talking only to his subordinate elements. During the afternoon, the American advisor remained in the adjacent hut and responded to a continuous barrage of inquiries from his senior in Xuan Loc.

Once, he had attempted to talk to the L-19 pilot when he saw him orbit a small field to his front but he had been cut off by the pilot as he was requesting an artillery fire mission. Rebuffed in his one attempt to engage himself, he fell silent and returned to the incessant chatter of his amplifier.

By midafternoon, Trinh had visited all his units and returned to the thatch hut house for refreshments. He stepped carefully from the jeep and placed his polished American jump boots squarely on the small rocks that lined the path from the village road to the hut entrance.

He stepped inside and waited a moment for his eyes to adjust to the dark. His aide was seated at a small ebony black table to his front. The wood possessed a remarkably high sheen from a combination of its great density and hard use. It reflected the available light in sparks and flashes and emphasized the blue swirling wisps of dust and smoke that eddied across the intermittent light shafts leaking through gaps in the thatch.

A large cat sat dozing on the bench to his front and a small beaker with a tiger lily rested at the center. The flowers had been placed there by the homeowner, who despite the confusion of unprogrammed occupation, believed that some color and softness should be added to the center of this commotion. Her obligation having been accomplished, the owner retreated to the shade at the rear of the house and prepared rice while holding her child next to her. Despite the encouragements from the soldiers and the aide, she could not be persuaded to enter into conversation with them. After several attempts, the aide had stopped trying and retreated to the table. At a lull in activity, the husband sent his wife and child to a friend's house but she had returned reporting that it too was filled with soldiers. Noting the aide's attempts to write, she removed a small kerosene lantern from a box, lit it and wordlessly placed it next to the aide.

Now, as Trinh entered, he was writing in a small notebook overprinted with graph squares, the kind used by engineers and other people who enjoyed precision and order. It was filled with concise verbatim transcriptions of messages from Xuan Loc as well as from the American advisor next door. He had plotted the information on a map spread across the table and offered to brief Hien on its contents and meaning.

Trinh waved him away and requested that the advisor join him. Shortly, the American entered and saluted. Trinh offered him a cigarette and ordered glasses of beer. In the afternoon, the heat in the hut had become quite stifling. That, mixed with the smoke from the cooking fire, had irritated Trinh's eyes and he began dabbing at them with the white handkerchief usually reserved for sweat beads. The beer was brought in large tea glasses. The glasses were filled with ice chunks and the beer poured inside. At the surface, pieces of wheat husk from ice chest insulation matted and collected against the meniscus.

Trinh dipped a delicate finger edged with an exaggeratedly long nail in the Vietnamese fashion and extracted the detritus. Slowly sipping the beer, he closed his eyes and pulled on his cigarette.

The American, quickly gulping the beer, with anxious eyes, began to speak. Trinh waved his hand and leaned back on the bench. He kept this pose for almost a half-minute and then sat upright. He opened his eyes and in a calm, even voice began to describe his visit to the troops. He recounted each stop in detail and with no particular emphasis. Once, when the aide entered with his message book, Trinh glared at him and waved him away.

A U.S. sergeant visited from the adjacent hut every few minutes and handed his colonel a transcript of messages received from Xuan Loc. The American would try in a half-hearted manner to dismiss the sergeant as Trinh glared at the intrusion but finally succumbed to his professionalism and accepted the papers. He would read the note, scribble a comment, and then return the paper to the sergeant. As the sergeant retreated, the American officer would follow him out with increasingly nervous eyes. Trinh attempted to divert his attention with aimless discussions but failed to overcome his growing anxiety.

As the afternoon light played into greater obscurity, Trinh became a small ebony oval face glowing in the heat of his cigarette. His aide brought a small plaster jar from which he spooned a thick brown liquid into a clear glass. Trinh slowly sipped the liquid and smoked cigarettes. The American attempted to leave on several occasions but was always exhorted to stay. Increasingly, Trinh was irritated by the Americans' attempt to engage him in the operation to the west. Unable to cause him to either drop the issue or lapse into comradely drinking, Trinh eventually allowed him to gracefully exit on the excuse of a latrine call.

The American left the room and hastily went to his communications setup. He talked to the senior advisor in Xuan Loc and provided hesitant responses to the barrage of questions that flowed over the radio set. At last in frustration, he returned to Trinh's room and went inside. The room was utterly dark with only the residual glow of the cigarette embers. Unable to find his counterpart, the American went to the rear of the structure and found the aide. Without responding directly, the aide pointed to the retreating lights of a jeep losing itself in the folds of the open farmland in the distance.

The American returned to his radio and reported that the regimental commander was not available to issue movement orders. Within the regimental perimeter, the obscuring sky was a signal for the rain sheets to be placed over the hammocks and the evening rice to be quickly prepared. The soldiers settled into the encompassing folds of the nylon and listened to the muttering sounds in the distance, glad they were not there.

30

Softly in the Night

The night, coupled with the rain and fog, permitted the soldiers from both sides, equally exhausted emotionally and physically, to rest. This was not possible for their leadership. In huddled groups on both sides, from the most senior to the squad, they attempted to understand what had happened and what remained to be done.

As night fell on Xuan Loc, the advisory compound and the division headquarters retained their activity level. As the afternoon wore on, both the advisors and the division began to realize that a tragedy was close to unfolding. The steady voice of the L-19 pilot had, all day, been describing the darkening events.

As the situation deteriorated, the senior American advisor's demeanor went from euphoria to agony. Enthused as he was with participating in a major operation with potentially significant reward, his mood turned increasingly from concern into frustration. His repeated attempts to gain activity from the 48th Regiment had been unsuccessful despite his continued badgering of the American advisor on the spot. Finally in frustration, shortly after 1730, he drove to the 18th Division Headquarters.

The division, though a flurry with energy and reports, was all process and no product. The available artillery was unable to move into supporting locations as its commander was concerned about being ambushed from the many small villages it had to traverse east of the combat area. He had convinced the division commander that two battles were worse than one. The division commander then requested that the cavalry reposition its artillery.

Earlier in the afternoon, the cavalry command post had already shifted its 155mm artillery to support the relief column and alerted the entire Second Squadron to begin road movement to join the advance forces. The artillery, trailing the maneuver column, had established itself at the side of the highway to the south while the remainder of the squadron worked between the French Fort and the ambushed column to extricate the engaged forces. Darkness came quickly upon this effort and the now released forces gathered next to the 175mm battery to reorganize and await daylight. These dispositions were observed by the ubiquitous scouts and carried to General Thanh, several kilometers west.

Resting in his underground bunker, away from the incessant chatter of the Morse key, Thanh interviewed the scout. He rose from his cot and climbed the steep stairs leading to the briefing area above ground. Here he found the Caucasians talking to the communications officer in French who was plotting the situation on a captured American map.

Thanh reinterviewed the scout, offered him a cigarette and small glass of hot tea. He then requested the presence of the Binh Tram commander. Thanh, now engrossed in the situation, retreated into his own world of activity and instructions. The Caucasian and Oriental visitors, usually treated with the greatest of deference, were ignored as specks upon the sea. His energy moved him between the radios and the map.

The Binh Tram commander reported to Thanh. Thanh, without looking up, issued several quick orders and retreated to his cigarette and map study. The commander attempted to question what he was told but was waved away. Quietly but with great agitation, he began to round up all available personnel and assemble them in the center of the compound. Once formed, he ordered them to move east under command of the regiment. Some soldiers protested and were surprised to find Thanh rebuking them in the dark. Later, Thanh traversed the entire Binh Tram with several sergeants and vacated the base camp of all but the most essential personnel. At the head of this last group of recalcitrants, he placed the Binh Tram commander. By 0300. he was satisfied and returned to his cot.

By 0700, the Ranger perimeter had shrunk to an ellipse. The command group was located roughly equidistant between the front and rear and close to the flank that abutted the Suoi Long Creek. The hand-generated HF radio, a U.S. standby from World War II, had been working continuously. Since the unit left the landing zone, it was the only communications link the battalion had with its superiors. Above, the L-19 had maintained a radio relay for the Americans but even their modern FM radios could not penetrate beyond it due to the great attenuation caused by the foliage.

The communications section had rigged a long wire antenna barely a foot off the ground parallel to Xuan Loc. The operator, afraid of attracting attention, used only Morse mode, ignoring the voice capability. His assistant, laying on his back with the generator handles between his legs, provided a steady slow power surge sufficient to send the low power signal off the ionosphere and back down to the 18th Division.

Throughout the battle, the radio was able to keep the division engaged. Concurrently, the division was able to question Hiep. By late afternoon, General Tanh had wished the communication link had been less effective. He had sent a message requesting Hiep's personal assessment. Hiep had responded that unless the Americans or 48th Regiment joined them by daylight, the Rangers would be overwhelmed. Disengagement by retreat was not an option. Tanh knew that surrender was equally out of the question. The emotions felt by both sides and the intensity of past conflicts had rarely provided prisoners. Rather a sweep of the battlefield would reveal small head wounds on the remaining soldiers of both sides.

The senior American advisor, now having joined General Tanh at his headquarters, read Hiep's message. He phoned the cavalry commander who indicated his inability to press the creek at night.

This situation was briefed to Tanh who asked to speak to Colonel Trinh at his field location. Trinh could not be located. Tanh ordered the regiment to move immediately toward the Rangers. Trinh's aide, well-schooled in this situation, acknowledged the message and wrote it in his notebook. He did not inform the American of the order.

The Ranger radio operator informed Hiep of the order. He lay on his back and smoked slowly, his uniform still well-creased. After approximately an hour, Hiep asked if the regimental radio was still working. Upon receiving an affirmative reply, Hiep smothered his cigarette and began to move forward to his closest company commander.

Throughout the night, the sharp click of bamboo sticks coursed across the perimeters. These sticks, wielded by the VC scouts, marked their traversing of the Ranger perimeter and fixed the locations for the machine gunners staking their barrels. The clicking served to give both sides pause—one knowing that they defined their exposure limits and the other to define just how small and weak they had become.

31

The Plan

Before he left, the battalion commander whispered quiet orders to his bodyguards behind the large tree trunk that now lay across the ground, parallel to the assaulting forces. So far, it had absorbed a large quantity of small-arms and several RPG rounds. The bark had been thoroughly scored and the impact of each round was easily transmitted through the spongy wood to the command group on the other side. The commander could judge the intensity of the conflict more from the vibration of the tree than the hoarse quick voices he heard from the radio.

By evening, the commander had known that his unit was in a major battle. By 0200, he knew he was in a battle of survival. By 0400, it was clear that annihilation was highly probable. Now, at 0430, he assembled his company commanders and reviewed the situation.

They were surrounded. They were reduced to half their strength and pinned between a creek and a river, with an overwhelming force to their front and a superior force to their rear. The usual support they had historically relied upon could not be brought to bear.

The artillery was too inaccurate. The armored cavalry had failed to push through. The 48th Regiment had refused to move. The Spooky was useless in the heavily fogged jungle. They were totally and utterly dependent on their own weak remaining devices. Their assets were reduced to the spirit of the unit which was as individually and collectively aware of the desperation of its condition as was he. In this mental framework, Hiep met with his subordinates and planned the next few hours of what could well be the remainder of their collective lives.

The commanders crawled into the shelter of the tree trunk amid the eerie quiescence of the battlefield. The fog had shrouded the area with a heavy blanket of silence. Laden with moisture, the heavy hanging air muffled the low tones of those alive between the lines and the quiet patient progress of the VC scouts.

The scouts moved around the Ranger perimeter, marking their positions with quick clacks of bamboo stalks. The Rangers noted the sounds and mentally reflected on how close the sounds appeared from across their flanks and rear. In any other environment, they would have fired at the sound. Now, they huddled in absolute stillness, held their breath and hoped the scouts would not penetrate to their position. No man wanted to be identified as the flank element of a very small line.

Amidst the quiet continuous clacking notes, the group huddled behind the fallen tree to take solace amongst themselves and to decide upon their final act.

At their rear, fewer than 50 feet from the tree and protected by the defilade of small depression, the command group radio team was steadily working. By early afternoon, the battalion communications team had realized that contact with their higher headquarters could not be achieved. All calls on the FM had been unanswered. Only the U.S. radios connected the battalion with the outside world and that only through the airborne relay. Accordingly, the commander had ordered that the heavy and unwieldy HF communications net be established.

This was a World War II-vintage piece of equipment that operated with a hand-crank generator and Morse code. The antenna was a long wire strung between two trees broadside to the station desired to reach. This means of communication invariably worked as the system could just as easily reach Saigon as Xuan Loc and therefore its signal could not be ignored. The communications team stoically ground the generator crank and tapped out the unit situation on a knee pad key as the bullets chewed leaves and bark over its head.

The team steadily informed the outside world of its situation. The casualties. Requests for reinforcement. Ammunition. Medical aid. The reports were briefly acknowledged between transmissions. As the afternoon wore into evening, the sight of the team gave way slowly to only the sound of the steady revolving generator crank and the weak clicking sound of the Morse key. The command group, huddled next to the trunk, could distinctly hear the difference between the Morse clicks and the bamboo clacks of the VC scouts. These sounds provided a subliminal sense of urgency to the discussion.

The commander lit a Pall Mall and reviewed the situation. The 52nd Recon Company to the front was apparently nonexistent. Several members had joined the center rifle company but that was all that was known. The 48th Regiment, only a few kilometers away, had refused to march. An entire squadron of the 11th ACR was stuck in an ambush 5 kilometers south. The 175mm artillery had to be cut off as it was too erratic. The Spooky could not effectively support due to the fog and its inability to pinpoint the now microscopic Ranger position. The four Ranger companies had lost most of the original seized base camp and were reduced to fewer than 50 men per company. The center company, Second Company, was believed to have fewer than 30 men left.

Still, some bright spots remained. The four machine guns remained intact. Though they attracted a great deal of fire, they effectively reduced the ability of the VC to mount a sustained frontal attack. This became more telling as the Ranger perimeter was reduced and the effect of the guns accordingly more pronounced across the front. The lines, though steadily reduced, were still coherent and enjoyed the benefit of interior communications. This was somewhat negated by the fact that a RPG fired at the front of the Rangers could easily impact past its rear and any indirect fire would hit something of value. Of greatest comfort was the continuous link with the rear through the L-19 relay flying above. It brought the outside world to the Rangers' side and provided some spark of hope, however small. The commander realized that the predawn period would be the ultimate and last test of the unit. His orders were born of desperation and the knowledge that they had only a single card left to play.

He did not ask for suggestions as was his usual method. He had already made up his mind as to the necessary actions and knew that the relative immaturity of his subordinates could not conceive of such a plan. Quickly he sketched out the concept, his mouth and moustache occasionally accenting his words in the warm glow of his cigarette. His subordinates said nothing but listened intently, fully recognizing that obedience held the only possibility of survival. With quiet, short comments, they indicated their comprehension and acquiescence and moved quickly back to their units. Through this all, the omnipresent clicks of the Morse and clacks of the bamboo provided a background tone.

His plan was quite simple and depended on a combination of ordnance and audacity. He knew the VC would attack at the very first light at the weakest point of the line—which he judged they believed to be the center—flanked by the two ubiquitous VC machine-gun bunkers that chattered throughout the night. This attack would be conducted with the greatest possible strength mustered throughout the night and designed to overrun and split the position before support could be brought to bear.

Hiep, through the American lieutenant, had asked the L-19 pilot to secure the maximum amount of air support possible, beginning just before dawn. He wanted a steady stream of bombs to be dropped from his own right flank position on the shortest route possible to the previous afternoon's landing zone.

The remnants of the Rangers would follow this bomb line to whatever safety could be afforded from that location. He also knew that his force had only a small percentage of the strength that was rapidly mustering on the other side. To redress the balance, for just the shortest period of time, he would have the center company conduct a frontal assault against the VC to coincide with the first air strike.

He hoped that the combination of the surprise Ranger frontal assault into an ongoing VC assault, combined with the air strikes, would permit some portion of the remaining Rangers to escape alive. He ordered the attack to coincide with the first bomb run. Within the range of a normal voice, similar preparations were being undertaken on the other side of the sheltering trees.

32

The Shoal of Fish

Once across the river the VC moved with definition to the forward edge of the unengaged portion of the base camp. The cadre took positions in the lead and end of each boatload and made every man hold the equipment straps of the man in front. Silence was rigidly enforced with open palm slaps to the head. Cowed and frightened, the soldiers moved with heads down and shallow breath to the welcome cover of the trench system. The convivial camaraderie and looseness of the long march down the trail from the north had been quickly replaced by the necessary discipline and anxiety of soldiers on the cusp of combat.

Initially, the soldiers were hot and sweaty from their fast-paced march to the embarkation site. As they backed up in the assembly area awaiting the crossing order packed like so many fish, the men became clammy and cold. They huddled together for emotional and physical warmth and listened anxiously to the mutterings of warfare across the water.

As the heavy fog settled in, the soldiers were gathered in small groups by the cadre and moved forward to the raft sites. Rising from the damp acid earth, each body triggered a phosphorescent explosion as it rose from the dirt. Small sparks and tangles of greenish light danced across the just-vacated depressions in the soil. The accumulated light reflected in Vermeer-like dispersions across the sweat and metal of the soldiers still laying into the earth and exposed their anxious faces and muscle-tensed ivory parchment skin.

This quiet tense motion went on all night until every trench line was filled as densely as could be packed. The last units simply lay on the ground between the last trench line and the riverside. By dawn, the camp could hold no more without exposure to direct fire. The First Regiment commander ordered a halt to the transit as the first light of dawn began its creeping infiltration of the night. By his count, more than 1,500 soldiers were jammed into an area of less than three acres.

Crouched in the trenches, the soldiers, bound by association but yet unblooded, clung to the earth and awaited the welcome light and warmth of the day. Untouched by the reality of war, they, like their counterparts, welcomed the light. Unlike those opposite them, only a few yards ahead, they had yet to realize the consequences of attacking a desperately defended position in daylight. Kept utterly silent by the cadre, they passed the remainder of the night much like the Rangers. Listening to the click-clack of the scouts' bamboo markers and the random shout or shot, each man tried to visualize reality beyond the dark and control his emotions and disciplined compliance to the group.

In the initial light, the cadre could see the anxious deer-like eyes of their charges as they fixed on every move or new event that crossed their view. The cadre moved quietly along the trench tapping weapons and adjusting equipment, providing the degree of assurance and confidence they knew was essential for the next critical step, the prelude to death.

Gradually, the light became distinct enough to gauge shapes within several meters. The shadows and substance of the camp composition gradually took hold as the veil of night lifted. When he could see both ends of each trench as they abutted the river banks, the regimental commander motioned to the cadre in the trench closest the rear.

On the sign, the cadre stood their soldiers in the trench and directed that they lay on the top of the ground facing forward. This act was repeated in a slow ripple until all but the three most forward trenches were vacated. Here, the remnants of the two original battalions had spent the night. Their positions were filled with the flotsam of the previous day: dead, wounded, and living. Now, all veterans and aware of the consequences of the dawn, they huddled in the depths of the trenches fingering their triggers and anxiously glancing at the leaders in the flank and middle of each position.

In a shattering tear to the fog-shrouded curtain that had softly fallen across the land, the heavy VC machine guns broke the abiding tenseness. From the flank and center bunkers, the weapons rattled and chewed their way across the front. Birds rose and screamed and eyes opened wide as the sound and energy of the bullets passed overhead.

With the sound of the guns, whistles blew from the flanks of each trench. Urged by the cadre, the new soldiers rose like so many shoals of fish, reflecting the morning light on the sweep of the chromed bayonets as they surged with ignorant driving energy blindly toward the trench immediately to the front. As a huge choreographed ballet, every trench line arose, flashed its bayonets in shimmering unison and lunged toward the sweet protective cover of the rented earth just so few steps in front.

Bullets danced and drove through the massed bodies like divers through schools of fish. Like fish, the force of the impacting objects diverted some of the silvery school away from the whole and drove them to the ground where they reflected some passing slivers of light to mark the passage of the whole.

In the forward trenches, the firing was too fierce to broach. Here knowledge and experience mitigated the fear of discipline. Stepping on bodies for purchase and shielding eyes against the constant rain of dirt, bark and cordite, the most exposed soldiers lay their weapons on the protecting parapets and fired blindly into the gloom.

The regimental commander could now see the entire front and noted that in many cases, the muzzle blasts from the Rangers and his forward elements overlapped. The air was alive with noise and death. The heavy odor of metal and cordite built across the front in a cloud of inversion. Trapped by the lifting fog and the heat of the weapons discharge, the expended detritus of the bores obscured the acts of death from all but the closest of observers.

As the shoals of fishes coalesced, broke and reformed, they began to flesh out the forward area until a solid mass was formed. Stopped by the wall of fire, the attacking soldiers built up in the forward trenches until there was no room to accept another. Dead and living in all configurations paved the earth and filled every wrap and wrinkle of earth. Some found cover in time and breathed in anxious relief joyful to inhale dirt and smoke and view the world from half an inch. Others found it only long enough to breath shortly and bleed, deeply sinking full face into the soil.

The time had arrived to press forward the phalanx. The rearmost units, filtered by their comrades from the stream of bullets to the front, moved several trenches forward relatively unscathed. Now, the final moves had pressed them against the human shields halted by the inability to overcome the most primordial of fears and instinct.

At the rear of the regiment, the commander had assembled his most veteran soldiers. These were a mix of sappers, scouts and cadre. Old faces, worn and lined but with relatively young bodies and hard animal-sharp eyes. They crawled slowly forward on line, never rising more than necessary and taking deliberate continuous movement, they positioned themselves at the rear of the packed formation. The school of fish were about to be pushed against the dam.

33

Fire Support

Just beginning to assist their brother VC soldiers, the regimental mortar crews poised their rounds in the tubes and began to interdict the battlefield. Approximately a kilometer south of the base camp, the 82mm mortar gunners had established a position on the edge of a small clearing. Due to the distance between the crossing site on the river and their intended support position, the regimental commander had placed them among the first groups to cross the Dong Nai. In the dark sweltering shroud of fog and humidity, they had left the growing cluster of massed bodies on the eastern shore and with their burden of weapons and ammunition, moved south skirting the river's edge and then east along a loggers trail. After an hour's slow pace, the mortar gunners, a group of 23, found their location. This was a small open area created by the local loggers who had cleared sufficient land to permit the logs to be trimmed, stripped, and loaded on the long flatbed trucks. The truck trails connecting to this open spot in the otherwise unbroken green carpet, snaked across the small patches of relatively dry ground to the east until they broke through to the raised plateau that connected Highway 20 with the rest of Vietnam. These trails, increasingly indistinct through disuse, were common connective tissue for communist units threading their way between secretive concealment and their populations of interest.

In the small turn around area, less than a hundred meters square, the crews had established their positions. With five tubes, an unusually large number of weapons for such a small area, they were very close together. They oriented themselves just inside the tree line with the tubes pointing into the obscured sky almost due north to the base camp battlefield. Once the position had been found, the commander, a senior sergeant, sent his runner back to the crossing site to inform the regiment. Now, in the waning hours of the night, coolies began arriving bringing more ammunition which was stacked just to the rear of each tube.

The regimental commander had provided brief concise instructions. At the first sign of dawn, the mortars were to begin a saturation firing of the Ranger position. They were to fire all their ammunition as fast they could and then evacuate back to the crossing site. To accomplish this task absent a map or optical sights, common and essential material with Western gunners, the mortar crew commander had relied on traditional methods gained from experience. He sent out two scouts with compasses to seek the regimental scouts who were tracing the Ranger field position. They drew a precise drawing of the entire trace of the Ranger position, width and depth. Each then departed separately from the flanks back to the mortar position noting the compass azimuth. From this information, the sergeant was able to accurately judge the range, azimuth, width and depth of the target. He carefully drew this information in the form of a schematic drawing on clean graph paper and divided his position into five equal columns stretching from each mortar to the maximum depth of the Ranger position.

Moving to each tube with the drawing, he carefully aligned the tube toward the Rangers, sighting his compass over the top center of the barrel. Once all tubes were aligned by azimuth, he called all the gunners to a conference. Huddled in the edge of the jungle, swiping at mosquitoes and illuminated by the light of a small shielded candle, they gathered around the small paper map, now tacked to a piece of cardboard and tilted next to the candle.

Hunched in a circle in the traditional Vietnamese squat, their sandaled feet almost touching the cardboard, the sergeant quickly briefed the concept. As experienced veterans, many assumptions were possible and many procedures had become rote so the discussion was efficient and short. On his command, the gunners would begin firing as fast as possible. After every five rounds, the gunners would shift the tubes on target adjusting to the left three full turns on the small brass crank. Then they would depress the tube one turn on the elevation and complete the process for three sequences. After that, they would reverse the process until the ammunition was expended. In this manner, they would saturate the Ranger position from flank to flank and front to rear in less than 10 minutes. The sergeant, wiping his glasses, consulted the card that accompanied the ammunition and determined that three of the wafer propellants would be sufficient and five complete turns from the bottom of the elevation screw would place the rounds on the target. In less than five minutes, the meeting was concluded and the gunners returned to their positions to make the necessary preparations. Throughout the process, the crews could hear the steady circling drone of the L-19. Shrouded by the fog and the deep heavy velvet darkness, the crews went about their invisible work.

Moving away from the crews, the sergeant sat down on the western end of the small clearing with his back against a tree facing the east. From this position, he could judge the first precursor rays of the dawn and begin his task. Perpetually smoking a French Gauloise, he sheathed his head in smoke and desultorily waved away the mosquitoes that clouded around him with a constant buzzing roar. Slightly before 0500, he sensed a subtle change and stood up. Aware more by intuition than consciousness, he walked to the center of the open field and saw for the first time that the enveloping fog layer had risen. He could see a distinct meniscus of purple-black light between the top of the tree line and the hovering gray-black fog bank above it. Allowing a moment for his eyes and mind to coalesce, he sensed that dawn was fast approaching as the purple gained increasing intensity. Anxious for the loss of the comforting fog layer against the eyes of the airborne pilot above, the sergeant quickly strode across the field toward his companions. Like most people who have lived on the edge of survival, the crews had been alerted by their own internal mechanisms and were shuffling around their positions in readiness. Amongst them, dawn subtly entered and was more sensed than noticed. By the time the rough pattern of the rapidly dissolving fog could be discerned, rough hands held the first rounds down the maw of the tubes.

In the Ranger perimeter, tar black and hidden from the changing light by the canopy above, the soldiers were still immersed in their own internal anxieties and efforts. The clacking bamboo signals of the scouts had ceased and the only rent in the blanket of sensual deprivation was the breathing of the closest companions and the occasional sharp cry of a wounded man. From an undetermined direction, several dull clunks could be heard.

The clunks were shortly followed by sharp clattering in the canopy above and quick loud blasts. Mortars. Fully aroused by the initial bursts, the Rangers became fully awake and clung to whatever elevation of protection could be found—tree trunk, log, or earthen shield. The clunks now became very rapid as the gunners slammed rounds continuously down the tubes in practiced rhythmic fashion. These arched their trace and disappeared through the light leafy canopy. Immediately, they encountered light and heavy branch material that struck the side of the projectiles and diverted them from their mathematically predictable path. Strong enough to influence the flight path but too light to initiate the nose fuses, branches brushed aside the rounds and caused many to impact sideways as duds. Others struck large branches and detonated harmlessly in the trees well above the combatants. Some small numbers followed their course and exploded on the ground but with little effect. The mud and shocked terrain absorbed most of the damage. Still, the fear of the recipients was heightened by the anticipation of the rounds and their possibility of success as the preceding clunks of the discharging rounds were distinctly transmitted through the still heavy still jungle air. Each Ranger huddled in his position, mentally tracking the time from the clunk to the canopy penetration to the explosion. Quickly, it became apparent that if the canopy noises could be discerned, the round would probably fail to ignite. Instinctively, soldiers huddled even deeper into the ground if no sound succeeded the heavy metallic sound of the discharging round. The sensory lesson was learned by all in less than two minutes from the first rounds in flight—such are the rapid instructions for survival on the battlefield. Their positions built to defend against horizontal assault, vertical missiles left them defenseless and unshielded, mentally as well as physically. The lieutenant recalled the books he had read about the terror of artillery on the battlefield and ironically noted how fortunate he was to have a slow small indirect fire weapon used against him rather than the faster larger artillery he was so used to employing against his adversary. From a state of torpor to an adrenalin charged high, all this took less than five rounds to achieve.

In about that time, Hiep and the lieutenant were aroused out of their individual melancholies and immersed into the larger requirements. Hiep knew this act to be the overture to the final VC assault and so to the concurrent initiation of his last desperate plan for survival. Once cued to the rhythm of the mortars, the lieutenant spoke to the L-19 pilot between explosions to seek the guns. The pilot, lost in bored orbits above the disappearing fog, was only vaguely aware of the dawn and was now snapped awake.

Advantaged by altitude, he could see the initial yellow-red shafts of light creep across the emerging band of the horizon and reflect in a yellow-gray tone against the blobs of moisture-laden clouds below. Beneath him, he could see little of the ground definition as he swung from east to west hoping to recapture some of his night vision. He asked the lieutenant for an azimuth to the guns as his aircraft bisected the river and the center of the Ranger position. Absent a fixed-position location, the pilot hoped to scare the gunners into silence with a low-altitude pass. Immediately after the low and loud pass, the lieutenant again heard the mortar discharges. Now standing up out of a combination of emotion and desperation, the lieutenant swung his compass around in what he perceived to be the direction of the sound and relayed the azimuth to the pilot.

While receiving this information, the pilot, his back now to the increasing dawn, saw several small pinpricks of light to his lower right. Instinctively, he swung the stick over and did a sharp pedal turn to the flickering lights. In less than two seconds he was upon the small clearing, now illuminated by the slowly growing light on the contrasting vegetation. The gunners, immersed in the smoke and noise of their assembly-line firing, only briefly glimpsed the plane as it roared overhead less than a hundred feet from the ground. The sergeant, at the eastern edge of the clearing and the flank of the unit, clearly saw the plane from the beginning and shouted for his people to fire faster.

The pilot now distinctly saw the flashes of the tubes as they silhouetted the loaders poised beside them. Abruptly cutting off the lieutenant's transmission, he rolled the aircraft around to the east and gained altitude. When he was about 3,000 feet above the scene, he slowly arced the aircraft nose down and traced a path from the northeast that placed his wings parallel with the gunners' location. Operating on instinct and experience, he fixed his eyes on a small piece of desiccated bubble gum that was affixed to the lower center portion of the canopy. He had stuck this on the glass almost a year prior as his aiming point and he knew that at exactly 2,000 feet, his marking missiles would hit the ground on the gum spot. He had learned this from an old warrant officer who had flown fighters here against the Japanese and was now the unit maintenance officer. Together, they had flown to the old French resort at Vung Tau and gauged the range against the tide line–zero altitude. It had cost him a crate of ammunition and a lot of bourbon for the warrant, but he now had a very precise knowledge of the ballistics of his missiles. Though not designed to be an attack platform, the white phosphorous-loaded rockets on his slow aircraft could be deadly if precisely applied. Now, charged with the abrupt end to his orbiting reverie combined with the urgency in the voice of the lieutenant, he saw an opportunity to personally physically engage himself for the first time in this combat. He had not even considered calling for the artillery that lay less than 6 kilometers from the repetitively firing mortars.

Keeping the bubble gum squarely on the center of the wood line and the flickering flashes, he ignored all but the altimeter as he drove the aircraft on an invisible line between the gum and the guns. He judged that at 2,200 feet, the rockets would impact just within the flanks of the mortar position. As the green-yellow phosphorescent needle indicated that altitude, he pressed first the right trigger button and then the left, igniting two rockets fixed to launchers under his broad wings. Following the course of their flight, he noted their white flashing streak toward the tree line. Fixated, he followed them directly toward the ground and as they exploded amongst the VC. At the moment of impact, he was less than 500 feet from the ground. The combination of sound and light awoke him and he instinctively pulled his stick back and to the right while applying full power.

On the ground, the explosions effectively covered the entire position with burning material and thick white smoke. Some of the phosphorous settled on the unused powder charges lying on the ground and on the ready ammunition neatly stacked just to the rear of each tube. The thin cheese-like wafers burned with great intensity, their heat concentrating on the thin metal skins of the mortars. By the time the L-19 had recovered altitude and the pilot had renewed his spatial orientations, the clearing began to rock with successive explosions of detonating rounds. The coolies and the sergeant, somewhat removed from the initial impacts, instinctively retreated into the cover of the jungle. The less fortunate gun crews were immersed in smoke, fire and shrapnel and were dissected in place. Some, with terrible burns, crawled to the interior of the protective jungle and hid behind the closest available trees. To the north, the lieutenant noted the abrupt end of the discharges but could not hear the explosions of the ammunition, it being on a less cooperative harmonic wave. Very quickly though, Lieutenant Tri gained his attention.

34

Infantry and Air

Lieutenant Tri, the center company commander, had absorbed Hiep's instructions with the fatalism inherent to any veteran soldier. Despite his relative low rank, he had been engaged in combat since his 16th birthday. Now, at 24, he was a graduate of the Dalat Military Academy and had never enjoyed a month free of combat in his entire adult life. He fully recognized the gravity of the immediate situation and the necessity to properly execute his commander's guidance.

He had served briefly under the French cadre and deeply resented the separation between the French and their native soldiers. He vowed that he would always be part of his soldiers' lives and went to extra pains to immerse himself both physically and emotionally in their situations. This was an attitude and approach that was not the norm within Vietnamese units and made him somewhat isolated from his peers. His soldiers recognized this and paid him back with an unusual degree of loyalty and responsiveness, acts also not the norm in an army tired and spiritually adrift.

Moving slowly from tree trunk to deadfall to depression, Tri made his way back to his company. Small as the perimeter of the contained unit had become, Tri was able to find his radio operator in less than three minutes of relatively slow movement. His task was greatly simplified by the VC machine guns that would routinely cross-stitch his center position with green tracers. The lieutenant would place his back to a tree trunk, observe the tracers' course on both sides of the trunk then move toward the joining of the engaging green lines.

Finding his position, he then crawled to the left flank position. It was important to Tri that he saw each man from the company and personally instructed him on what would shortly be required. This was a task that could not be delegated to almost nonexistent subordinate leadership, nor one that he would be comfortable with being transmitted by others.

The men were strung along a series of depressions, deadfalls and trench portions. In some areas, the soldiers occupied the ground in pairs. In others, an isolated soldier would be filling a large void comforted only by the knowledge that his comrades were on the flank and that there was no security to the rear. Each man knew from experience the desperateness of the situation and the lack of alternatives. When Tri briefed them, it was a message of possible salvation as much as a requirement for probable destruction. Actionless, they knew their deaths were but a matter of time. With action, there was some slim possibility for the saving of a few. Having known no gambling but war for a lifetime, each soldier accepted the odds as even.

In this ground, even desertion was not an option. At the slightest sound, the VC line, now less than 10 meters from the front and comforted by numbers, would fire in great volume. Any exposure above the marginally protective logs or dirt was invariably fatal. Only the period immediately following a grenade shower provided safety. In an almost nanosecond of time after the explosion, the Rangers would place their weapons at ground level and fire. They knew they had less than a full second from the explosion to achieve fire supremacy and knock down the attacking wave that threw the grenades.

Tri could see the very controlled but tight mental state of each man. He recognized that the soldiers had reached the point of ultimate mental exhaustion. Each man greeted him with a look of anxious hopefulness and an outstretched hand or arm in recognition. No words were passed initially. Each soldier hoped that Tri would bring the message of delivery. Instead, he brought a requirement for death.

Tri would grasp each man's hand tightly and pull his face close to the soldier. He would then bring his mouth to the soldier's ear. Unable to acknowledge the emotional attachment he held for each soldier, some of whom had been with him for several years and dozens of engagements, Tri spoke in an intense but controlled, scripted delivery. He quickly reviewed the situation and the orders. He asked if the soldier understood. Gaining some form of positive feedback, Tri would then move to the next soldier in the line and repeat the script. In this manner, he was able to complete his task.

He welcomed the few locations where there were pairs of soldiers as that permitted him to brief both simultaneously with less opportunity for direct personal engagement. Always, he came across wounded soldiers either behind or next to occupied positions. In each case, he would change his demeanor, smile and shake the soldier's hand or pat his head and offer a quiet word of personal encouragement. No mention was made of either the situation or the new requirement. Both he and they recognized that whatever occurred, they, the wounded, would be left to their own devices and ultimately death in the hands of their VC discoverers. In a dishearteningly short time, Tri had briefed his entire company. He had talked to fewer than 35 soldiers.

Tri now returned to the center of his line and rejoined his radio operator to wait for the dawn and the first shriek of the supporting aircraft. Desperately as he wanted a cigarette, he knew its ignition would bring a hail of fire. Instead, he contented himself with closing his eyes and listening to his own breathing and the intermittent clicks of the VC scouts as they measured the miniscule perimeter and prepared for their own dawn assault.

Tri, balanced between sleep and wakefulness, was able to track the progress of the scouts and the futile attempts by his own side to use the Spooky. He felt the sticky wet blanket of the fog and realized its implications. He heard the 175mm artillery crash in the distance and eventually grow silent. Occasionally, a wounded soldier would groan or make some noise that initially attracted fire. In time, both sides seemed to reach a point of exhaustion and lapsed into an undeclared armistice.

As the evening began to creep into dawn, the noises changed. The wounded became quiet. However, there was an overriding sound of low shuffling movement against the heavy air. Large bodies of people were moving in a disciplined purposeful way.

Tri was abruptly wakened from his mental analysis of the noises of the night by the sharp whopping sounds of a helicopter. The light now permitted him to see 10 or 15 feet and it distinctly glowed through the canopy overhead. The lieutenant realized that the most important moment of his life was about to unfold.

The helicopter, one of a pair of gunships launched by the cavalry, had just reached the operational area. The cavalry commander had been extremely frustrated by the failure to breach the ambush to the south and had ordered an all-out relief attempt at dawn. Still, a tank as well as several ACAVs and soldiers were isolated on the far side of the stream that marked the initial ambush. In addition to his other responsibilities, the L-19 pilot had maintained a radio watch with one vehicle that housed the survivors. Around them, Thanh had instructed that a small force remain to insure that their presence was always felt.

For the morrow's effort, the cavalry commander had pushed a reinforced squadron to the French Fort as well as two additional 155mm batteries. Frustrated by the lack of decision on the part of the 18th Division, he stopped assuming their presence and developed an assault plan based solely on American participation. He had relayed this point to the senior American in Xuan Loc. He, in turn, had requested the L-19 pilot to place the U.S. advisors with the Rangers on a separate frequency to permit a relayed conversation with them. He informed the advisors that they should feel free to do whatever they felt appropriate under the circumstances and that if they could join the Americans to the south, they could do so without prejudice. The American lieutenant acknowledged the comment and suggested that if artillery was with the 48th Regiment, its help would be useful. This went unanswered as he and the pilot returned to the operating frequency.

Though it violated standing safety of flight instructions, the cavalry pilots, without orders, had launched in darkness and vectored themselves to the L-19 with its blinking strobe lights. The pilots wanted to take advantage of the dawn and to engage those targets too slow to seek cover as the light crossed the termination from darkness. The pilots were well aware of the failure of the Spooky and the relief column. In an unusual concession to the circumstances, they had kept the L-19 pilot's frequency on all night on the speaker box in their sleeping hutch. Unlike previous evenings of laughter and drinking that closed the day, the pilots returned from dinner, lay on their bunks, and listened to the quiet steady voice of the pilot talking to the remaining ground elements. They could not hear the other transmissions but spent their waking moments interpolating what was said based on the pilot's response. Eventually, they dozed off and waited fitfully for the opportunity to make a difference.

By the time they arrived over the river, the fog had shifted into large patches that gathered between the tallest portions of the canopy like lint on a rug. The gunship pilots arrived just as the light separated the L-19 from its background. Quickly, they talked to the lieutenant on the ground as he attempted to determine their location and direct their fires by sound.

Their sudden appearance awakened a sense of purpose within the lieutenant and caused a burst of energy. Now, filled with a false hope, he stood behind the large protecting tree folds with his compass and spoke softly into the radio.

He made several adjustments to their flight as they crossed the canopy and achieved an initial attack path. The first bursts of red tracers began in the rear of the lieutenant's position, bisected a line within a foot of Lieutenant Tri and continued on into the main VC position. The pilots, alerted by the L-19, broke from their treetop run and swung well north.

At this point, several events occurred at once. Tri heard the VC whistles to his front and held his breath for the near-immediate grenade shower. Almost concurrent with its arrival, the first air-delivered bomb burst in the canopy just ahead of him. Tri, like an automaton, pulled his pistol from the holster, placed the barrel on the frequency dial of his radio and pulled the trigger.

The Vietnamese officer then stood up, blew his whistle and moved quickly forward. As if driven by unseen hydraulics, the miniscule company arose and moved forward into the acrid black smoke and intermittent green streaks and spilling flesh that rained through the lessening gloom.

35

Air Strikes

The first F-4 made a lazy 5-mile circle from 7,000 feet as the pilot struggled to spot his target mark. He could see the L-19 3,000 feet below making smaller circles over the jungle canopy carpet but could not see the yellow smoke the spotter pilot said was drifting up through the leaves. He throttled down the F-4 until he was just above stall speed and requested a re-marking of the target. The light wind and promise of emerging sun had begun to burn off the early morning haze and fog over the Dong Nai. The pilot could clearly pick out the winding water snake below. The L-19 pilot reported that he had expended his marking rockets but would run a suitable angle of attack and tightly circle the desired impact point.

The pilot swung out over War Zone D, west of the river and picked a straight line from a bend in the river to the last wisps of yellow smoke now dissipating within the cottony morning fog. As he crossed the river, he began to take green tracers from both banks of the river and informed the F-4 pilot. The VC gunners were surprised by the low and slow pass and did not take time to properly aim. The pilot proceeded to the target point as best he could recall its location and executed a tight left turn until the F-4 pilot acknowledged his fix.

Concurrently, the wingman for the first F-4 broke off and flew several kilometers south of the spot and aligned himself along the river run. He reached down with his thumb and flipped on the arm lever switch for his 20mm Gatling gun and settled the aircraft into a flat slow descent to 2,500 feet bisecting the river as he flew north. He and his partner then began a twin run. The low bird saturated the river bank across from the aircraft's angle of attack with the Gatling gun while the higher aircraft ran fast and straight toward the canopy marked by the L-19, which had now swung a mile to the east.

Underneath the higher F-4 were slung twelve 750-pound bombs. Additionally, it carried a belly canister of cluster bomblets. The pilot toggled a release switch with his left hand when he reached 2,500 feet and pulled sharply back on his stick. This action sent two 750-pound bombs on a high arcing trajectory parallel to its mother craft.

Slowly, and then with increasing speed, the bombs and the mother craft parted company as gravity overcame flight dynamics and the bombs entered the canopy top. Both bombs were flying about 15 feet apart and penetrated the leafy top growth simultaneously. The yellow-fused noses brushed aside the light green canopy material and proceeded toward more substantial matter below at about 320 kilometers an hour.

The first fuse nose hit a branch approximately 50 feet off the ground and mashed its nose firmly into the firing chamber of its green bomb casing. The second bomb continued unimpeded on its course. The first fuse, now activated, sent a message to a small charge at its center set back from its nose and resting tightly within the fuse well. This charge exploded and began a chain reaction with the explosive residing within the dark-green bomb casing. The chain reaction generated a tremendous amount of heat and energy that separated the iron bomb casing into hundreds of technically designed shards.

The metallurgists had specified the type and form of alloy to be used in the casing to insure a maximum amount of sharp edges and angles to provide for the greatest tissue damage. Their efforts began to reap their reward.

Beneath the initial bomb line, Major Phu, the First VC Battalion commander had assembled his men for a flank attack against the thinned Ranger line. He had specifically picked this spot because he knew that regardless of the success or failure of his attack, it would place the Rangers in a critical position.

He sat astride their only avenue of withdrawal and it was now impossible due to losses for the Rangers to cover themselves from both the front and the flank.

Accordingly, he had massed his entire 500-man force in a very small space directly flanked to the right of the Ranger line. His men were aligned in six waves to wash over the remaining Ranger positions while his sister units assaulted the depleted Ranger defense from the front. He had just ordered the first two waves to stand up and move out when the first fuse buried itself in a tree limb above his head.

The low fighter strafing the river bank had provided a seconds-early warning for the VC assault force. Upon hearing the sewing-machine sound of the Gatling gun, the assault line looked over its shoulders and slightly up as the attackers strained to recognize this new sound on the battlefield. As they did, the first bomb burst like a miniature sun over the left portion of the VC line. Concurrently, the second bomb track registered in the minds but not the consciousness of the third wave, which was sitting on its knees about 15 feet below the first bomb.

The initial force felt by the VC was energy that was without form but was quickly followed by a rain of metal shards moving faster than sound that rent the flesh apart from the human structures and finally by a great wave of heat that blew the steaming blood vapors along the air current's blast path.

The atmosphere became a vacuum as it was exhausted of its oxygen. The surrounding air rushed in to fill the void and swirled the leaves and loose smoke and dirt into its vortex, covering the just-expired corpses with its fine white-gray dust. The entire sequence took less than a full second.

The effect on the jungle and its inhabitants was striking. The initial energy blast pushed all but the largest material items back from the center, the metal shards then began to strip away all living organic material. Shirts, skin, bark, feathers, carapaces, and leaves were quickly atomized into nothing. Layer by layer, flesh and material were stripped, sliced, and flogged into gas and minute organic matter. The wave of heat that followed merely reinforced the act but it was inconsequential as the desired effect had already been achieved.

Where the bombs had burst, large craters replaced the previous level organic matter. The crater for the initial airburst bomb was quite small, a little more than a ring of cleared ground marked by still discharging steam, cordite, and burning wood. The earth itself was turned over exposing fresh soil and streaks of black where the red-hot iron had violently collided with the earth. Ringed around the crater were dozens of lumps of black and blue marking the spots where the VC had died of overpressure or shrapnel.

The bodies had no particular symmetry about them other than that they were stretched out facing away from the blast. A number were in trees and branches and one was married to a large tree trunk as if cut in bas relief. The attack had been halted before it could properly begin.

Stunned by the blow, the American lieutenant picked himself up from the center of his tree root mass where he was thrown by the blast and looked over the chipped and jagged edges of the roots. His first sight was that of a half torso bolt upright two feet from his front. Neither the head nor the legs were attached. Yet, the blue canvas grenade vest and the shirt were neatly buttoned and pulled tight over the torso.

Beyond the torso, the lieutenant could plainly see the newly opened jungle and the myriad bodies that ringed the open sky lit area. He also saw the remainder of the VC assault line revealed to him for the first time, frozen in shock and the suddenness of death.

The assault line, what was left of it, was transfixed as if in stone. The first three lines no longer existed. They were part of the smoke, steam and gasses that had been converted from organic matter by the suddenly released heat and energy.

Several of the lines behind those in front had been blown and scattered like leaves. Somewhat protected by their peers, these soldiers retained their whole shape as they dangled from trees like so many Christmas ornaments while others were violently flung to the earth and were partially imbedded in the soft wet earth.

The last assault line, while alive, was incapable of action. Its members lay on the ground or sat partially upright. Most were bleeding profusely from the ears and nose while some even bled from the edges of their eyes. All were comatose and immobile with half-open eyes that stared straight ahead with fixed microscopic pupils. For at least the moment, the attack on the right flank had ceased.

The L-19 pilot placed his plane in a right aileron dip and slowly traversed the newly opened jungle. He immediately saw the lines of blue edged against the trees and radioed to the F-4s to hit the tree line again on the northern side. He recommended that the first strike be with 20mm to take advantage of the exposed force and that the second aircraft follow with a ripple of four bombs.

As the two fighters completed their attack orbit and fixed their eyes on the newly revealed contrast to the green carpet below, they heard the calls from other aircraft inbound to their orbit spot from Bien Hoa. "Graybeard 03 with a flock of four from Yankee," "Possum Six from Clay Bird," "Tango 12 with two from Thunder," "Victor 09 with two from Hardcore."

The L-19 pilot vectored each of them to an orbit point and deconfliction altitude several kilometers to the west until he could clear the first working aircraft. His intent was then to shuttle the rapidly stacking aircraft toward the objective as fast as he could clear each preceding aircraft. He made short notes as to each newly arrived group's fuel, weapons, and home base status to insure he expended each load before having to break their station for home base. He then called home base indicating that he had spotted the main force and would need all available assistance. Bien Hoa control converted this request into 72 separate sorties that would expend their ordnance within a 45-minute timeframe. Timed to take full advantage of this support for the greater good and salvation for the remainder of the battalion, Lieutenant Tri, the center company commander, had already begun to move forward cued by the sound of the first jets of the morning.

The American advisor, now partially recovered from the initial blast, spoke to the spotter pilot. He hastily outlined the action that was unfolding below.

Lieutenant Tri's center Ranger company, at this moment, was assaulting the middle of the VC position. Concurrently, and absolutely essentially, the fighters would have to make a ripple drop on a line from the last craters toward the original insertion LZ. The remaining Rangers were gathering what wounded they could and were moving from crater to crater toward safety staying one bomb strike behind. The L-19 pilot was to gather as many aircraft as possible and keep the strikes going continuously until the remaining force was free of the trap.

Below him, in the newly opened canopy, the pilot could see small groups of brown-clad men moving between trees and deadfall into the sheltering lips of the bomb craters. He could also see, ringing the ground like frosting on a glass, small specks of blue scattered in windrows outside the blast radius and speckling the exposed trees.

The L-19 pilot relayed the requirement to Bien Hoa with a good deal of urgency in his voice. He had seen the VC assault line revealed and estimated the strength and finality behind it and he had heard the catch and breathlessness in the lieutenant's voice. He instinctively knew that his ability to gather airpower would decide if the unit engaged had a hope of surviving the next hour.

The newly cleared ground showed as a beacon for the circling pair of Phantoms. Waving off the spotter pilot's suggestion of a marking run, the flight lead nosed his aircraft over, made an arcing run with his back to the growing sun and switched his far wing external stores to release the remaining set of bombs.

36

Bomb Burst

The twin bombs nosed their way down from the outside wing stations of the Phantom and followed parallel courses toward the ground separated by fewer than 30 feet. They were 750-pounders with a small yellow circle six inches from the nose that outlined the fuse well. The fuses were extended rods of aluminum with blunt ends called daisy cutters. The rods were four feet long and ignited the bombs before they impacted in the earth, thereby providing the maximum blast effect in heavy vegetation. They were the last two bombs on the aircraft and the F-4 was already headed toward Bien Hoa airfield before they exploded.

The pilot had aimed for the edge of the newly opened clearing thinking that the VC would be hiding under the woods rather than in the cleared area. This was true. However, the Rangers were using the cleared area as they went from crater to crater right behind each burst. Thusly, they wove a line of retreating soldiers from the jungle, through the clearing and back in the jungle again. The L-19 spotter pilot was no longer able to judge friend from foe and his radio contact with the ground elements was very spotty. Accordingly, he opted to stitch a straight line of bombs from the original burst to the LZ and hope that minimal friendlies would be injured.

The twin bombs, flying at over 160 kilometers an hour, were unimpeded in their rush to earth. The trees, which moments before had towered a hundred feet in the air, were reduced to splinters, ash, gas, and smoke. Their organic material was destroyed and hidden by the newly gouged earth of rapidly formed pits and concentric ovals of large walls of soil and churned mud. By the lip of each crater, Rangers in small groups would hug the mother earth, wait for the next overwhelming shock and overpressure and then dash for the newly formed crater while the steam still rose from the rented earth and the shrapnel had not yet fully flown to earth.

The daisy cutters impacted simultaneously into the soft mud of the lip of a just-formed crater. On the edge of this feature, the battalion commander, closely attached by Comrade Hu to his rear, was half erect with his two radio operators flanking and fronting him. The commander was holding the handset of the flank operator as they dashed to the next exposed hole.

Due to the very soft and newly turned soil composition, the fuses did not gain sufficient pressure to ignite them until the yellow fuse nose ring was almost in the dirt. At that moment, the ignition series, taking less than a hundredth of a second to run its course, ignited.

The effect of the explosion was to create an arc over the lip of the original crater. The heat and metal of the exploding bomb followed a course from the nose almost vertically up to a height of six feet and then peeled over and slammed toward the ground. Under this protective arc and hardly aware of the explosion itself was the battalion commander. His mind had lost its cognitive awareness several minutes prior and he, like the rest of his remaining soldiers, was operating on pure visceral instincts and reactive ability. He had ceased to be a normal human being as his mind acted to blot out the events that it saw.

The flank operator was totally unaware of the burst. Before his eyes or ears could inform him of the event, a large piece of tempered jagged steel, one-side colored olive drab with a portion of the yellow fuse well stripe, neatly sliced him in half at beltline. The upper torso kept moving forward with the last neuro-muscular message from the body's momentum but the lower torso remained firmly standing on the edge of the crater, the left leg stepping forward from the right as blood and viscera poured over the exposed belt.

The battalion commander did not notice the release of pressure on the handset cord as the cut line snapped back to hit his ear. He landed on top of the radio operator to his front, rolled over and waited for the next bomb burst. The handset still remained firmly grasped in his hand. Neither did he notice the small green, red and white wires protruding from the mud where the severed radio cord lay next to his knee.

Resting momentarily, he looked around for his companions. He saw the Americans, a remaining radio operator pulling the radio off of the shattered torso of his companion, and a single bodyguard. The bodyguard was pushing Comrade Hu in front of him. In a very compact group with less than six feet separating them all on the lip of the freshly sifted earth, they awaited the next screeching run that would be the starter's gun for their next dash to safety.

37

Bien Hoa Control

In a large concrete building on the northeast edge of Bien Hoa Airfield, Tac Control managed its business. The building was very solid, less than two years old, built by Philco-Ford with all the amenities. It had air conditioning, paneled walls, carpets, and subdued lighting. The atmosphere was very corporate.

It was manned by a crew of 20 personnel, mostly enlisted, wearing well-starched jungle fatigues. The crew was supervised by an Air Force major. In turn, he was supervised by the Director of Operations, the DO, a lieutenant colonel who was sitting behind a large glass partition looking into the work area.

The center of the operation was a large clear plastic map of South and North Vietnam where all aircraft were plotted once aloft. On a wall to the rear, was a board that outlined all the aircraft and missions that began or ended at Bien Hoa.

It was the mission of this room to integrate the available air assets with the requests from all the competing users. If a conflict arose, the team chief consulted with the DO and if he couldn't resolve it, the DO called on the red phone to the DO at Seventh Air Force at Tan Son Nhut. This was a form of warfare that appeals to the technical mind.

All the assets were tracked by radio and radar and the control system was redundant and calm. Regardless of the situation, a calm, corporate atmosphere prevailed with shifts coming on and going off like so many stock analysts. The emotionalism of the requestor on the ground or the intensity of the situation requiring resolution were never transmitted into the decision-making process of the team by the map that calmly marked the comings and goings of its multimillion dollar assets.

The initial flight of two F-4s for the first morning strike was a diversion from a strike near the Cambodian border. At 0300, HQ MACV notified Bien Hoa Control that a Ranger battalion was in heavy contact near the Dong Nai River and that Spooky was unable to effectively engage the targets.

Bien Hoa was asked to stage some dawn sorties to the area once the fog cleared and the situation better developed. The tech sergeant took the mission board for the Cambodian flight and wrote in Dong Nai with the latitude and longitude grid zone designator. The pilots, who didn't know they were originally programmed for the border area, simply took their revised mission sheet, confirmed the ordnance loads and took off.

The DO, as was his usual habit, requested that the radio in his office be connected to whatever air controller was reporting troops in contact. This morning, he was drinking his first cup of coffee and listening to the L-19 that slowly circled over the Ranger battalion and directed the initial morning strikes.

When the first sortie revealed the massed troops, the excited narration by the pilot alerted the DO. He pressed the button on the microphone on his desk and asked the team chief what other aircraft were available for diversion to the area.

The team chief studied his mission board and responded that a sortie of four A-7 attack aircraft could be pulled from a strike in the Delta and that two alert aircraft on the ramp could also be used. The DO directed that all six aircraft rendezvous on the L-19.

Almost immediately, the red phone on his desk rang. It was the duty officer at Seventh Air Force indicating that MACV had requested all available air to operate in support of the Rangers in contact. The duty officer was unsure as to the nature of the contact, only that MACV was directly involved and had asked for help. He further indicated that he had six uncommitted aircraft available and requested instructions.

The Bien Hoa DO looked at his watch and made a rapid calculation in his head regarding station time of the present committed aircraft, travel time to the strike area and loiter time required to make a quality strike. He requested that the aircraft reach the orbit point in 30 minutes, flying in pairs 15 minutes apart. He further asked that they load up with 500-pound bombs and 20mm.

He knew from his own days as an air controller that napalm was generally useless in the jungle, that a 500-pounder was just as good as a 1,000-pounder, and that ammo loaders were too lazy to load 20mm unless forced to do so.

The L-19 pilot now had aircraft beginning to stack up in the rising morning sun. He would alternately brief the strike crew as to adjustments and then brief the newly arrived pilots regarding the strike location and target nature. Each arriving crew would do a large corkscrew orbit at prescribed altitude and inform the FAC as to ordnance and loiter time available.

In the midst of the initial morning strikes, the L-19 pilot had relayed the Ranger plan to Bien Hoa Control. He tried to do this matter-of-factly while coordinating all the other actions. However, the sense of urgency in his voice and the desperation of the situation clearly permeated the transmission.

The DO, in an unusual move for him, preempted the team chief response and talked directly to the pilot. He informed him that he was moving all available aircraft to his orbit and asked for time intervals of arrival.

While this conversation was going on, the Commanding General of U.S. Air Force elements, Bien Hoa, had stepped into the room and was listening to the conversation. After a few seconds, he picked up the red phone and began talking earnestly into the speaker. He also wrote a short note and passed it through the door to the team chief while still talking on the phone. It said "All available in range to Dong Nai—Now. Wide area alert." This meant that all strike air assets under command of Seventh Air Force could be flowed to the site unless otherwise supporting troops in contact.

The team chief showed the note to the tech sergeant who began to erase the mission boards. The team chief then quickly briefed the duty crew on the radios and telephones and they began to activate the Urgent system. Phones began to ring in mission control rooms in II, III and IV Corps and in the Navy CIC in Saigon.

Pilots, en route to designated strikes within the radius of the range circle plotted on the Bien Hoa plastic board, were given divert instructions. At Tan Son Nhut Airbase, a tanker was rolled out with instructions to assume an orbit track over D Zone and service the diverted aircraft. The corporate system of warfare was going to work.

38

Light

The efforts of the Air Force began to arrive in a continuous stream. Very quickly, the L-19 pilot had to seek additional support for the mass. A second spotter aircraft was launched to manage the crews orbiting to the north awaiting their turn to run. A third aircraft, this one an Air Force controller aircraft from Bien Hoa, arrived to spot targets for destruction for those aircraft that had to expend ordnance before they could strike the primary target.

Soon, the newly exposed sky showed the black smoke and hanging fresh density currents of a just-passed aircraft. In the American lieutenant's eye, he saw the pair of green-skinned torpedo-shaped objects with flat square tail wings extended. They seemed to hang just over his head as if both he and they stopped to watch the space between them. He rolled over and prepared to run forward into the now comforting swell of noise and smoke that would soon enshroud him with its promise of security, if he and his companions could time its arrival with precision.

Slowly, for what seemed an eternity, the survivors followed this pattern. Blast, run, hide. Blast, run, hide. Singles and pairs and occasional groups repeated this halting staggering pattern through the field. Each blast brought new openness to the ground and space nearer to safety. The unit was no longer a unit but a scattered assemblage of small bits and pieces of reactive soldiery struggling toward survival. As moths to the light, they followed the direction to survival through the heat and energy of directed death.

Finally, the pieces converged on unrent jungle. The groups coalesced together in a stunned silence broken only by heavy insistent breathing and the quiet gasps of the wounded. The lieutenant stood upright in the jungle edge and looked to his rear. He could see only the narrow rip in the fabric of vegetation that marked the trace he and his companions had just come. In the all-encompassing and lightning-like silence that suddenly enveloped the group, the lieutenant mentally counted 32 soldiers, including himself. For the first time, he heard no rifle fire and saw no blue/black uniforms. He looked at his watch and noted 45 minutes had elapsed from the first strike to where he now stood. Wordless, he picked up a dying soldier and moved into the welcome light of the woods' edge and the landing zone he knew was just beyond his vision.

39

The VC Prisoner

The lieutenant, determined to recapture some part of professionalism other than individual survival, made a walking tour of the new perimeter. Rising from behind a large log that faced the previous day's landing zone, he sucked on a Pall Mall, looked at the sky and began to walk amongst the soldiers, counting in a low voice as he went.

The walk took a shockingly short time. He had traversed fewer than 30 yards and had counted only 32 people. He found the battalion commander and a bodyguard. He saw the radio operator but no radio. He found two of the Montagnard machine gunners quietly puffing on their short-stemmed pipes overlooking the barrels of their machine guns, ever alert and anticipating, unflappable, and unfailingly under control. He recalled that in a year, he had never heard one of them raise his voice.

The soldiers were dazed and quiet. Almost all nursed some form of wound. Many had multiple bandages. Little conversation was heard. Some soldiers, too injured to assume a position on the perimeter, lay on their backs and occasionally uttered a sharp short sound as pain overcame control. The lieutenant saw several whose pale, near-alabaster skin was lightly beaded with dew-like sweat. They were perfectly quiet and reposed in the quiet drifting sensual borderland of imminent death. Rangers quietly smoked and looked with glassy eyes to the sky or to the ground. Some of the healthier tended the more fearfully wounded. Neither ferocity, anger, fear, nor animation presented itself. Instead, a heavy cloaking curtain of physical and emotional exhaustion engulfed them all.

The perimeter formed a half circle with its back to the landing zone just within the edge of the jungle shade. The spot had been the last concealed portion of their explosively guided trek when they had finally revealed themselves to the L-19 spotter pilot. He had seen the first pair of Rangers emerging from the smoke and venting mud at this point. He shouted into the mike that he had them in sight and performed a near-standing turn and dive swooping toward them at treetop level waving as he inverted his fuselage. The Rangers, moving into the sunlight from the still curling remnants of the last bomb run, stopped looked up and numbly stood transfixed. Other Rangers began to pile up on them until a small body of men like so many newly forming statues, stood on the edge of the open clearing following the small aircraft as it did slow circles above them.

Finally, breaking the trance, the battalion commander, quietly gestured with his swagger stick toward the wood line. The soldiers wordlessly lay down along his indicated mark and looked quietly with glazed eyes back from where they had come. Unnoticed by them, a tall very young man dressed in black pajamas approached from their rear.

The man was a VC soldier. He was slightly more than 15 and had been used as a messenger by the scout element. He had moved between assault units passing messages and keeping the flank units aware of their respective positions. Constantly moving, he had a unique perspective on the action. Unsupported by membership in a unit, he was always alone, physically and mentally.

Initially this did not bother him. He was exhilarated by the opportunity to participate in a great and seemingly successful adventure. The nature of his job gave him emotional prestige as he was entrusted with maintaining communications between critical units. He was always greeted with smiles and appreciation by senior commanders and offered hot tea or cigarettes before he left. This made him feel important and useful.

Lately, as the tempo of action increased and darkness enclosed him, he began to realize the reality of the situation. Everywhere he went, there was deep anxiety and intensity in the units he encountered. The smiles and tea were no longer present. He saw quantities of dead and wounded and often found different commanders issuing instructions within an hour of revisiting a unit. Everywhere, cries of wounded, shouts of soldiers, and the constant chatter of bullets and grenades greeted his arrival. By late afternoon on the first day, he gained no respite as the din of death continuously assaulted his consciousness.

At the moment of the first air strike, he was between the creek and the principal assault unit when the initial dawn bomb strike hit. The strike threw the middle torso of a soldier, still fully clothed with light blue canvas assault vest, across his legs. The explosion and its newly created missile threw him against the nearest tree and disoriented him.

When he regained consciousness, he became aware of the continuous explosions and rippling waves that coursed across the jungle floor and the constant rain of debris, mud and occasional human parts. He arose from the dirt and began to follow the edge of the stream. He was unable to find any friendly personnel. Everything he saw was either burning, dead, or a disfiguration of its natural state. Bodies draped the trees and the juice and matter of life lay splattered against the smooth mottled trunks of those trees not totally destroyed. The shriek of jets and immersion in the detritus of their wake washed all sense of residual duty from his mind. At this point, he realized that the most important thing in his life was to live.

He reasoned that if the enemy could bring such destruction and continuous death to bear on his forces, than safety must reside with them. To this point, he had seen almost no enemy dead, mentally attributing to them some form of invulnerability. Accordingly, he traced their path as it moved north. By staying close to the river, he was able to avoid both his own forces and the death created by the bomb strikes. He moved quickly, hesitating only when the strikes fell silent. At those rare moments of quiet, he would drop to the ground and rest within the covey of a tree or plant.

At the first high-pitched shriek of a jet, he would quickly stand up and move north. Eventually—actually after fewer than 30 minutes of elapsed time—he found himself at the western edge of the clearing that was the Ranger landing zone the day prior. He could see the scout aircraft slowly circling the open sky and edged himself toward the clearing. Just where the last tree line stood, he dropped his weapon and equipment, sucked a deep breath and walked into the warm sunlight of the open field.

He crossed the open clearing with great hesitation and the fear-filled eyes of a deer caught in headlights. Summoning an inner strength, he walked with great discipline and purpose until he was fewer than 10 feet from the rear of the small semi-circle, his head in sunlight and his torso blended into the shade. Private Nguyen Phu had surrendered himself to the only force at this time that was probably incapable of capturing him under any other conditions.

Phu was a presence that was initially felt but not seen. Only with the greatest of discipline did Phu remain standing, quiet and stoic until recognized. Finally, a soldier, reaching back to re-bandage his leg, saw the black-clad statue silhouetted against the sky. With an initial reaction of fear, the soldier quickly swung his rifle around and leveled it at the figure. This act caused the soldiers in the immediate vicinity to swing around and fix their attention on the lone standing man. The abject fear registered on Phu's face quickly allayed their anxiety and most turned back to the jungle and returned to tend to their wounds.

From a short distance, the lieutenant observed this and like the others, quickly raised his rifle toward Phu as initial visceral fear overcame mental and physical exhaustion. Like the others, he quickly recognized the fear and exhaustion in the man-statue to his front and lowered his weapon. The battalion commander's bodyguard moved slowly toward Phu, held out his hand and tenderly gestured him toward the small circle of soldiers. Phu, his confidence restored, moved toward the command group and settled down next to Comrade Hu and the radio operator. Though without a weapon, he physically and emotionally assimilated into the small body of men recovering at the edge of the clearing. In less than five minutes, he was sound asleep next to Comrade Hu.

40

The Ranger Prisoners

They were glassy-eyed and moved in a trance-like walk. Their uniforms, barely discernible, were caked with mud and blood. Their arms were trussed behind their backs and their necks were connected with a single long rope. The rope was held by two soldiers at the head of the column moving with almost the same somnambulant pace and expression. All were at the limits of human exhaustion as they entered the principal base camp. These were the sole prisoners captured by the assault force after the final morning clash. The remaining 444 Rangers were either dead, missing or had escaped. This point was extremely vexing to General Thanh and the regimental commander as they hoped to have a good bag of prisoners for news reporters. Not only had they planned on a good quantity of prisoners, but they also counted on catching several of the officers. As it was, all the prisoners, less one, a sergeant, were lower-ranking soldiers.

Thanh ordered that the reporters be kept away from the area until the next day. Hopefully, more prisoners would develop. Perhaps the unit could move back into the area after the planes departed and recover more bodies to be claimed as Americans. He sent word to the Binh Tram for a photography crew. Specifically, he requested the French news team that routinely worked along the trail, gravitating between Tchepone and the rest tour at Phnom Penh.

Without instructions, the guards staggered with their prisoners to the creek bank and led them into the water. In their dazed state, the guards went into the water without really thinking about their larger responsibilities. As they greedily immersed themselves in the cool fresh water, the prisoners followed them along like dogs on leashes and followed their example. When the regimental commander first came upon the scene, all he could discern were eight soldiers drinking like so many horses from a trough. Deciphering the assembly, he issued sharp instructions which brought the guards to a dazed dripping attention. Reluctantly, they led their charges from the water to several small bamboo cages on the periphery of the camp. To an observer, the guards seemed to have a closer kinship with their prisoners than with their leadership. Both had shared a great deal that the camp population could never appreciate.

The guards placed each man in a cage and closed the chain binding the bamboo door. Done, the pair wearily sat against a large tree facing the cages and shared a cigarette. The prisoners, exhausted, ignored their surroundings and individually fell to the floor and like dogs in a fetal position, soon were fast asleep.

41

The Arc Light

The command briefing room of COMUSMACV (Commander in Chief, U.S. Forces Vietnam), though configured as a theater, was very quiet and corporate. The color scheme was a neutral beige with swatches of camouflage highlighted by the campaign-bedecked flags of the Services and the United States as well as the blood-red general officer flag of General Westmoreland, COMUSMACV. A major and master sergeant, responsible for the arrangements of the theater, insured that a flag with the appropriate amount of stars was part of the panoply for each subordinate attending flag officer.

Every morning, General Westmoreland received a situation report of the previous night's activities, proposed operations and relevant intelligence in the theater. These briefings were presented by a variety of officers in clean, starched jungle fatigues and shiny black boots. They were rehearsed several times by a nervous lieutenant colonel prior to the main event and read their remarks from 3 by 5-inch cards illuminated by the soft glow of the light shielded by the podium.

Behind the briefer and hidden from view, was a master sergeant who manipulated the stack of slides to be projected on the screen, cued by the briefer's remarks. There had been several rehearsals for today's morning brief but they had never been particularly good as the intelligence and targeting portions underwent constant changes. The master sergeant's last guidance was to do the best he could to match the slide with the narrative.

The briefing began at the entrance of the general. The scene had been fully lit as the room began to fill with staff officers, guests and interested hangers on. As in all things military, the seating arrangement was a direct reflection of rank. The most important people sat next to the CINC and the remainder fanned out into the distance recesses until all the seats were taken.

This presented some problems and difficulties for the lieutenant colonel as he had to determine the relative importance of civilian guests as well as drop-ins from the U.S. These were particularly troublesome as he was not politically astute and the general often wanted to ingratiate himself with visitors from Washington by giving them prime seating. This often resulted in some momentary confusion and embarrassment as another general would have to shift to accommodate the anointed visitor.

As they filed in from early breakfast, the normal attendees, augmented by visitors, talked to each other in low tones but all had a catch of anxiety in their voices and reserve in their actions as they awaited the entrance of the principle player. Precisely at 0730, the general entered the theater, preceded by a loud, "Gentleman, the Commander in Chief" shouted by the sergeant major. This brought all discussions to a complete halt as bodies snapped to attention and personnel scurried to their designated seats.

The general strode to the front with short side comments to personnel standing in the aisle and then took his place at the center front seat. He made a few quick handshakes with people to his immediate sides and flashed a smile and a hand wave to those outside of his personal reach. The lights came down and the briefing began.

The briefing followed a rigid sequence and pattern. As much as possible, the presentation had been standardized to present the information in a form that the general had found comforting. The briefers had learned to gauge the general's mood and interest and cued the master sergeant to change the slides with a small light button at the podium. The guidance was to move through the briefing as quickly as possible and leave any interactive discussion to the appropriate staff officer in the audience.

This approach had presented a problem for some of the subordinate generals. After three years in Vietnam, the CINC was extraordinarily well-informed about all aspects of the situation. He knew units, areas, and personalities better than any one-year-tour officer could hope to accumulate. This placed great pressure on each staff officer to be thoroughly knowledgeable on the background of each briefing piece.

This situation meant that each briefing officer had to brief each staff principal several hours before the main event. In turn, this translated into innumerable phone calls between the briefing officer and primary source of information. By briefing time, the CINC was refreshed and ready to attack the day and his staff and briefers were ready for bed.

The briefers went through the routine litany: time, weather, incidents, enemy actions, friendly actions, friendly casualties, planned operations, and other items of interest. The briefing was concluded by an Air Force officer who presented the day's recommendations for the Arc Light strikes.

Arc Light was the term used to describe the B-52 strikes allocated to the theater. In any given 24-hour period, the CINC could depend on a minimum of three strikes with a maximum of six if he notified the Air Force 48 hours in advance. Each strike consisted of three aircraft.

Due to the devastating effect of these strikes and the very limited number of sorties available, the Arc Lights were viewed as strategic assets and required the personal management of the CINC. The purpose of this portion of the briefing was to determine which three Arc Light proposals would be flown the next day. It was a process where in theory, the units in the greatest danger or in the most important engagement would be augmented by the most devastating weapon available. In truth, the quality of the briefing and the ability of the various intelligence sections to place red dots in the target box often carried more import than the blood on the ground.

The targeting officer presented a series of rectangular boxes filled with a variety of red dots. He presented each box with its title as Case One, Two, Three, etc. Each presentation was accompanied by a description of the friendly forces involved, the enemy dispositions as they were known, the intended targets and the projected effect if the Arc Light was approved.

The presentation was made in a quiet emotionless monotone. The briefing officer was able to make no emotional or verbal connection between the dots in the box and their representational human beings on the ground.

The general permitted all the possible choices to be briefed before he entered into substantive discussion. He had learned that targeting officers often became fixated on available intelligence rather than the strategic value of the action and often made the presentations out of logical order. He had long since given up hope that his J-2 could provide such value judgments. As an intelligence officer, the J-2 felt most comfortable recommending the box with the greatest amount of red dots and the most dramatic field report rather than rely on subjective judgment.

Seemingly inconsequential buildups in I Corps were often overlooked in favor of direct confrontations in IV Corps even though the strategic significance of I Corps was far greater. Concurrently, the staff had a tendency to downplay Vietnamese actions in favor of U.S. engagements. The general was acutely aware that Vietnamese units carried about 75 percent of the combat load and a disproportionate share of the casualties. The small, carefully manicured Vietnamese general by his side every morning rarely spoke to remind him of this. This time he did.

General Minh was short, polished and spoke in a soft voice. It was highly unusual for the Vietnamese to speak unless directly questioned. Usually, he offered some insight into Vietnamese units or local conditions of a battlefield area. Rarely did he volunteer to speak and even more rarely, do it with emotion.

This morning, General Minh had been talking to the 18th Division Commander and to the III Corps Commander. Neither conversation had left him satisfied. It was obvious to him that both had no real handle on the situation with the Rangers and even less interest in committing troops on their behalf. If the unit was to be salvaged, he would have to intervene.

General Minh had known General Westmoreland for several years. He understood the pressures and sensitivities on him and also understood how to take advantage of them. Six of the possible Arc Light choices involved U.S. forces in direct contact and two others were in strategically sensitive areas. Only two of the twelve choices involved Vietnamese forces. One of these encompassed the largest portion of Binh Tram 42, derived from a combination of radio intercepts and intuitive judgment regarding the origin of the forces presently engaged by the Rangers and the Cavalry.

Before the briefer could request the decision slide, General Minh turned to his counterpart and began to speak. Minh was a full foot shorter than the principal. To the audience, the pair looked as much like a father and son out to the movies as co-equals responsible for the lives of over a million armed men and the destiny of their nation's respective strategies.

Minh spoke in intense short sentences looking directly into the eye of the listener. He quickly outlined the situation on the Dong Nai and the criticality of the action. Occasionally in the discourse, Minh's emotions raced ahead of his language ability and he would stutter to a halt. When this occurred, he would close his eyes abruptly, stop talking and then begin speaking slowly. This morning, there was an intensity and interest that General Westmoreland had rarely seen.

Only the closest audience was able to listen as the pair intently conversed. After a period, General Minh stopped talking and remained looking at Westmoreland. The CINC abruptly rose from his seat, directed that Case Seven be approved and strode out of the room. The staff was left with the task of selecting the remaining two strikes. The Rangers would get their Arc Light though perhaps not in time enough to make a difference and at a location that would not provide them immediate relief. In the manner of lofty decisions, such a strike would provide a modicum of cosmetic comfort at the senior level while its effect would go largely unnoticed by the people responsible for initiating the process.

42

The B-52 Strike—Air

Lifting slowly off from Okinawa, the three great dip-winged aircraft trailed gouts of black smoke marking their climb to altitude. From the ground, the trio appeared to be barely moving though in fact each was going more than 400 knots at this point in the mission. As the aircraft climbed higher, they achieved an ideal fuel-oxygen mixture and the black kerosene smoke transformed itself. First to brown, then to gray and finally to nothing at all but invisible heat and water. Only the occasional contrail at level altitude revealed their presence. Slowly and almost with majesty, the three camouflaged aircraft headed initially east and then turned south toward their targets leaving the hazy iridescent outline of the island beyond view.

The aircraft were heavy winged. At takeoff, the small bicycle tire wing wheels kept the tips off the ground as the aircraft struggled to achieve translational lift, overcoming the combined weight of the full fuel load in combination with the array of 750-pound bombs that nestled in the belly and hung tightly clasped to the under wing hard points. On takeoff, the joining of engine thrust and wing flex combined to alternately dip and spring each aircraft off the ground just as the final stripes of the runway closed under the cockpit.

Each aircraft lumbered to its start point in the hot humid tropical air and achieved necessary thrust while the pilot stood on the brakes. To the rear, the convection currents roiled with the pent-up exhaust gasses to diffuse the air and obscure the runway vegetation and nearby structures. As the pilot judged the generated thrust, he released his feet from the top of the pedals and directed the aircraft down the centerline. Assisting him, the copilot held the throttles at full open against the forces of gravity and vibration while the flight engineer studied the fuel flow gauges as the great turbines hungrily sucked their greediest ingestion.

Slowly, at a rate a man could almost run, the aircraft moved down the runway accompanied by a roar of engines and clouds of partially combusted fuel. Initially imperceptibly but with increasing awareness, the mass began to gain speed. The small runway lights began to flash past the crew faster than could be individually registered. Those of the crew not directly occupied with the takeoff grasped their seats and observed somewhat blankly the experience they had felt dozens of times before. The tail gunner, watching the scene unfold opposite to the direction of flight, found it easiest to look at the sky or momentarily close his eyes to avoid loss of focus.

Initially, the tires of the aircraft were solidly on the ground and transferred each contact with the concrete expansion bays directly to the crew. Each man's thighs could recount each bar that was crossed. Soon however, the bumps became a dip in vibrations as the invisible lift began to take effect. Then, the vibrations became a smooth sensation as the rubber barely touched the runway. Finally, the transition from driving to flying was achieved as lift replaced gravity and sky replaced the ground in the mind's eye.

At 40,000 feet, the sky was clear for the 160 plus kilometers the crew could see from its positions. Above, the sky was a dark blue fading to a deep blackish purple. Below, one could see the blotchy scud of the first cumulous layer that faded into a mixture of blue and white haze as it was married far below to the ground.

At flight altitude, man-made features were almost imperceptible. Nature could only be recognized at the macro. Water, land, and rivers revealed themselves as much by reflection and color as by specific definition. The struggles and issues of infinite personal import to those on the ground lay far beyond the perceptions of the crew. Reality to them was the radar map overlay, the time chart and communication instructions.

A B-52 is a system. It agglomerates the finest aspects of synchronized technology that money can buy. It is a system devoid of warmth and aesthetics but filled with devastating efficiency. The crew had never heard of Soui Long and knew nothing about the rationale for target selection. Their knowledge was restricted to the radar map provided to the bombardier and the flight route charted by the navigator. On the charts, the mission was refined to a series of numbers, latitude, and longitude indicators, codes for orbit or change of direction points and communications instructions, geographical place names and ground tactical descriptions did not intrude to identify a connection with human endeavors.

The aircraft flew in pods of three. One at the center lead and the other two just to the rear and beyond the wing tips of the first. This permitted the best possible bomb dispersion pattern while insuring the most thorough effect of the combined loads at the point of impact. Occasionally, a particularly adventurous or bored flight commander would permit formation dispersion or rotate flight lead. However, by the time the trio was near to the target, it would have returned to the mother formation.

The crew settled back into a bored and systematic execution of duties as the long distance between Okinawa and Vietnam unfolded. Some smoked, others read or wrote. The cockpit crew stretched, performed necessary communications and discussed past or future events.

Should anyone look out, he would see his sister aircraft fading against the misty blue sky. Occasionally, a thin white contrail would emanate from each extended wing tip fading beyond sight to the rear. Nothing else broke the scene. Just the silent passage of the great metal birds through the thin invisible atmosphere.

As time wore on, land came into view and the time from normal transit to bomb run compressed. The crew began to act instinctively at some imaginary point, putting down its desultory tasks and anxiously began to focus on the task at hand. The horizon soon took on the small dark streak that alerted the mind to land. Quickly, the streak became a slash and then a clear transition point between the bluish white beaches and the deep blue green land.

The bombardier closely studied the sweeping amber scope as the electric arc showed the relationship and proximity of the aircraft to the impersonal degree and minute marks well below. At an electronically predetermined spot on the video screen, the doors covering the great maw of the aircraft quickly popped open revealing a series of dark clustered cylinders suspended on swaying conveyors.

The bomb racks instantly felt the pressure of the air and reduced the swing of their loads as commanded by the sudden rush of air. The bombardier continued to study the covered scope and to track the displayed data and his position. A small line marked the flight path and the target release point in a correlated picture. At the point of coincidence, he flipped a small red switch and notified the pilot. This was an unnecessary gratuity as the pilot was informed instantly by a large green light on his fire control panel when the switch was activated.

The initial bombs came in clusters of three from the outside wing stores stations. These were mated with a portion of the bombs from the internal racks. This insured that both the width and depth of the target box was covered. Under ideal conditions, a box of 3 kilometers in length and 1 kilometer in width could be transformed in less than one minute into a very uncomfortable place.

Once activated, the electronic system took effect without regard to human intervention. Flying the aircraft, gauging the winds and airspeed at both altitude and target and sequencing the destructive load, the electrons insured that each bomb would achieve maximum programmed effect. The crew waited quietly and with some anxiety as the system performed its tasks and then turned the instrument back to its human handlers. The transition from human to system to human control required less than three minutes to cycle.

At first, the bombs retained their metallic marriage. Each cluster of three would initially nose down with the wider portion of the casings mated by gravity. Then, as air began to pillow and lift underneath the narrow yellow-tipped green cylinders and flow across the small rectangular tail fins, the bombs began to separate and float apart with a slight waffling effect as the metal shimmied against the invisible pillow underneath.

Some of the bombs had been fitted with long chrome daisy cutters insuring a detonation well above ground level. These bombs took slightly longer to achieve a stable level descent. As the lead bomb in each trio, they seemed to be the band master pointing the way for the remainder to follow.

As each aircraft moved ahead, the steady stream of threes filled the sky below and trailed slowly away in graceful arc toward the blotchy green and blue haze below. At flight altitude, the bombs seemed a huge mass of droppings like so much rain.

Further away, their mass and definition was lost against the great blue-gray sky. Specks became streams, black against light as they slowly arced their way toward the earth. Soon, by the time it took the aircraft to release their burdens, a series of broad dark arches grew gracefully from earth to sky marking the light backdrop like a great J. M. W. Turner skyscape.

The first bomb fell through the hot green canvas and was momentarily lost to the spotter's view. The L-19 pilot, slowly circling several kilometers from the target box, was still tracking the aircraft contrails when the bomb re-emerged in his consciousness.

He first noted a small burp in the canopy quickly followed by a white-hazed shock wave that grew like a ripple on a pond as it spread across the green carpet. This was immediately followed, almost too fast to judge the separation, by twin blast wave rings emanating from the canopy just slightly ahead and to the sides of the first impact as if they formed some giant triangular explosion of heat, light and pressure from some unseen Zeus on Olympus. These too spread across the canopy and intermixed as they sped in ever wider circles until they dissipated into nothingness.

These were joined in an instant by dozens of similar triangles as the vegetation heaved, waved and spread apart across the path of the gently arcing dark streaks from above. Quickly, the canopy grew dense with blue-black smoke and widening shock waves. They alternately impacted on each other and shattered the stillness. The canopy top wavered, staggered and opened its skin to reveal the dark red earth underneath in the brief brilliant yellow-white light of explosive force.

Boiling and fuming, the earth rendered great hunks of laterite and vegetation out and up as each shock wave expanded, struck its sisters, and, reinforced with the newly created detritus, disintegrated the elements of nature that lay in its heat-laden path. The steady march of triangles continued across the jungle floor for approximately two and a half minutes as the small dark arcs, at first a great series of nestled lines, reduced themselves to a perceptible few and finally a lone arc. Finally, nothing disturbed the blue-white haze of the hot tropical day. The spotter pilot then executed a slow left bank, dropped the nose and set a course to exactly bisect the newly rendered earth exposed in its fresh rectangular box.

The jungle air that flowed into the cockpit space was damp and dank. It smelled of heat and cordite and fresh-cut wood and rotting vegetation. Even at a thousand feet the air roiled and tumbled with convection currents and disturbed invisible turmoil. The trail of destruction was wickedly clean and obvious. A ragged-bordered rectangle lay newly exposed to view. The earth below was clean and full of fresh crumpled definition like a new plowed field not yet settled by weather and time.

Craters delineated the new exposure and even in the immediate freshness of their creation began to show small quantities of water puddling in their centers. Craters overlapped craters and heaved double helpings of earth at the edges. Among this disorderly array, the pilot could see vestiges of what had been before. Whole trees were rent upside down with root masses sticking in the air shading their nest like huge umbrellas. Trunks lay scattered and splintered across the ground. Some buried half in the edge of the exposed earth and others lay shattered in pieces around the more discernible fragments. Occasionally, several clean cut ends could be seen announcing their previous use as manmade structures.

The pilot, as had been his past practice, made his first pass across the long axis of the strike at less than 200 feet. Experience had taught him that the first pass, if accomplished immediately after the strike, could be done from a low altitude. After that, a higher pass was necessary to avoid the fire from those soldiers on the periphery that had escaped the strike and had regained their cognitive powers. On his first bomb-damage assessment, he had been rudely awakened on a third pass by converging green tracers from several positions on the chewed edges of the newly created wood line.

Nosing through the smoke, steam and still settling leaves fluttering back to earth, the pilot did a slight aileron flip and viewed the left side of the box. He could see nothing of note existed in the rectangle, his intent was to determine what lay just beyond the grasp of the strike that may have eluded the targeteers.

The newly freed light shown into the edge of previously pristine terrain. The neat rows of bunkers and sleeping areas now lay exposed to direct sunlight. Among them he could see piles of bodies and pieces strewn across the structures and tree limbs like so many Christmas ornaments in a storm. He saw several individuals moving slowly among the charnel ruins with no apparent purpose or direction.

Having traced the entire rectangle, the pilot proceeded on for a short distance to watch for strays—those bombs that had been last out of the aircraft and landed outside the principal destruction pattern. Often, these were the ones that did the main damage if the intelligence analysts had been just a little bit off mark. He enjoyed it when he found such a situation because he could then bring in tactical air strikes with some precision rather than the usual blind guessing and dropping as was so often the case.

A sharp right bank and 180-degree turn recovered the aircraft back on the tracing path. The other side of the box revealed little. Apparently, the mass of the base camp was along the target line and slightly to the west. He observed some light structures through the edge but no sign of solid construction. As on the other side, considerable flesh and viscera shown in the bright sunlight. Less than halfway through the course, the pilot spotted a lone naked human standing in the sunlight.

This man was standing on the edge of a crater as it met the jungle. He was holding on to the side of an upright trunk. Both he and the trunk were stripped bare. The tree was shaved to the cambium layer by blast and shown wet and sticky in the sunlight absent its protective leafy cover and umbrella limbs. The man looked upward at the pilot with a blank stare and unmoving stance. The blood coursing from his ears and nose was clearly visible to the pilot. Seeing no other items of interest, the pilot made a second long, low pass and throttled the plane to gain altitude. The wind created by his pass stirred the edge of the woods and sent a small photograph of Private Ngo's family gliding on a phantom of air toward the brown-red puddle forming several feet away.

With a sense of satisfaction, he noted the position on the map and shifted the plane to the Ranger location. He wanted to brief the damage assessment from a position he knew the Rangers could monitor. He simultaneously called Bien Hoa Control for additional sorties to work over the newly exposed camp. For those on the ground, depending upon their disposition, it was either a very short day or would be a very long one.

43

The B-52 Strike—Ground

It was midday, prior to the strike. Under the fetid canopy General Thanh and Private Ngo were engaged in the same diversion: sleeping. Thanh was exhausted from a night of moving forces, briefing commanders and writing dispatches to Hanoi detailing the previous night's actions and future intentions. His rest platform was carved into dirt walls a full 10 feet below the dark clay earth. A single bare light bulb hung outside his sleeping niche covered by an empty U.S. C-ration fruit can. The light was barely bright enough to read by but Thanh preferred it over the bright gas lantern as it produced neither heat nor noise.

Unlike many people native to the tropics, Thanh was sensitive to sweating and was always seen with a handkerchief in his hand mopping his head and the backs of his hands. Regardless, he much preferred being in the field and avoided urban areas with their inherent bureaucracies. Here, he could make his own schedule, wear his own uniform of choice, usually an open shirt and shorts and summon unquestioned obedience over the entire Southern effort.

Ngo, having marched all night from a border camp as part of the constant replacement stream, was stretched in a hammock swung between the corner posts of a cooking hut. The air was hot and still. The torpor was broken only by the steady drone of flies and mosquitoes endemic to any occupied position rich with the warmth and scent of blood.

Ngo was clad in a pair of dirty cotton shorts. His hair was closely cropped and coarsely black like a fresh-trimmed horse mane. His feet were darkly stained with months of direct exposure to mud and his toenails black from constant battling. Seen alone, they would indicate an age far greater than actual. His skin shimmered with sweat and, hairless, revealed delicately exposed sweat beads from each naked follicle pit. The sweat gathered in rivulets and coursed down his body until it met the nylon of the hammock. Here, the flies and mosquitoes gathered to drink at the edge of the expanding salty wet rings.

The base camp, Binh Tram 42, that Thanh and Ngo occupied, was an entrenched encampment that wound its way across several small hills in a roughly rectangular pattern creating a box of approximately 600 by 400 meters. This was somewhat deceptive, however, as the camp was not laid out as a single entity. Rather, it was a series of interrelated parts designed to accommodate transiting packets of companies and battalions as numbers would dictate. Only the center, the command heart, bore any resemblance to an integrated whole. It was designed to be a place to sleep and eat, not to fight. There were more than sixty of these Binh Tram complexes along the Ho Chi Minh Trail and they very efficiently maintained the North–South lifeline that sustained the war effort.

As a standard design feature in the Binh Trams, each occupied area had a series of well-developed bunkers and trenches off of the primary trail. Within each complex, several cook shelters, instructional areas, and command huts were built. These were flimsy but adequate shelters consisting of little more than four stakes, a roof frame with dried palm fronds and a light log floor.

On the periphery, the remains of many transiting units was indicated by the large amount of fire-blackened bamboo stakes driven into the ground. Each group of three shafts marked a location where several men had heated their rice over small black pots or captured helmets. Over time and hard use, some tips had burned off and new green shafts were substituted. These stood out from the rest and could be seen by contrast from some distance.

The camp was protected along its long length by a creek on the low side that separated it from the Dong Nai. Two smaller steams bisected the camp laterally and were used solely as a fresh water source. All bathing was done in the large creek, the opposite bank of which was well-outposted. A headcount would show over a thousand souls residing within its borders.

The salient feature of the location was its invisibility. Not a single major tree had been felled in the camp development. Rather, the underbrush and new growth had been cleared, leaving the protective tall canopy to shade the facility from the sun and technological intrusions.

The discipline of under-clearing was well-regulated through habit and experience. Only the brush in the living interior was cleared. To the limit of the first bunker line, nature remained untouched. This insured that the camp could not be seen until an intruder presented himself in the opened perimeter, already deep within the carefully calculated interlocking lanes of fire.

Guides brought transiting soldiers across the ridge tops perpendicular to the camp axis and opposite of the creek-guarded low ground. Only very important people such as General Thanh were permitted to transit directly between the camp and the Dong Nai.

General Thanh's command post was at the camp center. It consisted of several large log bunkers, a classroom area with sand table and several palm covered rooms. Several deep rooms were accessed from the interior bunkers.

Several wire lines emanated from one bunker and fed small lights from a generator slowly puffing blue smoke through an exhaust hole.

Another log shelter displayed several strands of small black wires. These connected General Thanh with his immediate commanders and a larger switch board with the local Binh Tram (a logistic support facility) several kilometers away. This arrangement permitted Thanh to pass coded traffic back to Hanoi or to subordinate elements without exposing his location to radio intercepts. Central to this facility were four soldiers working quietly under a palm frond shelter.

One soldier sat on what appeared to be a dark-turquoise-colored bicycle frame absent the wheels. He was slowly turning two crank handles attached to the axle where the front tire normally would have been located. Sitting on a chair next to him was a second individual intently working a small instrument attached to his knee.

Attached to his right thigh was a tin-plated Morse key device that he intently worked with the index finger and thumb of his right hand. In his left hand, he held a small school notebook filled with graph paper on which his message had been meticulously written. The script was very small but precise, reflecting the careful disciplined habits of the female author to his side, a school teacher by previous training.

General Thanh had selected her to be his primary communications officer as she possessed a very quick mind and was exceptionally organized. In a headquarters that traveled light and with minimal support, her ability to maintain a vast library of codes and addresses in her head was invaluable.

Several times a day, she would take notes from Thanh, reduce them to the shortest possible words and convert them to three-letter code groups. These groups were then transmitted at prearranged hours by the quick-fingered sergeant intently manipulating the key. Rarely did these transmissions take more than two minutes to dispatch, the minimum time it was assumed the Americans needed to make a reasonable directional intercept.

The fourth individual sat somewhat apart from the three. He smoked quietly on a pipe with his back against one of the support shelter's posts and absently tormented an ant with a twig. This was General Hien, the ranking political officer with the headquarters. He was required to read all messages from the organization and to render political advice to Thanh.

Hien recognized the difficulty of his position, providing strategic guidance to what was almost always a tactical situation, and that to a man who reveled in ignoring superior headquarters. Over time, he and Thanh had reached an accommodation of necessity: Thanh would brief him on intent and decisions,

Hien would render opinions and suggestions and record the history, but he would not appeal decisions to his superiors.

He did, however, make a fetish of listening to every briefing and monitoring every message transmitted. Thanh appreciated this as Hien returned the courtesy with a requirement for minimal support and attention.

The radio team had strung a long-wire antenna for HF transmission across the center of the classroom. It was quickly erected about 10 feet above the ground and insulated by a U.S. white plastic C-ration spoon at each end. A connecting wire, perpendicular to the antenna, joined the small box at the front end of the bicycle. From practice, the team could erect the antenna, send its messages and repack the antenna in less than five minutes. Now in a static position, they maintained their transmission discipline but did not dismantle the antenna.

While the radio team was quietly performing its task, more than 800 soldiers occupying the camp dozed with the torpor of a tropical midday. The two Caucasians, overweight and profusely sweating, sat on canvas lounge chairs and desultorily waved at flies with handkerchiefs. The Chinese liaisons with Thanh lay on the log floor of the classroom head to head, quietly smoking Gauloise cigarettes and blowing smoke toward the groups of hovering mosquitoes seeking a cooler shade. At this moment in time, the first bomb indicated its presence.

Striking the thick overhead canopy, the long chrome-coated daisy cutter was activated by a large branch approximately 50 feet from the ground. The built-in delay mechanism permitted the bomb to travel another 25 feet before it detonated. This event was unrecognized by the slumbering perimeter for the briefest of moments.

The first precursor of a deviation from the daily regimen was a loud clunk followed by a terrific blast. To those nearest to it, the bomb's presence was noted only by the tremendous noise and pressure that washed over them before they disintegrated into atoms. Igniting in the air, the explosive pattern expanded in an inverted funnel shape traveling in the direction of its flight before it dissolved in a climax of heat, noise, expanding gas, and technologically designed metal shards.

In less of a time lapse than could be recognized, the initial bomb's sisters exploded. These, however, were assisted by the path of the first that cleared much of the thicker vegetation in the several nanoseconds before they ignited. The effect was to provide a clearer path for the explosive force which now streamed and generated a focus of force to the now-exposed soldiers below.

The three bursts were quickly followed by similar pods over the length and breadth of the camp as it was transformed into a charnel house of overpressure, heat, and destroying gasses. Mixed in the marriage of bursts were increasingly greater amounts of earth, metal, trees, and indiscernible portions of body parts rapidly dissolving into elements of oxygen, steam, calcium, and other chemical components.

In near instantaneous fashion, this scene was repeated in a rectangular box a kilometer by three kilometers—the heart of the Binh Tram. To those on the leading edge of the strike, none of this was known. The time between explosion and the comforting white light of death was immeasurable. To those in the center, there was only time to be aware of something amiss before they too were dissolved into organic matter and returned to the earth and air. The greatest torture was reserved for those at the trailing third of the strike. They were fully awakened and mentally aware of the event well before the inevitable arrival of the overwhelming heat and light that they knew would be unavoidable.

Structures, trees, equipment, and flesh comingled in the orange flames and heaving earth. The jungle floor would rent open, consume the material on its top and then vent it away as the trailing blasts overwhelmed the initial penetrator's efforts. Huge chunks of ground were uplifted and thrown against the still-standing trees. That which lay open to the new sky reflected the blue-black burning and steam that evidenced their close proximity to the heart of the reinforcing explosives.

Private Ngo was vaporized in his resting position, his body lost to the rapid expansion of heat and gasses that combined to vaporize him before passing through the sheer nylon of his final resting place. Below the spot where Ngo had lain, the white pages of a letter gently rustled in the alternating blasts unharmed save for the microscopic covering of dust and powdered cordite.

In less than three minutes, the rain of heat, gasses and screaming metal shards ended. As quickly as it had begun, the scene was rendered into a still and awful silence. Save for the fierce calls of frightened birds diving toward the canopy, nothing stirred or reflected life. The earth steamed and stank of its new-found combinations. The air was filled with thousands of newly released leaves and dusts as they rained down from their just executed freedoms.

A hundred yards outside the newly formed rectangle and sheltered by a small hillock, the bamboo cages housing the prisoners were ripped and tipped by falling trees and large clumps of earth. Split asunder, they had fallen apart and dispersed their human charges onto the earth. Farther back from the blast and sheltered by the trees, the isolated swampy portion of the camp was a salvation to the prisoners. Dazed and spent, they had recovered individually resting on the shattered pieces of the bamboo walls. Awakening to reality, several of the Rangers arose and quietly brought their comrades to consciousness. Taking advantage of the situation, they quickly recovered their capacities, hastily gathered some loose weapons, rice, and canteens and slipped quietly into the still reverberating jungle to seek their way to the east and freedom. The last Ranger took a Makarov pistol from a large Oriental in civilian clothes, seemingly asleep under the windblown picnic table resting across the remains of one of the bamboo cages, and moved purposefully toward another form barely regaining consciousness, and pumped five bullets into the just-conscious guard and moved quickly toward the undamaged jungle. Turning away, the Ranger tucked the pistol into his pocket and rapidly trotted toward his disappearing companions.

Farther away, the Rangers in the hasty perimeter near the original LZ felt the earth swell and roll from some giant subterranean tide. The lieutenant could see the folds of the earth move and ripple with the background sound of the strike. Extended by time and distance, the explosions rolled into a single long mutter and continuous rumble that lapped over the resting soldiers. Though imprecise as sensations, both the sound and the physical tremors clearly explained their root cause. The survivors of the recent struggle looked toward the new intrusion and imagined its effect but with at least as much reflection as satisfaction.

44

The Return

The termination of the air strike was coincidental with the arrival of darkness. The Rangers, now fortified by an additional 40 soldiers who had trickled in through the awful charnel house to the south, slept as if they were in winter quarters. Their laxness, even if atypical of the unit, was reinforced by a combination of recent information and exhaustion.

Hiep had dispatched four soldiers to retrace the battalion's path and to ascertain the state of the VC force. Experience told the soldiers that such a heavy pounding would cause the VC to retreat from the base camp for fear of attracting a major American assault. Their intuition was rewarded as they carefully moved in the shadow land between the craters and the pristine jungle. No sign of a living foe was visible. Everywhere, the open areas were garnished and highlighted with the remains of the struggle. Bodies and parts of bodies were scattered in a variety of visible forms. Some were intact as seemingly untouched in sleep. Others were evident only as parts and pieces protruding from the rented earth or hanging from an opportunistic tree branch. In other places, the evidence of a previous life's presence could only be discerned through the red misty stain on a water's edge or a dark streak against the smooth white blasted cambium layer of a just-flailed tree.

The path to the camp was a sinuous blasted trace that exposed itself to the harsh sunlight. Into this brilliant exposure, the teeming insect life of the jungle host gravitated to feed upon the newly discovered detritus. The cleansing tools of nature had begun their task even before the bomb-induced heat had left the crater's edge. Working their way to the edge of the original camp, the Rangers everywhere were met with deafening silence and visual chaos. They came upon the camp unexpectedly quickly. Lulled by the unique sensory stimulations, they walked into the original perimeter before they realized it—much like the action began. Instead of the intense chatter of the machine-gun fire that greeted their first incursion, here was only silence. Concentration broken by an occasional squalling bird, they gingerly stood on the edge of the perimeter and peered at the ground that had so recently defined their lives. Like four statues on the edge of a park, they gazed into the interior for several moments.

The inner perimeter closest to the river was virtually intact but stripped of its overhead vegetation. The leading edges, the last portions of the Ranger perimeter, as well as the flanks, were blasted into huge mixed mounds of interlaced craters and churned earth. Only the occasional presence of a sawn log or palm thatch betrayed the previous human endeavors. Not a living thing was seen, almost as if by design to pay homage to the many dead.

Everywhere the team looked were bodies. Ranger dead. VC dead. Intermixed forces. Parts and pieces scattered throughout the exposed earth and dangling blasted vegetation. Equipment and material, harder and heavier than flesh, settled itself inside the craters while the more delicate remains were heaved in windrows at the crater edges or buried between overlapping dirt mounds—known only by the sight of a protruding appendage or identifiable body part. Toward the northern flank and the rear of the camp, bodies lay in neat rows where they succumbed to overpressure in parade-ground cohesiveness. Toward the center of the perimeter and tracing the course of the bomb line, bodies were scattered as the forces of ordnance dictated. Those that could be discerned as humans were uniformly disfigured and rent by the whole panoply of explosive force that was brought to bear. The quartet remained immobilized by the sight for some passage of time and then as if on a common signal, wordlessly turned their back and returned toward their companions.

Further to the south, the cavalry had begun to extract itself and had begun movement toward the Chinese Farm. The Cav commander's intent was to join the Rangers at their location and to provide both relief and reinforcements. As L Troop closed on the open fields of the farming land, it passed through the perimeter of the 48th Regiment and was halted by Colonel Trinh's jeep and an array of regimental APCs.

Trinh sought out the troop commander and suggested that his vehicles lead the formation the short remaining distance to the Ranger perimeter. While the troop commander conferred with the command post, Trinh motioned his vehicles forward and left the Cav to follow in his tracks.

Placing his jeep well behind his last vehicle but well in front of the leading Cav carrier, Trinh followed the unit trace as it crossed the northern edge of the old landing zone and halted just inside the brushy shade that marked the rear of the Ranger position. Slapping the accumulated dust from his boots with his swagger stick, he swung out of the jeep, straightened his fatigue shirt and with a broad smile sought out Hiep.

Hiep, his face masked by an impassive emotionless exterior, met him at the edge of the position, formally shook his hand and without speaking, walked into the sunlight toward the advancing American unit. The troop commander had halted his track just prior to running over Trinh's jeep and motioned with outspread arms for the trailing elements to fan out in an arc cocooning Tanh's element with the Rangers. Into this miasma of dust, noise and belching exhaust, Hiep emerged as a small dark shadow. The commander halted his orders in mid-sentence as if struck dumb by this inconsequential yet imposing apparition.

With a broad smile, Hiep went to the side of the track, extended his hand and vigorously shook the commander's hand. In excellent English and with great intensity, he thanked the officer for his efforts of the previous day and suggested that he join his unit in the shade. The captain ordered the tracks to shut engines, dismounted and followed Hiep into the cool dark shade.

Shortly, a messenger from the Cav entered into the perimeter and spoke softly to the captain. He whispered quickly to the messenger who departed to the sunlit open ground. Very quickly, the exhausts of the Cav were reignited and the vehicles moved off to box the LZ. The captain found it hard to speak in a normal voice as he visually reviewed the small dappled clump of soldiers. He sat beside the command group and without meaningful engagement contented himself with absorbing the scene. The American lieutenant spoke in short abrupt sentences of welcome and inquiry and then retreated into silence smoking a cigarette. The NCO ventured into the sunlight and shortly returned with two cans of C-ration peaches that he and the lieutenant hurriedly opened and devoured.

Before the fruit was consumed, the sound of helicopters crept into the group's consciousness and heads involuntarily turned toward the noise. Soon, the air was filled with a variety of sounds, dirt and flying material as visitors descended on the spot. The Cav commander arrived, followed by the Province Senior Advisor accompanied by General Tanh. Behind them, several groups of news correspondents, alerted by the Saigon press briefings, flooded across the ground seeking interviews. Among the last to land was a highly waxed helicopter from Saigon carrying the Vietnamese Corps Commander and a representative of the Joint General Staff. Colonel Trinh made a point to greet every newly arriving party and to usher it into the Ranger perimeter. Hiep, responding to some inner guide, never met the visitors but instead rose to greet them once they entered his perimeter.

Accompanying the senior advisor was the L-19 pilot. He had forced himself on the party when he heard they were going to the LZ. Dressed in a sweat-soaked flight suit and a loosely strapped .38 pistol, he trailed the official party and stood in the half-sun half-shade while the Vietnamese general and American made their overly aggressive greetings to Hiep and the American advisors. The lieutenant, though momentarily distracted, noticed the pilot, anxious and sweating on the edge of the light. He dropped all pretext of polite conversation and moved immediately toward the pilot, wrapping his arms in a tight embrace around his body and wordlessly hugged him. Hiep, now distracted by the activity, recognized the visitor and his significance and joined the pair. The three exchanged comments with intensity and disappeared into the depths of the perimeter leaving the distinguished guests to converse among themselves.

Soon, the visitors gathered together by accumulation into the Ranger perimeter and continued desultory conversation amongst themselves. Too inhibited to force deference for rank and precedence on their hosts and too intimidated by the circumstances to depart, they contented themselves to rest, reflect, and cross-complement each other and their organizations. By this time, Tanh had established a CP and mess by his jeep and was dispatching tea and cold drinks to the group. Just in the darker shadows adjacent to a large tree, the two prisoners, Hu and Phu, viewed the scene, safe in anonymity from recognition. By some instinct, they recognized the virtue of isolation at this time and lay on their stomachs feigning sleep. Hu rolled his head slightly and took note of the jungle growth and its proximity to the Rangers. He would exhibit patience and cunning. This was his home.

Shortly, Hiep emerged from the shadows and stood before the group. He had just spoken to his scouts and had coalesced his thoughts. He spoke forcefully to the group. Without selecting a target for his comment, he stated that he wanted to return the unit to the battlefield with the Cav's assistance and recover the Ranger bodies. For a moment no one spoke. Then breaking the hanging silence, General Tanh inquired if the Rangers were up to such an operation and suggested that they be returned to Xuan Loc and that Colonel Trinh's unit recover the bodies. Hiep stood silent for a minute and then, selecting his words carefully, stated that the Rangers could not return without their dead and the possibility of finding the many wounded and missing. Sensing the tension, the Cav commander suggested that a mixed force of American and Vietnamese vehicles carry the Rangers to the camp. When Hiep did not object, the party, sensing an appropriate break, arose and moved to their various means of transportation. Shortly, after a cloud of noise and dust, the perimeter was left to its near original composition.

With minimal discussion, the designated Rangers were distributed to the five ACAVs the Cav had shifted into the last shadowy precursor to the trail of craters that beckoned in the sunlight. Walking behind the tracks, Hiep and his command group, with both prisoners in tow, slowly traced the route they had so recently followed. Colonel Trinh's carriers, though in the lead, were empty of all but the assigned crews. With some hesitation and inquiring looks to the rear, the tracks began their slow traverse over the churned landscape. Watching their progress, Hiep stopped and sat by himself on a fallen log, pulling long, deep draughts on a cigarette until the force could only be discerned by its sound. Slowly, he arose and followed his senses.

The lead APC lurched its way across the bomb craters and belched a clot of blue white smoke as it abruptly stopped at the edge of the base camp. The driver had maneuvered around the fallen trees and craters and picked his route carefully to avoid the various bodies and other obstructions that impeded his path.

His tracks had cut a wide meandering ribbon of new-turned earth to their rear that resembled a puzzle answer to a maze problem. The vehicle threw its passengers forward and then quickly backward as it came to an almost immediate halt. The passengers sitting on the deck held onto whatever purchase was available and rode the armored bronco as it weaved its way through the jungle from the LZ to the base camp. Upon its halt in front of the first major bunker, the passengers jumped off the top of the APC in crumpled little heaps and looked around with anxious and cautious eyes.

In daylight and without benefit of feat, the base camp had a totally different view to the observer. The camp was almost uniformly covered in a light pale turquoise coating of leaves. The leaves had fallen from the topmost portions of the trees as they were blasted off their stems by the combined efforts of the artillery, tactical air strikes and the just-completed B-52 strikes.

The vague shapes of the bunkers projected above the overall level ground and married themselves to the geometric slashes formed by the trench lines that bisected the viewers' eyes. Where before the entire area had been shaded in constant shadows and dark, it was now lit by brilliant sunlight. The dozens of trees that protected the camp from aerial view lay scattered and atomized all around. In some cases, only bare trunks existed.

Some trees had been reduced to small splinters of the original giant host outlining its position on the jungle floor. The exposed wood had been thoroughly burned and laid bare. It had a wispy odor of charcoal and cordite and was coated with a light grayish black powder from the immediate heat of the explosive charges. Portions of the base camp were interdicted by huge piles of exposed mud and earth material thrown up by successive bombs that exploded on the jungle floor no longer impeded by the tree canopy above.

Scattered throughout the area were small segments of limbs, trunks, and once threading vine mass. No piece was bigger than a man's arm though thousands of board feet had been processed through the explosive mill. The observers were totally silent as each man was lost in his own initial impressions.

In response, the jungle too was dead still. The normal animal and bird sounds were missing. Present over the entire scene was a heavy penetrating odor of cordite and a light atmosphere of bluish-gray light as the sunlight worked its way into long-neglected corners through the prisms of rising moisture and the small threads of heat and smoke still emanating from the day's ordeal.

The crews stood still for a moment, transfixed by the scene, each man collecting his thoughts and registering his impressions. The American lieutenant broke the mood with a soft comment to his Ranger counterpart and the soldiers began their work. Each man went to the back of the APC and donned rubber gloves and aprons that had been hastily provided and took a large Vietnamese straw broom in his hand. The soldiers broke up into individual elements and went silently about their work.

A man would come upon a lump in the leaf cover and sweep at the lump with his broom. Underneath, a scene of life in death would be revealed. Each form disturbing the level turquoise floor was a man or men revealed in their last moment of struggle for life. Like the plaster casts at Herculaneum, the graphic facts of the last 24 hours were laid out to view.

Next to a portion of a log were three soldiers—one was a Ranger, the other two were VC. The Ranger had the bayonet and muzzle of an AK-47 buried in his throat while the VC lying on top of him had a short brush machete protruding through the small of his back. The sweeper attempted to separate the two but was unable to do so without placing his foot on the Ranger's head and pulling up on the VC with a half Nelson hold. The second VC lay across the back of the legs of the first VC and had clearly been killed as he tripped across the log protecting the Ranger. The top back portion of his skull had been neatly channeled by a machine gun that continued to draw a neat line through his buttocks and heel. Further along, a sweeper called out and asked for assistance. His partners joined him and watched as he slowly and with care brushed the leaves from his find.

Satisfied that he had been sufficiently thorough, stepped back and joined his partners in viewing the scene. Revealed in front was a drama of human service. A Ranger medic, clearly marked by a Red Cross armband was draped across another Ranger and a VC. The Ranger and VC both had bandages on their chest and head. The medic covered both bodies and had his hands firmly wrapped around a hemostat and muscle spreader on the wounded Ranger's thigh. From afar, it looked as if the medic was closely examining his patient. However, his helmet was several feet off to the side. Instead, his skull was covered with a heavy brownish mass of matted blood that had clotted on his thick course hair. The sweeper stroked the skull with the broom and revealed three blue black holes neatly on line from the bottom of the hairline to the center of the skull to the top of the skull. The latter bullet had carried an exit force sufficient to remove the top portion of the medic's forehead.

This activity went on for several hours. Each sweeper would reveal his find, reflect on the action and continue his work. If a particularly interesting or confusing find arose, the discoverer would call for his companions and they would move to the site, discuss and decide and then move back to their task. By midday, the initial work had been completed.

At midafternoon, the team removed itself from the camp and returned to the armored guards to rest and reflect. Food, though offered by the drivers and security force, was seldom accepted. Rangers quietly smoke and drank from their canteens and settled into individual brooding moods. The scene of the battle in deathly still life had been laid out. The fighting positions were apparent by each body's presence. The individual deaths and group efforts were outlined by clots of corpses or individual physical statements outlined in the soft earth. Small mounds of spent cartridge cases from both sides, intermixed with American-made grenade rings and VC pull strings, marked the ebb and flow of the tide of previous battle. Particularly contested ground was indicated by multiple bodies in both uniforms arrayed on confined terrain.

The progress of the battle was traced by the layering of powder-blue uniforms across the Ranger fighting positions as clearly as flotsam marks the progress of the tide. Here and there were signals of a soldier's failure to maintain his cohesion with the unit, as he lay dead pointed in the direction of his own lines instead of his enemies. There were very few of these from either side. Most of the uniforms, blue and camouflage-patterned, were melded into each other in a mutual grasp as if in the final steps of some deathly minuet.

This had not been easy ground for either attacker or defender in light of the spirit of both parties. Still in spite of the sunlight and elapsed time, silence was the loudest sound to accompany the quiet exertions of effort as the participants were arranged in rubber cocoons or arranged on the bright ochre of newly turned earth.

The clearing party rested a second time and ate from necessity. By now, the emotion had been wrung from them as heat and numbing repetition exacted its toll. Drained of energy, the soldiers ate the rice and cold tea provided by the drivers. The rice came in clear plastic bags that were thrown into a nearby trench when emptied. After smoking pungent Army-issued cigarettes, Ruby Queens in a pink wrapper, the soldiers reached into the back of the APCs and replenished their supply of body bags and dropped them off by each ground-bound statue of life's last moment. The sun had begun to do its work and all personnel placed gauze masks over their faces and wetted them down with cheap shaving lotion.

Slowly, now operating as a single team, they placed each Ranger in a bag and zipped it tight. The VC were rolled into the closest fighting trench but with some care and regard. By 1500, the Ranger bodies had been stacked next to the girdling APCs.

The lieutenant had counted 206 Rangers and 302 VC—all KIA. He made a mental note that the last portion of the engagement must have been tremendously intense as it was highly unusual for the VC to leave a battlefield without clearing their dead, particularly in the numbers evident. He had walked around the base camp during the day's work and observed portions of human appendages and pieces of both sides' uniforms showing through the numerous bomb craters and newly expunged earth.

Toward the end of the day, as the clearing parties had worked their way to the inner portions of the base camp, a soldier gave a shout and the others raced toward him. He was standing on the edge of a fighting trench peering down with his hands on his knees. His companions joined him and quickly lapsed into silence as each was lost in his own reflection of the scene. At the bottom of the trench, approximately 4 feet deep and 2 feet wide, was a crumpled bundle. Under the bundle was a dead VC. He was wearing the standard powder-blue grenade vest and black pajamas. His bare feet, wrapped in rubber sandals, protruded beyond the bundle with his toes pointing straight up. His feet were a dark bruised color, lined with dozens of cracks and coated with a light glaze of red laterite. The large toenail was almost a butternut brown and mauve where it had been bruised in life. The top of his head shown from beneath the bundle with his black hair neatly thrown backward on the floor of the trench. His face was partially covered by the bundle but was exposed enough for the careful examiner to see his half-opened eyes as they dully reflected through the long silken strands of the bundle's own hair.

Resting on top of the VC was the rigid and partially turned body of a nurse. She had fallen on top of him in a half profile that showed her feminine soft features. She appeared to be resting on her human mattress until awoken to continue her tasks. She was considerably smaller than her patient and covered him with a partially curled body. However, fully a third of the patient was covered with her flowing hair. The hair had many long parts in it that revealed segments of her patient as a rippled veil. The hair complemented her extreme femininity and gave the scene a grace the workers had not felt to this point.

They silently drank in the scene. The lieutenant, after a minute, grasped a body bag and softly dropped into the trench. With slow and deliberate movements, he straightened out the nurse, rolled her over to face the sky and slipped her body into the bag starting with her feet and working to her head. He pulled her pant legs and sleeves to their fullest length and reached into the bag and pulled the shirt bottom down all around until it was fairly tight and uniform. Unlike all her philosophically aligned companions that were pitched into the common graves of shell craters, she would be formally buried with the Rangers.

His last act was to grasp her hair in repeated handfuls and place each strand carefully cleared from her left ear across to her waist. After all her hair had been neatly arranged, he slowly closed the zipper, keeping his hand running along the inside of the zipper trace to insure it wouldn't tangle. Without a spoken word, another soldier joined him in the trench and lifted the body to the waiting hands of their companions. They carried the body to the APC, placed it inside the carrier, started the engine, and without a word, began to retrace their tracks through the jungle floor. The evening had begun to fall. Still, save for the rising and falling of the engine pitch, the jungle remained silent.

Hiep had watched this from the edge of the blasted jungle and had made no move to participate nor exercise curiosity. His bodyguards had separated themselves slightly from him and rested nervously in the shadows, uncertain whether to assist in the clearing process or minister to their commander. Choosing neither, they opted to sit quietly around a small rice-cooking fire and wait for the day to close. Comrade Hu and the other prisoner had placed themselves between Hiep and the fire and had spent the day largely unnoticed. Distracted by the intensity of the scene, the guards lost interest in their charges. As darkness descended, no one noticed Comrade Hu as he slipped quietly into the jungle to trace in reverse the path being blazed by the just-released Ranger prisoners to the west. Phu, his much younger companion, charged with fear, could not be persuaded and crawled quietly to the interior of an APC, forcing himself into the rearmost corner of the vehicle, hidden by the stacks of bodies and their rigid protuberances.

Awoken from his deep trancelike state by the sounds of the APCs, Hiep moved toward the retracing trail. His bodyguards, anxiously searching for their prisoners, scuttled from tree to tree. Oblivious to the situation, Hiep resignedly motioned them to follow with his swagger stick. He was lost in obscurity when the last group retreated toward him from the rim edge of the blasted clearing. The young prisoner, now jammed against the bulkhead wall of the APC and immersed in body bags, was fast asleep in an amniotic sack of emotional fluid.

45

Reconstitution

The UH-1H flew across the canopy just barely missing the topmost limbs. The crew leaned out of the craft looking intently at every opening in the canopy and riverbank. It was a hot and sweltering day and much too early for the cooling afternoon thunderstorms so the crew extended themselves as far out of the hull as possible. They were looking for people, any sign of people.

Small groups of soldiers had begun to make their way back to friendly lines. On this, the third day after the action, the battalion was now able to muster almost 150 people. The helicopter, on a recon mission from the 11th Cav, was tracing a path across the trackless green hoping to find some of the soldiers who had separated themselves from the unit in the last 45 minutes of the battalion's existence.

The commander of the Cav didn't have to do this as he had no responsibility but the brotherhood of arms and the shared aspects of this action. The previous action caused him to view those soldiers as his own. From now until the Cav commander returned to the U.S., he would employ the reconstituted Rangers at every opportunity and they would reward him with exceptional service. In one action in relief of an ambush of an entire Cav squadron on Highway 20, the battalion would receive an American Presidential Unit Citation. One of the reasons for this relationship was just beginning to appear out of the left side of the helicopter.

The helicopter crew chief had tied himself in the craft with a monkey strap, a long nylon strap attached to the passenger and then snapped into the metal rings on the floor. This arrangement allowed the man to lean well out of the aircraft and in some cases stand on the struts without fear of falling. Gunners particularly liked this arrangement because it allowed them to stand on the landing struts and operate their machine gun fully from the 12 to 6 o'clock firing positions. Some gunners who had spent a great deal of time in-country would wash the pilot's window—while still in flight.

Today, at 1051, the crew chief thought he saw something moving in the bamboo field they had just passed. He asked the pilot to turn around and buzz it again. The pilot, knowing that he was without escort and deep in

War Zone D, executed a 180-degree pedal turn and increased his speed to maximum obtainable and both dove and slipped sideways concurrently in retracing his steps across the small open space in the jungle carpet. Standing on the northern edge of the clearing was a man, waving both arms.

The pilot quickly gained altitude out of small-arms range and called back to his base camp. The radio operator briefed the watch officer who went to the operations officer for instructions. The ops officer noted the location on the map and issued instructions.

Lying in the shade of the rubber plantation bordered the Cav base camp was a platoon of soldiers. They were the Blue Platoon, an infantry reaction force designed to provide protection for downed helicopters or reinforcement missions for troops in contact (TIC). TIC was a term that everyone immediately understood and reacted toward. Mess personnel stopped stirring, clerks stopped their typing, and all within earshot stopped walking and looked toward the combat control center. The hesitation and halt to the routine lasted only a moment but it effected everyone. TIC meant lives at stake. The next moment's actions and orders determined the extent of the bill that might have to be paid.

Each man in the Blue Platoon instinctively placed his hand on his rifle and looked toward the platoon leader. He arose from the shade of the trees and moved toward the radio operator. The lieutenant took the handset and listened to the operations officer's description of the mission. He gave the handset, black and sweat-coated at the earpiece, to the operator and waved his troops toward the waiting six helicopters that were rapidly warming their engines.

The squad leaders moved directly over to the lieutenant and got their maps out of the cargo pockets on their pants. One squad leader dropped his copy of *Playboy* that came out with the map and another lost his cigarettes that had caught in the folds of the map. He stepped on the edge of the pack with his jungle boots and reached down with his left hand to retrieve them while shaking the map flat with his right. All the time looking his leader straight in the eye with a gaze of anxious anticipation.

The lieutenant quickly sketched the situation over the noise and dust of the helicopters and indicated the landing zone with his finger. His finger nails had a reddish black tone from the laterite and the quick had been worn down well below the edge of the finger. For months, the lieutenant had absentmindedly worked the nail down through biting it off and then honing it even lower with the edge of his ballpoint pen.

The rotor wash was so strong that it was impossible to accurately see the spot on the map. The paper kept flapping wildly in spite of the lieutenant's efforts to hold it flat. He then placed a black grease pencil mark on the LZ and gave the map to each squad leader.

When each man had his map marked, the lieutenant gave them a quick mission order. They would orbit over the LZ while a chase bird landed to check out a possible sighting of Rangers lost during the battle at Soui Long. They go in if the bird is downed. It could be a trap.

The squad leaders returned to their aircraft and got onboard. They gave a very short précis of what was happening over the sound of the helicopters but most was lost as the birds rapidly gained power and drove into the sky. The soldiers, though interested in what their mission was and with unfulfilled curiosity, soon returned to a semi-trance watching the countryside flow beneath the aircraft as it bore its way across the sky.

As the Blue Platoon lifted off, another empty Huey also was airborne. Because it was unloaded, except for a medic and the door gunners, it was able to catch and surpass the infantry-laden helicopters. It quickly reached the open area where the scout helicopters were circling back and forth at an elevation that kept it well above potential small-arms fire. Below, the small black dot that brought them all there and had caused all the energizing of purpose and effort remained motionless.

The dot realized that it had accomplished its mission and waited patiently. From 2,000 feet, the scout pilot could still see the object of his interest, once a man and now a small black shadow against the bright green of the new bamboo and elephant grass.

Shaking him out of his concentration, a radio call signaled the pilot that the main body was about to close on his position. He turned to look out of the right window over his armor plate and saw the sinuous black line that marked the sister ships closing on his position. He switched his finger to the external transmit button on the collective and vectored them to his position.

Once the entire body was orbiting the open field, the scout bird had the empty helicopter trail him and ordered the gunships to precede them both to the field. Still, the black dot remained motionless.

Breaking away from the Blue Platoon force, the scout bird, empty bird, and gunships quickly dropped power and bore straight toward the field. The scout bird pilot, concentrating on organizing the force, had failed to push his right pedal far enough when he dropped power and the gunner on the left had called him that his tail was not aligned with the direction of flight. He quickly corrected and noticed that the black dot now became a man with some sort of large lump near his head.

The scout bird, upon reaching 100 feet, gave aircraft maximum power and raced across the LZ, letting image of the standing man register in his brain without taking the time to actually rationalize the entire scene consciously in his mind. After 17 months in Vietnam, the pilot had prided himself on his ability to intuitively sense a trap. He did not have that sense now. He could see the figure standing stock still in the field with two lumps on his shoulders, one looked larger than the other but he could not make out specific detail.

He did an abrupt full-power pedal turn and told the empty to fly in and pick up the soldier. As the empty Huey floated toward the earth, the gunships positioned themselves on the flanks of the LZ and slowly moved across the open field. The pilots realized they could not hover due to their overweight condition so they chose to slowly drop altitude over the LZ, maintaining visual contact with the overgrown flanks of the open field. The inside gunner fixed his bullseye sight on the lone standing figure while the outside gunners fired on the trees that marked the edge of the fields for telltale movement, shining objects or new trails. The mixed tracer and ball ammunition feeding into each machine gun rattled and scratched the C-ration fruit can that they lay on as they disappeared into the maw of the feed tray cover. The cans kept the ammo level with the feed tray and had been worn to bare silver tin over time. Watching the ground, the gunners could see out of the corner of their eye, the tips of the bullets rise and fall on the shining tin surface as the wind ebbed and flowed across the linked ammunition. The standing soldier remained perfectly still.

The rescue helicopter cut in quickly at a perpendicular angle from the scout bird track to lessen its exposure in the open field. The pilot performed a full-power flare and dropped the skids less than 20 feet from the soldier. He stood impassively while all this was going on and braced his body against the impact of wind and blowing debris and vegetation from the surface of the elephant grass. His hair was blown straight back and he had to take a half step to the rear with his left foot to brace himself against the air pressure.

At the moment the skids impacted with the ground, the medic jumped off the helicopter, himself touching ground before the helicopter came to a complete halt. He needed only four steps to reach the object standing in the field. He almost immediately realized why the man had remained so impassive and immobile throughout the aerial acrobatics.

The man was a Ranger sergeant. He had no boots on his feet, which were clearly bleeding through the mud that had caked to his ankles. It had baked itself to a glue-like texture that became more clearly red as the mud and glue mixture thinned out toward his shin. He had no headgear. However, his coarse black hair had matted down across the scalp with a shiny black viscous material of blood and scalp that both dried and oozed in the tropical sunlight. Over his right shoulder, he held a fellow soldier who had on only a pair of shorts. The man had several major wounds that had been bandaged with his personal clothing and was unconscious. Over his left shoulder, the sergeant had two weapons and two sets of equipment.

The medic took the unconscious man from the sergeant and placed him on the aircraft floor and then returned to half-carry and half-pull the sergeant to the aircraft. While reaching for the sergeant's arm, he first noticed that the sergeant had a major sucking chest wound as well as a small black hole in his side.

The chest wound was bubbling a small froth in synchronization with the sergeant's breath. It had been covered by the sergeant with the plastic sheeting from a radio battery and tied to his chest with boot laces. The small black hole in his side was quivering when the medic examined it. The medic pinched the wound with both hands and squeezed out five fat brownish white maggots.

With both the sergeant and his wounded comrade lying on the floor of the helicopter, the pilot quickly pulled up on the cyclic and rapidly gained altitude. The sergeant stared impassively at the gray plastic quilt ceiling. The medic was inserting an IV in the unconscious soldier and talking to the pilot, describing the situation. The door gunners stared at both Rangers with a mixture of curiosity and amazement.

The sergeant looked toward the gunner on his side with an imploring gaze and raised his right hand and extended his first two fingers and moved them in a scissors motion. The gunner stared transfixed for a moment as this signal registered and then fumbled in the sandbag behind him. He extracted a Pall Mall cigarette from its red container, shielded himself from the wind by turning his upper torso into the compartment and lit it after several attempts.

The gunner placed the hot-red glowing cigarette in the sergeant's mouth and returned to watch over his gun barrel. The sergeant locked the cigarette in his dry lips, took a deep pull and fixed his eyes to the ceiling. The plastic sheet on his chest exuded a mixed gas of light red vapor and grayish-blue smoke around the small tiny bubbles that escaped their protective cover. Two more soldiers were going home.

46

The General Returns

Masked by the sound of the retreating APCs, the scouts from the remaining VC force still monitored the ebbs and flows of the opposition's movements. The surviving cadre had undergone many previous waxing and waning of fortunes and proceeded with a dedication born of fatalism and experience. During the principal air strikes, they had retreated to the edge of the river bank and avoided opportunities for inclusion with the greater mass. As dark succeeded daylight, they retraced their steps to the main battle area and retreated to the Binh Tram with the survivors, portering what wounded and dead as they could.

On one of their first forays, Comrade Hu was encountered waiting patiently by the familiar east bank crossing site. Though his identity and significance was lost to the scouts, they accepted his presence and escorted him to the base camp, retaining him on its edge until his relationship could be confirmed. Upon an excited approval from General Thanh, he was ushered into the command post and given a place of honor amongst the other traveling guests. Unused to the attention, Hu felt uneasy with his more polished and clean companions and excused himself. He found an unoccupied hammock and was fast asleep under the large tree shading the shower unit, less than a hundred feet from the Ranger prisoner cages.

Over the next few days, as the only residual coherent force left, the scouts provided a covering screen for General Thanh, who was now concerned about the possibility of a major Allied offensive against his depleted force. It was during one of their absences that the scouts missed the B-52 strike against the camp.

Hearing and feeling the massive concussions telegraphed through the plastic jungle floor, the scouts waited for its conclusion and then assembled on the eastern shore of the Dong Nai, less than half a mile from the original battlefield. There, the scout captain left a small contingent and moved the remainder toward the Binh Tram.

More than a kilometer away from the camp, the unmistakable signs of the bomb strike began to appear. Portions of trunks and flailed root strands were scattered along the jungle floor. White trunks were spotted with clods of mud that streaked the bark and lay in profuse mounds to the range of the human eye. Occasional portions of milled logs could be seen strewn on the jungle floor with an accompanying hole in the canopy where they had smashed their way through.

Within several hundred yards of the Binh Tram, the signs of the strike and its results were unmistakable. Trees were lain like windrows on the dirt pointing away from the blast. Many were flat against the ground while others leaned upon their stronger neighbors. Everywhere, the soft leaf and vines had been disintegrated into a giant snowfall of green detritus that covered tree and dirt alike with a blanket of tiny particles.

Now, occasional reminders of the frailty of human flesh came into view resting on an elevated tree crotch or protruding from the green blanket. Borne by the waxing and waning explosive winds, the manufactured material of the owners descended last, resting in shreds and tears upon all else, incongruous in nature's recycling process.

Standing on the edge of what was their base camp, the scouts saw a huge undulating naked field of craters, water and smoking vegetation. Across this sea of destruction, they could see some undirected but distinct human movement. Retreating to the physical and emotional peace of the jungle, they rested and began a long circuit around the ploughed earth to the remnants of humanity they had spotted on the other side.

After an hour of difficult movement, the scouts came upon the western edge of what remained of the base camp. Within this small area, the residual forces had gathered to recover themselves. They were barely coherent and only capable of concentrating on returning their mental equilibrium. The captain estimated that fewer than 300 personnel remained within the site, constituting a polyglot of forces. He found an NVA lieutenant colonel, a Chinese advisor and the two Russians but no senior division or COSVN leadership.

By chance, the bomb strike had missed the shaded mortar crew camp and stitched its line of destruction just west of General Thanh's location. Safe by distance from the effect of heat and shrapnel, he and his command group had been killed by the immense overpressure that had swept across them.

Standing and smoking a cigarette, his mind sensed the bomb strike, but his body had not yet reacted. Within a millisecond, a huge cloud of invisible force blew through his position—the cumulative effect of overpressure, shockwave and heat turning his internal viscera to a jellied mass but leaving his external features, less a light coat of dirt, largely untouched.

Next to the Chinese officer who was quietly smoking a foul-smelling cigarette, were the bodies of Thanh and the immediate group, neatly aligned and without a mark save for the small trickles of blood that had dried in their ears and nostrils. The faces had been covered with a hammock to protect them from the flies. Yet the captain could still discern two of the identities from the feminine nails and fingers of one and the uncalloused palms of the other.

Night settled quickly upon the camp and its members quietly went about their necessary personal tasks in the last vestiges of daylight. The survivors, remnants of shattered units with the memories of that experience still fresh in their minds, acted more as individual campers than members of a disciplined military force. The scouts, uncomfortable with the situation and the unshared experience, retreated to their own isolation in the jungle. Everywhere, the beginning whiffs of the sickly sweet smell of rotting flesh began to pervade the atmosphere.

Soon after everyone had settled into the early morning hours, a large group of people arrived at that portion of the camp that had been General Thanh's command post. Several were dressed in full formal uniforms of the North Vietnamese Army. They were accompanied by several Chinese in plain khaki cotton clothes. Absent a guard or greeting party, they woke the first people they could find and ordered that a fire be built for light.

Shortly, both the original Chinese and Caucasian visitors were awoken on order and proceeded to the fire. There, still confused and half-awake from the combination of the bomb strike and the hour, they met in hurried and intense consultation with the new party. They abruptly left the group, returned to their hammocks, packed their now minimal belongings and returned to the fire. In their absence, the new leadership had ordered that General Thanh's body be washed and placed in a large American body bag that had been brought by the new arrivals. When everyone had returned to the campfire, the senior leader, a small man with a distinct overbite, gave a short order and the party, now augmented by the body and the visitors, disappeared into the jungle.

The funeral party proceeded through the center of what remained of the Binh Tram base and followed a small trail that eventually expanded into a single-lane hard-packed earth roadway. Proceeding on this path for several hours, the group emerged onto a much larger main road. This was a primary conduit, one of seven, that created the Ho Chi Minh Trail. There, the body and the accompanying group mounted two Zil trucks and headed initially north and then, on a smaller road, due west.

Halting at daybreak in one of the many way stations that supported the trail complex, the trucks parked beneath a finely woven canopy of living trees and brush. The group dismounted and was led into comfortable sleeping quarters for the remainder of the day. Throughout this period, the senior general restlessly walked around the small camp and constantly dictated messages to the North. Here, in a more sophisticated and isolated location, he felt relatively free to communicate by radio and did so with a Chinese HF radio with secured transmissions. Only in the last part of the afternoon did he indulge himself in a short rest before he woke the group and ordered them to load the trucks.

Once loaded and with the sudden seep of twilight into darkness, the trucks departed and headed further west. In less than an hour's transit, the convoy had moved into the relatively open terrain that skirted the border between Laos and Cambodia. Here, the fetid smell of the jungle was left behind and the air, clear and cool, was markedly less humid. The passengers, rolled and shaken into a perpetual torpor, were revived and gazed across the rolling terrain as they drank in the unusual experience of transiting open terrain in broad daylight. A sensory explosion excited them into wakefulness and they began to animatedly chatter among themselves. Even the Caucasians, now cooled by evaporation, began smiling and offering their cigarettes to their much smaller companions who had been squashed against the truck canvas by their hulking guests.

Once the NVA general felt secure in his navigation, he directed the driver to turn onto a semi-paved portion of highway and proceed at breakneck speed to a small village contained between two low-lying hills, less than 32 kilometers into Laos. There, as the late afternoon sun bent its golden light across the village silhouette, several guides emerged from the village and directed the group to what had once been the house of the French administrator. In the hissing brilliant light of the Olympus gas lantern, the general dictated a short message to the guide and then went soundly asleep on the square ironwood plank bed, his body obscured by the encapsulating white mosquito net.

Near midnight, the guides awoke the general. He issued several short orders and directed that the foreign visitors pack their gear and join him. Woken from a fiercely hard sleep induced by the combination of altitude, cool air and exhaustion, the group assembled in the brilliant glare of the hissing lamp. Here, they were told to follow him and do as instructed. The group departed the light of the house and after adjusting their eyes in the dark, moved off toward the hill closest to the village.

When they arrived at the top, a small fire had been established. Several feet away, in the flickering shadows, the bundled remains of General Thanh could be seen resting next to a much larger pile of split bamboo and several plastic bottles of kerosene used for cooking stoves. The group was directed to sit on the elephant grass that had been previously beaten down by the villagers. Now, it was damp and ran with water on its spiky edges where it had trapped the evening dew. The moisture quickly passed through thin cotton pants and most began to shiver in the light wind. One of the Caucasians attempted to protest but caught himself when he saw the flint-edged gaze of the general reflecting off the small red glow of his cigarette.

Within an hour, a runner approached the group and spoke briefly to the general. He sprang to his feet, gesticulated toward the large mound and waved the group to the edge of the larger wood pile. Quickly, it was ignited and began to burn with a series of loud snapping cracks as the bamboo-trapped water exploded out of its confining cells. The area was increasingly illuminated as the fire grew and bathed the grass in its light and heat. Initially welcoming the warmth to ward off the damp chill, the party now retreated to the edge of the grass where it stood straight and untrammeled. Masked by the fire's noise, the group was unable to discern the sudden appearance of a visitor until it descended upon them, coating them with burning embers and windblown splinters.

As suddenly as it appeared, the French-built Alouette helicopter came to a complete halt and slowly idled its rotor blades. As soon as it reduced its main power, Thanh's body was snatched from beside the beacon fire and hauled across the slippery wet grass where it was tied to a medical evacuation basket attached to the outside landing struts. The general then gestured the Caucasians and one Chinese to load themselves inside the helicopter. As soon as the door closed, the helicopter gained maximum power and quickly lifted off in a whirl of ashes and wind-driven embers that beat themselves through the rotor wash and back onto the standing bodies. Before the ash had settled, a second Alouette landed. The general ordered the remaining Chinese into the helicopter, secured the door for them and mounted the left front seat. The helicopter quickly took off and left the remaining personnel to stand in the darkening gloom of the now dying fire.

The helicopters followed the line of hills as they their way toward the North. Aided by a bright half-moon, the aircraft flew less than a hundred feet from the ground ducking and weaving their way through the Laotian hills, marking their way with well-memorized landmarks. After an hour's flight, they arrived at a long flat stretch of road that bisected the Plain of Jarres. Here, they settled down on a roadside turnout that had been marked by several truck lights. Trucks also marked both ends of the flat road.

While the party was still stretching their legs from the cramped helicopter ride and relieving themselves in the bright moonlight night, a much louder sound penetrated their minds causing them to simultaneously look up into the sky. Quickly, they could discern the large silver aluminum shape of a Soviet-built Antonov 124 transport plane. It swooped down the road on a long, low recon pass, conducted a sharp turn and landed abruptly on the roadway, less than 75 feet from the truck at the leading edge of the ersatz airport. At no time did the aircraft ever fly higher than 300 feet off the ground.

The plane rolled down the road and halted amidst a shower of dirt, rocks and trash. As it slowed down, the ramp was lowered to the point where it began to kick up sparks just before the plane halted. The general picked up his party and with the assistance of two bearers holding General Thanh's sacked body, mounted the aircraft. With the general's entrance, the ramp was raised and the plane swung around and began its takeoff roll. It departed the ground before several of the passengers could take their seats. Gravity and speed pushed them on the floor where they remained mixed with the body bag and personal effects until the plane leveled off a minute later.

Still less than 500 feet off the ground, the plane banked sharply east and ducked through the wide gap between the Annamite massif marked by Laotian Highway 5 and the rolling hills introducing North Vietnam. As dawn was breaking, the aircraft landed at a small concrete runway at the juncture of the Red River and Yen Bay, the command post for the North Vietnamese Army at the siege of Dien Bien Phu. Waiting for the group was a small honor guard to retrieve the body. Waiting in the shadow of the wings were several senior officers, who took each Chinese and Caucasian traveler by the arm to a waiting vehicle.

Before noon, a large party of press was invited to the historic NVA command post. Thanh's body, freshly wiped with lemon juice and carbolic acid, dressed in full formal army uniform, was laid upon an open flower-covered bier. An announcement was made that Thanh had died of a heart attack. Many in the press remarked on how rested he looked. Less than a mile from where Thanh had made his winning argument, the official mourners and honor detail sat in a large room drinking cool tea and discussing strategy. It promised to be a long afternoon but there was plenty of time available. Time was a matter of choice and how it is to be used.

47

To the Work

During the funeral, the other side was in the process of making its own arrangements. Moving slowly from their position at the elephant grass LZ, the Rangers, now somewhat reconstituted by a combination of recovered missing and fresh replacements rushed to the unit by the Saigon High Command, slipped into the jungle and retraced their steps. Their continued field duty was a political ploy to establish the facets of victory for the press and a clear dislike by General Tanh of having the Ranger remnants barnstorm Xuan Loc in a series of survival celebrations.

The day prior, many of Saigon's ranking leaders were flown to the landing zone for an award ceremony. There, the Rangers were given flower leis and a variety of medals. For appearance's sake, elements of a sister battalion were arrayed to the immediate rear of the battalion survivors so that the recipients appeared to be a small part of a larger body.

Despite his objections to the concept, General Tanh was required to promote Major Hiep to lieutenant colonel after a direct order from General Vien, the Chief of the Joint General Staff. The advisors, though politely courted by the visiting Vietnamese and the many press, stood aside and spent the available time soliciting C-rations from the cavalry element guarding the scene.

The ceremony was mercifully short due to the combination of heat and distance from amenities. In less than an hour, the helicopters ferrying the dignitaries departed amidst a swirl of dust that coated the honorees. Quickly, as the sounds of the helicopters faded in the distance, the Rangers were left alone with the cavalry.

Shortly, another UH-1H appeared on the scene to land next to the cavalry. Before the blades could cease rotating, the cavalry commander leaped out and marched directly toward Hiep's command post, a grouping of soldiers and radios collected under a stretched poncho and the remains of a bent banana tree. He gestured toward his aircraft and four soldiers descended from the interior. They each carried two brand-new M-60 machine guns that they placed in a neat row in front of Hiep, now standing at a formal attention in his always immaculate fatigues.

Wordlessly, the colonel and Hiep shook hands. Hiep was unable to speak but gripped the Cav commander's hand tightly and looked him directly in the eye. Momentarily breaking the spell, Hiep gestured toward his bodyguard who produced a pack of Pall Malls and a bottle of Johnny Walker. Hiep took a swig from the bottle and passed it to the large American who unhesitatingly drew a large draught from it and returned the bottle. Hiep invited the man to sit under the shade of the shelter, which he did. Both now smoked quietly. Wordlessly, they watched the Montagnards recover the new weapons, examine the contents of the spare barrel bags and gesture thanks toward the pair with clasped hands against nose and forehead. The oldest Montagnard, with gold-capped teeth smiled broadly and rendered a formal French salute.

After a period of time, the colonel rose, shook Hiep's hand, saluted and departed. Hiep, for the first time in several days, smiled and waved farewell. As the dust from the retreating helicopter settled around him, he gestured toward his company commanders and outlined the next day's plan.

They followed the same path they had taken several days previously. However, this time, they were accompanied by the whine and security of the ACAVs from the Cav and the relief from the anxiety of what would greet them at their destination. Quickly, as all retraced paths seem to do, the unit came onto the scene of its initial engagement.

The area was burned, blasted, opened, and reeked of a combination of cordite and corpses. The soldiers slowly and without emotion placed themselves in the cleared perimeter outlined on the ground by the still visible mounds of expended cartridges, grenade pins, and articles of burnt and torn clothing and bandages. This time, they filled the spaces of their adversaries and positioned themselves much as their enemies had done scarcely a day prior. With a combination of emotion and professional interest, they privately reviewed the other side's perspectives.

The machine gunners occupied the angled bunkers and the command group requisitioned the remnants of the kitchen area to the rear. The soldiers, what remained of the reconstituted force, filled the available space. Buttressing the unoccupied territory, the ACAVs provided gap fillers. Without command, both units, Americans and Vietnamese, began to undertake the individual and collective tasks of soldiers that are common to all.

The lieutenant and sergeant occupied a position to the left of the line that connected Suoi Long stream with the base camp. Directly in front of them was a large banyan tree with spreading tree root buttresses. Facing them, held between two of the extended roots as if he were taking an afternoon nap, was the body of a VC soldier that had been missed by the clearing teams.

His head was slumped down on his chest and his arms were folded across his AK-47 rifle that lay atop his legs. He was directly facing the lieutenant, less than 20 feet from his position. By all appearances, he was fast asleep.

The lieutenant was initially shocked to see him. Thinking him a member of his unit, he approached the sleeping soldier to awaken him and noticed the small black line that traveled from the soldier's chin to his chest and the large amount of buzzing flies that swarmed around the hair and skin.

He carefully placed his M-16 barrel under the chin of the soldier and raised it with the large A frame sight. He saw the small black hole at the upper right portion of the forehead and the mass of black flies congregating around the eyes and lips. Now, he could clearly see the patch of blood and brain matter that discolored the light beige of the tree bark where the head rested against the white layer of fresh wood exposed by the exiting bullet.

The mouth had begun to open slightly and the teeth were visible tightly held together. The hair, black and evenly cut, barely reached the blue-black wound.

The lieutenant studied the body in an almost clinical manner and then let the weight of the head lower the rifle to where the corpse was again in natural repose. He returned to his position and spoke quietly to his sergeant. For the duration of their stay, the two closely studied the progress of the transition of the body from that of a soldier to its assimilation into the other organic matter of their surroundings.

Initially the body was as if in life. The skin and flesh retained their natural appearances. Though pallid, the body's outer covering retained its integrity and the composition appeared correct and natural. With great rapidity, nature began its inexorable recycling process.

The lieutenant and sergeant, as they had done previously, separated their sectors of responsibility. They established the corpse as the boundary and used it as the basic reference point. Initially, they could see no appreciable change to the composition and carefully studied its repose.

Small flies and insects were observed gathering at the soft parts of the face and other bugs began to traverse the clothing toward the head. The face itself was largely hidden by a combination of the drooping hair and downcast pose. Occasionally, one or the other would, in the course of normal business, pass by the body and examine it more closely.

By the evening of the first day, the eyes and lips were thoroughly consumed. The mouth was now fully exposed as the teeth provided the only guardian between the jungle's reducers and the inner sanctum of the soldier. With a fixed and shiny smile, the corpse provided a beacon to the local consumers.

The eyes, no longer in existence, became tunnels into the tributaries of the cranium. These various avenues were fully involved by an unceasing line of insects that coursed from the jungle floor, along the folds of the uniform, across the cold wood of the rifle, through the wrinkles in the shirt, across the increasingly dark and seeping skin and into the welcome womb and warmth of the newly exposed recesses of the flesh. Slowly smoking their cigarettes and drinking the last of the evening C-ration coffee, the pair watched this act of decomposition with a quiet curiosity.

By morning of the second day, the body had undergone a major transformation. The flesh supporting the face had disappeared. Instead a shaking brownish-black mass had adhered to the bone surface and gave the appearance of constant motion. The hair had fallen like snow across the shirt and ringed the area below the cranium. The top of the skull was now exposed and the wavering stitching of the bone was clearly visible, exposed by the quiet miniscule bites of its constantly moving guests.

The uniform appeared almost alive. Everywhere, the material moved in irregular jerky motions. Wrinkles filled and reformed. Lines and shadows traced their way across the gray-green material marking the trail of the small scavenging army. The legs, more difficult to penetrate, had swollen from gas and now pressed tightly to the limit of the tailoring. But, even here, small movements were becoming visible. The pair smoked cigarettes, warmed their coffee against the cold morning air and wordlessly observed the progress of the jungle's evolutionary process.

The third day presented a distinctly different scene. The previous evening's work had been thorough and the connection between the corpse and a human form became one more of imagination than reality. From the beltline up, the form was largely skeletonized. The shirt had been opened exposing a partial torso just above where the naval would have been.

Above that, the skeleton lay fully exposed. The bones were a gray yellow green with a shiny wet film. Though still held together by connective tissue, the joints were under steady attack by thousands of small burrowing dots. The larger insects had migrated to the more rewarding still available regions of flesh and left the smaller portions to their lesser companions.

The skull, now fully pared of flesh, lay drooped over the chest cavity. The larger opening to the rear of the skull, hitherto unnoticed by the pair, was apparent. The two noticed this and poked the dark spot on the tree trunk that contained the mortal bullet.

Around the mark, the cambium layer lay exposed with a dark blotchy stain around its circumference composed of bone matter and blood. This too was under unrelenting attack from the small insatiable lines of insects moving between it and the ground. Curious, the sergeant lifted the skull by placing a small stick in the left eye socket and aligning it with the hole in the trunk. He commented that the soldier had probably been napping.

Over the course of the night, rain had intermittently fallen on the corpse. The insects had eaten the flesh to the beltline but had been unable to press much below. Consequently, a pool of water had formed in the abdomen with the meniscus grasping the upper edge of the belt as coping on a swimming pool. Small patches of intestines broke the surface like small islands stranding unwary insects and animal life as it ventured to new exposed feast sites.

The pair noticed that a spider had formed a web between the rib cage and the spine on the left side and was stretched fully across the net, reaching for the early shafts of morning sunlight. The sun danced and glistened its light off the shimmering water in the torso and reflected the yellow-green tone of the spider's long arched legs. Several small mounds interrupted the orderly geometry of the web attesting to the intelligence of the builder.

By midafternoon, the pair noticed that the legs, once fully bloated to the extent of the available cloth, was now considerably looser and seemed alive with motion. Small traces and ripples of movement could be discerned across the material as if it were alive. The pool of water had become a welcome oasis for transiting scavengers as they paused to refresh themselves in the cool and unexpected liquid. A solid mass of vibrating brown circled the pool as the mass continuously substituted itself between the water above and the pleasures of flesh below.

The fourth night wrought dynamic changes. Sensing that a climax was approaching, the lieutenant and sergeant moved to the body at first light. Slowly drinking coffee and careful to sit outside the range of the converging insect armies, they noticed the changes.

The pool of water was now gone, drained by numerous punctures to the body vessel from below. The belt and pants now hung lifeless around portions of the pelvis, a hip bone that protruded gray green on the left side. The connective tissue holding the spine together had been largely eliminated. That, combined with the weight of bones had caused the structure to implode inward and the skull now rested in the lap with the topmost segments of the spine scattered in a small circle around the main heap. The pants clung loosely outlining the now fleshless legs. The white ankle bones shone brightly beneath the cuff.

The point most noticed however, was that the bones were now a soft and uniform white. Having eliminated the great mass of compacted flesh, the insects were forced to work the bone covering and viscera for sustenance. Through the night, the nutritional bone covering had been reduced to calcium. Now, the army of cleaners had reduced itself to squads and platoons of stragglers working the last remnants of viscera.

No longer a thing of recognition, the pile of bones and cloth lost its attraction for the pair, as it had for the insects. The lieutenant and sergeant recovered their equipment, grasped their rifles, and moved off into the obscuring filtered light toward the work that lay ahead. The lieutenant had slightly less than a year. His charges had a lifetime.